KEY GUIDES

The Charity Treasurer's Handbook

5th edition

Gareth G. Morgan

dsc
directory of social change

Published by the Directory of Social Change (Registered Charity no. 800517 in England and Wales)
Head office: Resource for London, 352 Holloway Rd, London N7 6PA
Northern office: Suite 103, 1 Old Hall Street, Liverpool L3 9HG
Tel: 08450 77 77 07

Visit www.dsc.org.uk to find out more about our books, subscription funding websites and training events. You can also sign up for e-newsletters so that you're always the first to hear about what's new.

The publisher welcomes suggestions and comments that will help to inform and improve future versions of this and all of our titles. Please give us your feedback by emailing publications@dsc.org.uk.

This is an introductory book. It seeks to explain the framework of charity accounting but it does not provide a full statement of the law. Where legal issues are covered, they are based on the position as at 1 January 2017, but there could be subsequent changes. Many accounting concepts are presented at an overview level only – particularly in areas such as accruals accounting, charity taxation and production of final accounts under the Charities Statements of Recommended Practice (the SORPs). It should be understood that this publication is intended for guidance only and is not a substitute for professional or legal advice. No responsibility for loss occasioned as a result of any person acting or refraining from acting on the basis of this publication can be accepted by the authors or publisher.

First published 2002
Second edition 2008
Third edition 2010
Reprinted 2012
Fourth edition 2014
Reprinted 2015
Fifth edition 2017

ISBN 978 1 78482 013 8 (print edition)
ISBN 978 1 78482 014 5 (digital edition)

British Library Cataloguing in Publication Data
A catalogue record for this book is available from the British Library

Cover and text design by Kate Griffith
Typeset by Marlinzo Services, Frome
Printed and bound by Page Bros, Norwich

Contents

About the series

This series of key guides is designed for people involved with not-for-profit organisations of any size, no matter how you define your organisation: voluntary, community, non-governmental or social enterprise. All the titles offer practical, comprehensive, yet accessible advice to enable readers to get the most out of their roles and responsibilities.

Also available in this series:

Charitable Incorporated Organisations, Gareth G. Morgan

The Charity Trustee's Handbook, Jacqueline Williams and Mike Eastwood

Effective Fundraising, Ben Wittenberg

Minute Taking, Paul Ticher and Lee Comer

For further information, please contact the Directory of Social Change (see page x for details).

Foreword

I was delighted to be asked to contribute a foreword for the fifth edition of this rightly popular publication. Charity treasurers need all the help they can get – and I mean that in the nicest possible way!

Across the UK, our diverse and vibrant charity sector is united by some common features: a sense of mission and a commitment to a cause; a reliance on voluntary inputs at all levels; and a requirement to display high standards of governance and stewardship in an increasingly complex operating environment.

The lion's share of the latter challenge sits with charity trustees: in particular with treasurers. Whilst charity finances sometimes come to the attention of regulators, or a wider audience, for all the wrong reasons, I am keen to remind commentators that for the great majority of the time, the great majority of charities run extremely soundly, displaying high standards of financial probity and operating to standards of transparency that can be very exacting. It is right that this is so – charities could not survive without the trust and confidence of their supporters and the wider public.

So, helping dedicated and sometimes long-suffering charity treasurers, and those who advise and support them, is extremely important work and this handbook is an invaluable resource in this respect. The book is written with the smaller charity and the volunteer in mind – it does not assume great levels of specialist knowledge on charity accounting or reporting. The language is accessible and the structure and indexing are clear. The handbook, however, also deals with issues in enough depth to be of value to more experienced readers, and in a world where the charities SORP changes on a regular basis, it is important that charities keep up to date with developments.

The book also recognises the realities of devolution of charity law and accounting practice to Scotland and to Northern Ireland, with areas of divergence appropriately flagged up and referenced.

I am sure that wherever you sit in the charity landscape, you will find the handbook a rewarding read and a frequent source of reference. I know it will make a valuable contribution to the sound management of charity finances in the UK – and perhaps beyond – and I congratulate the author on this latest excellent edition.

David Robb
CEO Scottish Charity Regulator (OSCR)

Preface

The aim of *The Charity Treasurer's Handbook* is to bring together many aspects of effective accounting and financial management in UK charitable organisations in a book which is short enough to be read in a few hours.

The role of a treasurer, finance worker or finance manager in a voluntary organisation can be a rewarding one if it enables the organisation to achieve its aims. It need not be daunting, but it does require an appreciation of those issues that make the finances of charitable organisations different from businesses.

The handbook will also be useful to those with financial experience in other sectors, who need a rapid overview of the accounting issues in a charity. The book is also intended for students on courses in charity and voluntary sector management who need an appreciation of the requirements of financial management in the sector.

This book outlines some of the key issues of charity law that affect the work of treasurers and finance officers in smaller charities. It explains a range of terminology, such as restricted funds, and the implications of the Charities Statements of Recommended Practice (the SORPs). It offers guidelines for day-to-day accounting procedures, as well as for year end accounts. It provides advice on topics such as appointing an auditor or independent examiner, and gives an overview of some of the specific tax issues affecting charities.

This handbook does not seek to cover the full detail of every issue, but simply to give enough information so that the reader will understand the main requirements. It is hoped that this will enable those responsible for charity finances to make sensible decisions and to enter into meaningful discussions with others when further guidance is needed. Where more detail is needed, the further reading list at the end may be helpful.

The book's main focus is on charitable voluntary organisations in the UK with total incomes in the range of £5,000 to £1 million – but larger and smaller groups will also find the book useful. Much of the content will also be relevant to voluntary organisations without charitable status. But, as explained in chapter 1, the impact of the various Charities Acts means many voluntary organisations that do not think of themselves as charities are in fact charitable in law. So the principles of this book apply to nearly all voluntary organisations, other than political organisations and private clubs.

One of the difficulties of charity law arises from the different legal systems in the countries of the UK. The book seeks to cover, at least in terms of key issues:

- the requirements in England and Wales under the Charities Act 2011 (including the latest changes from 2016);
- the rules for Scottish charities under the Charities and Trustee Investment (Scotland) Act 2005 (including amended regulations from 2016); and
- the rules for Northern Irish charities under the Charities Act (Northern Ireland) 2008 (including the regulations which began from 2016).

Legal and similar issues are stated as far as possible in terms of the requirements for financial years starting from 1 January 2016, covering accounts which will generally be filed with charity regulators from 2017 onwards (for earlier years, see the appendix on page 193). But a book of this kind can only give an overview of legal issues – there are often more detailed requirements, exceptions and special cases which cannot be covered here. When a charity is in any doubt, it is often wise to take professional advice.

For the second, third, fourth and fifth editions, I have also taken the opportunity to update many sections to clarify issues that have become particularly important to the sector over the last few years. These include the accounting issues when voluntary organisations get involved in providing public services, the differences between grants and contracts and the whole area of full cost recovery. I have also added some material on partnership arrangements in the sector. This fifth edition addresses many new issues which have arisen in the last three years. These include experience with the new Charities SORPs from 2015 and the further SORP changes in 2016; the increased audit threshold in England and Wales (widening the range of charities which can have independent examinations); and the start of the new charity accounting regulations in Northern Ireland. Other changes include updates to the Gift Aid regime, and advice on the practical issues of accounting for charitable incorporated organisations (for more on CIOs, see my other book in this series). This edition also includes an extensive glossary of terminology used in the field of charity accounting (see page 199).

The central message of the book is that being a charity treasurer or finance officer is an important and worthwhile role. It involves much more than keeping the books: the treasurer or finance officer is a key person in all kinds of strategic decisions and in ensuring the organisation meets the requirements of charity law. Contrary to popular belief, the role does not require massive accounting knowledge, or a brilliant head for figures: simply a commitment to the importance of financial resources, and a willingness to see them used effectively for the purposes of the charity.

About the author

Gareth G. Morgan has been involved in advice, research and teaching on charity accounting and regulation for 25 years.

Most of his time is now spent as the senior partner of the Kubernesis Partnership LLP, a small firm of charity consultants based in Yorkshire, England and East Lothian, Scotland. Through this work he helps to support charitable organisations across the UK and other professionals advising charities in the areas of accounting, formation of new charities, charity tax issues, and other aspects of charity regulation.

He is Emeritus Professor of Charity Studies at Sheffield Hallam University where he was formerly course leader of the MSc in Charity Resource Management and led the inter-faculty Centre for Voluntary Sector Research. He continues to support students researching the charity sector and is collaborating with international colleagues in charity-related research and policy work. Over the years he has worked on a range of research projects concerned with charity regulation and accounting including studies for the Charity Commission and major accounting bodies. He gave evidence in Parliament to the Joint Committee of both Houses of Parliament examining the draft Bill which became the Charities (Protection and Social Investment) Act 2016. He is the author or co-author of many research papers and articles in these areas.

Gareth is a Fellow of the Association of Charity Independent Examiners, a Full Member with Diploma of the Institute of Fundraising and an Academic Fellow of the Association of International Accountants.

He is also a member of the Charity Law Association where he has contributed to several of its working parties, particularly on regulations related to charity structures and accounting. He served for six years on the Charity Technical Committee of the Institute of Chartered Accountants in England and Wales (ICAEW) and is now on the Charity Expert Panel of the Institute of Chartered Accountants of Scotland (ICAS).

Over the years he has been a trustee of a wide range of charities, including serving as treasurer in both local and national organisations.

Acknowledgements

Over the years I have been enormously privileged to work with several hundred charitable organisations in terms of their accounting and financial arrangements, in many cases helping them to implement procedures to reflect the new charity accounting rules and in several cases acting as their independent examiner. Others have attended courses I presented, and raised significant questions which have caused me to reflect. Many of the ideas in this book derive from the insights of the people in those organisations, and I would like to dedicate the book to them.

I am also very appreciative of many individuals who have offered advice, listened to my questions and been willing to debate different approaches to charity accounting. This includes key figures in the Charity Commission for England and Wales, OSCR, the Charity Commission for Northern Ireland, academic colleagues, members of the ICAEW and ICAS charity committees, and leading figures in the Association of Charity Independent Examiners (ACIE).

I would also say a special word of thanks to my students over the years – all experienced charity practitioners – on the MSc in Charity Resource Management at Sheffield Hallam University. Their questions and challenges have been immensely valuable, both on technical aspects of the regulations, and on the practical issues of applying these principles in real charities run by real people who are not always keen to follow the official line!

I am also most grateful to the Directory of Social Change for inviting me (back in 2002) to produce a book on this topic and to update it at intervals thereafter including this new fifth edition. My wife, Sharon, who is also my partner in the Kubernesis Partnership LLP, has given a great deal of encouragement to this project and read many drafts.

Nevertheless, I must stress that all opinions expressed are my own (unless another source is mentioned) and any errors remain my responsibility.

Gareth G. Morgan
Dunbar, Scotland
December 2016

About the Directory of Social Change

The Directory of Social Change (DSC) has a vision of an independent voluntary sector at the heart of social change. The activities of independent charities, voluntary organisations and community groups are fundamental to achieve social change. We exist to help these organisations and the people who support them to achieve their goals.

We do this by:

- providing practical tools that organisations and activists need, including online and printed publications, training courses, and conferences on a huge range of topics;

- acting as a 'concerned citizen' in public policy debates, often on behalf of smaller charities, voluntary organisations and community groups;

- leading campaigns and stimulating debate on key policy issues that affect those groups;

- carrying out research and providing information to influence policymakers.

DSC is the leading provider of information and training for the voluntary sector and publishes an extensive range of guides and handbooks covering subjects such as fundraising, management, communication, finance and law. We have a range of subscription-based websites containing a wealth of information on funding from grant-making charities, companies and government sources. We run more than 300 training courses each year, including bespoke in-house training provided at the client's location. DSC conferences and fairs, many of which run on an annual basis, include the Management and Leadership Fair, the Charity Accountants' Conference and the Charity Law Conference. DSC's major annual event is Charityfair, which provides low-cost training on a wide variety of subjects.

For details of all our activities, and to order publications and book courses, go to www.dsc.org.uk, call 08450 777707 or email publications@dsc.org.uk.

List of abbreviations

BACS	Bankers' Automated Clearing System
Charity Commission	Charity Commission for England and Wales
CCNI	Charity Commission for Northern Ireland
Charities Act	unless otherwise stated this means the Charities Act 2011 (applicable to England and Wales)
CASC	community amateur sports club
CAF	Charities Aid Foundation
CBS*	community benefit society
CIC	community interest company
CIO*	charitable incorporated organisation (unless otherwise stated this abbreviation includes CIOs in any part of the UK, including SCIOs)
CSG	cost sharing group
CLG	company limited by guarantee
EEA	European Economic Area
EU	European Union
FPS	Fundraising Preference Service
FR	Fundraising Regulator
FRC	Financial Reporting Council
FRS102*	Financial Reporting Standard number 102
FRSSE	Financial Reporting Standard for Smaller Entities
GASDS	Gift Aid Small Donations Scheme
HMRC*	Her Majesty's Revenue and Customs
IFRS	International Financial Reporting Standards
NFP	not-for-profit organisation
NI	National Insurance
OSCR	Office of Scottish Charity Regulator
PAYE	Pay As You Earn
R&P	receipts and payments (when referring to R&P accounts/ accounting)
RTI	real time information (for PAYE)
SAP	statutory adoption pay
sch.	schedule (to an act of parliament or regulations)
SCIO*	Scottish charitable incorporated organisation
SMP	statutory maternity pay
SOAL*	statement of assets and liabilities
SOFA*	statement of financial activities

SORP*	Statement of Recommended Practice (unless otherwise stated this will always be a reference to the 'Charities SORP' – see chapters 2 and 7 for explanation)
SPP	statutory paternity pay
SSP	statutory sick pay
VCOs	voluntary and community organisations (some VCOs are charities but not all)
VCS	voluntary and community sector

* These terms are explained in more detail in the glossary starting on page 199.

Glossary terms

Terms which appear in **bold** in chapters 1–12 (when first used) are explained further in the glossary, starting on page 199.

References to endnotes

Superscript numbers within the text denote references to the legislation or further details – the corresponding notes appear on pages 221–222.

1 Finance in charities and voluntary organisations

Before taking on the role of being a **treasurer** or finance officer in a charity, you need to understand what is meant by a **charity**. Charitable status makes a huge difference to the need for accounting and financial management. But many more organisations are charities than people often realise and, as we will see, the term 'charity' actually includes a very large part of the voluntary sector.

Many people think that 'charity' applies only to certain types of organisations with a particular legal form, and which are registered with the Charity Commission: this is quite wrong. There are many possible legal structures for a charity, and there are many organisations which in law are charities, even though historically they were not generally required to be registered: churches are probably the largest such category. Also, the Charity Commission only covers England and Wales; in Scotland the Office of the Scottish Charity Regulator (OSCR) registers charities and in Northern Ireland charities are now registered by the Charity Commission for Northern Ireland (CCNI) – see page 13 for more on the different kinds of charitable status. Moreover, many larger organisations have been formed as charitable companies, which means they are subject to both charity and company law (although the emergence of **charitable incorporated organisations – CIOs** – has made the company structure much rarer for new charities).

The principles of being a charity treasurer, and most of the law on charity accounting, apply to almost all charitable organisations.

The third sector, voluntary sector, charity sector and social enterprise

To understand charities, we need to begin with the widest possible view of the sector.

People often refer to voluntary or **not-for-profit** (NFP) organisations as the 'third sector'. The government's definition of the third sector is organisations which are neither: (a) established primarily for distribution of profit; nor (b) part of the statutory sector. The third sector is usually seen in contrast to the other two sectors – the commercial sector (business organisations) where profit is the central aim, and the public sector (for example, government, local authorities and the health service), which, although NFP, is part of the work of the state. It is best to use the term 'not-for-profit' since many businesses going through hard times are non-profit-making in certain years. Not all third sector organisations are NFPs; for example, many cooperatives generate profits which are shared between the members. But while most people would class cooperatives as being part of the third sector, a profit-distributing cooperative could not be a charity.

The third sector is often (wrongly) divided into two main categories: voluntary organisations and social enterprises. However, this is highly misleading because many voluntary organisations, including many charities, undertake social enterprise activities (see below for more on this).

Voluntary organisations are established voluntarily to advance aims that are non-statutory and NFP. The term is normally used to describe groups and organisations with some definite constitutional form that are working towards a socially beneficial aim. Some are large national organisations (these almost always have charitable status); others may be small community groups with no paid staff. Voluntary organisations will always have volunteers in governance of the organisation (who may be called trustees or management committee members) and may have volunteers in other roles. Some people prefer to talk of voluntary and community organisations (VCOs), and hence the voluntary and community sector (VCS), but in this book the term 'voluntary organisation' is used to include small community groups, faith-based organisations and, indeed, any organisation which meets these criteria.

Many voluntary organisations are charities (see page 6 for the definition) but there are some organisations which, although voluntarily governed and with socially beneficial aims, do not meet the precise requirements of charitable status. An example would be a group set up to raise funds purely to support one person or family, or a group which operates purely as a club for the benefit of its own members.

Social enterprises, if separately constituted, are trading organisations where profit may be an explicit aim, even though the purpose of the trade is for the benefit of the community. They do not have to be voluntarily governed – they can have paid board members if resources allow. Since 2005, many social enterprises have been established using the structure of a community interest company (CIC). Others are structured as cooperatives. CICs are subject to an **asset lock** – this allows outside investors to receive a modest return if required but most of the profits must be retained for the social aims of the organisation. However, cooperatives and CICs are *not* charities and so they are not directly considered in this book.

Note that charities often undertake trading activities (see page 46), and many quite justifiably describe these activities as 'social enterprise'. It's perfectly possible for a charity which undertakes significant amounts of work funded by fees or charges to describe itself as a charity *and* as a voluntary organisation *and* as a social enterprise. Some kinds of government support for social enterprise can include trading activities undertaken by charities so such a label can be helpful. Also, as mentioned in chapter 11, some larger charities may have a subsidiary company that undertakes non-charitable trading activities (with the aim of making a profit for the charity), which are often classed as social enterprises. But a charity which describes itself as a social enterprise must still produce charity accounts and comply with all the other requirements of charity law.

So in this book we use the term 'charitable trading' to describe trading activities undertaken directly by an organisation with charitable status, as the term 'social enterprise' can include both charitable and non-charitable trading.

As well as voluntary organisations and profit-making social enterprises, the third sector can also be considered to include other kinds of NFP organisations, for example trade unions, political parties, trade associations and private members' clubs, but none of these can be charities.

The financial management of NFP organisations is obviously quite different from profit-making organisations: the central aims are usually concerned with providing services or making a positive difference to the world. Certainly NFP organisations must be non-profit-*distributing* – that is, if they do make a profit or surplus one year, it is retained to support the work of the organisation in future years, not distributed to owners or shareholders.

To most people the word 'profit' implies profits being taken out, so it is best to avoid this term in the NFP sector: occasionally you may want to talk about the profit on a certain activity, but you cannot meaningfully talk about the profit of a charity as a whole. If a charity's income exceeds its expenditure in a given year, we say it has made a **surplus** (or a **deficit** if the expenditure was more than the income). Of course the income and expenditure will never be exactly equal, and in most NFP organisations a small surplus one year will be balanced by a small deficit another year. Sometimes surpluses are needed for a few years to build up sufficient reserves (see chapter 4), but it can never be right for a charity to be making surpluses indefinitely, as it would mean substantial amounts of income were not being spent on the charity's objects. This is a big contrast to the commercial sector, where a profit is normally sought every year.

There are some similarities between the public sector and the third sector in terms of bidding for resources and managing budgets in a largely NFP context; the fundamental difference is that public sector organisations are under government direction (national or local), whereas organisations in the voluntary sector are regarded as independent and can set their own directions and priorities. But the specific accounting rules are generally quite different.

This does not mean that voluntary organisations are totally free of government control. They must obviously obey the laws of the land (including a number of specific issues of charity law and general issues such as employment and health and safety law) and many voluntary organisations get at least part of their income from the government, for example through **grants**, fees or Gift Aid tax refunds on **donations** (see chapter 12). But at the end of the day, a third sector organisation is primarily accountable to its own stakeholders, for example its members, trustees and **beneficiaries**.

A relationship of trust

This independence also creates a special relationship with funders and **donors**: a relationship of trust. Much income to charities (and to many other voluntary organisations) relies on money that is *given* to the organisation. Few people would make donations to commercial businesses or to the public sector, but people routinely give to charities and to other NFP organisations without seeking anything in return other than an expectation that their gifts will be used to advance the organisation's aims.

This does not just apply to personal donations; most grants, whether from the public sector or from other charities, are *given* to a charity. Grants and donations may be subject to specific conditions on the use of the money – this gives rise to restricted funds (see chapter 3) – but ultimately the relationship with the funder or donor is one in which money is given and the charity is entrusted with using it properly.

This is in complete contrast to commercial organisations, where most of the income is from sales, in which the relationship is contractual (for example, 'We will let you have this tin of paint if you pay us £5.50'). Charities can also have contractual income (trading income – see chapter 11), and for some charities this can be the main form of income, but for many charities money that is given is their main source of funds.

This relationship of trust is central to understanding voluntary sector finance, and is also the reason why much charity law has developed from trust law. For this reason, those who have the day-to-day control of a charity (for example, a management committee, church council or directors of a charitable company) are called 'trustees': they are entrusted with funds given by others to advance the charity's aims. However, the trust relationship can also apply elsewhere in the sector, for example with gifts to political organisations. Any grant or donation to a voluntary organisation implies some kind of trust relationship.

Trustees who fail to respect such relationships are guilty of a breach of trust, a serious matter that can result in court action. In extreme cases, a trustee who recklessly commits a breach of trust might have to reimburse the charity personally for money that was wrongly used.

In some NFP organisations it is common for board members to be paid; for example, in the public sector many people serving on trust boards are entitled to allowances or salaries, and this can also apply to non-charitable social enterprises. But a central issue of charity law is that **charity trustees** must not be seeking a tangible benefit from their role. They can, naturally, be reimbursed for their expenses, but the role of being a charity trustee is essentially voluntary. This clearly includes the treasurer, since a charity treasurer is normally a key trustee (except in rare cases where someone takes on the treasurership without having the right to vote at trustees' meetings).

There are some exceptions to this rule. A few charities have special governing instruments allowing certain trustees to be paid and, subject to very strict criteria, the Charities Act 2011 allows a charity to pay a trustee for specific services outside their role as a trustee. In other one-off cases a charity can apply for individual approval from the Charity Commission for a transaction with a trustee. But these are relatively rare and, excluding these cases, paying anything to a trustee other than reimbursement of expenses is a clear breach of trust. As shown in figure 7.2 on pages 112–113, to help safeguard against abuses, any payments to trustees must normally be shown separately in the charity's published accounts.

The principle of unpaid governance is at the heart of the voluntary sector, and even non-charitable voluntary organisations will find it hard to get grants if their committee members are paid. Some people question the term 'voluntary sector', pointing out that many charities nowadays do much of their work through paid staff, with limited use of volunteers. But all voluntary organisations rely on volunteers at the trustee level.

(For more information on trusteeship, see the *Charity Trustee's Handbook*, also in this series.)

What is a charity?

For any organisation to be a charity, it must clearly be a voluntary organisation with a group of people – the trustees – responsible, in most cases on an unpaid basis, for deciding on the use of the funds (subject to any conditions imposed by donors).

But not all voluntary organisations are charities. The test of charitable status does not depend on a certain structure nor on registration with the Charity Commission or OSCR or CCNI, but on the definition of 'charity' in law.

In England and Wales, it depends on two key tests, both concerned with the purposes or objects for which the organisation is established. This principle goes back to a 1601 statute of Elizabeth I, but from 2008 a new list of charitable purposes took effect – the list is now in the Charities Act 2011.

- The organisation must have exclusively charitable objects falling within one or more of the followings headings:
  - (a) the prevention and relief of poverty;
  - (b) the advancement of education;
  - (c) the advancement of religion;
  - (d) the advancement of health or the saving of lives;
  - (e) the advancement of citizenship or community development (this includes rural or urban regeneration, the promotion of civic responsibility, volunteering, the voluntary sector or the effectiveness and efficiency of charities in general);
  - (f) the advancement of arts, heritage, culture or science;
  - (g) the advancement of amateur sport;
  - (h) the advancement of human rights, conflict resolution or reconciliation or the promotion of religious or racial harmony or equality or diversity;
  - (i) the advancement of environmental protection or improvement;
  - (j) the relief of those in need by reason of youth, age, ill-health, disability, financial hardship or other disadvantage;
  - (k) the advancement of animal welfare;
  - (l) the promotion of the efficiency of the armed forces or emergency services;
  - (m) any other purpose which may reasonably be regarded as analogous to the above (including purposes under existing charity law).
- The organisation's purposes must be for public benefit. In other words, its aims must be to benefit a wide range of people (and there must be little or no private benefit; for example, except in very exceptional cases, the trustees must be unpaid): the Charity Commission has issued guidance on this which trustees are required to consider.

These charitable purposes apply to England and Wales (although the list above has been slightly paraphrased from the Act). However, there are some minor differences in Scotland (with slightly tighter rules on public benefit) and further small differences in Northern Ireland. If a charity is to operate throughout the UK, the objects need to be worded in order to meet the requirements of all three systems of charity law.

It is clear that a very wide range of voluntary organisations seeking to do work that most people would regard as worthwhile can fit into one or more of these categories if they word their **governing document** appropriately.

In England and Wales, the Charity Commission decides whether a particular organisation meets the criteria for charitable status (although in case of disagreement it is possible to appeal to the Charity Tribunal and ultimately to the courts). In Scotland, decisions are made by OSCR. In Northern Ireland, CCNI now has the role of registering new charities.

It follows that the governing document of the charity (its **constitution**, **articles of association**, trust deed or rules – see 'Legal forms', page 8) is vital in determining charitable status. In particular, the objects of the organisation (as stated in the governing document) and the range of beneficiaries are central to this decision. In theory it is possible to have a charity without a written constitution – occasionally people make the mistake of launching major appeals without any written documents. In such cases the charitable status of the funds raised would depend on witnesses testifying to what had been said at the time. But in the long term it is very hard to raise funds without a formal structure.

So in practice a very wide range of voluntary organisations are likely to be charities, if they have charitable aims and serve a wide range of beneficiaries, even if they are not formally registered as such. The main voluntary organisations *excluded* from charitable status tend to be:

- those whose aims are deemed in law to be primarily political or linked to self-interest: for example, political parties or campaigning organisations whose main aim is to achieve a change in the law, or trade unions working for the benefit of their own members; and
- those not offering sufficient public benefit, for example a tenants' group working purely with the tenants in a given block of flats or a club whose facilities are only available to its members (unless the membership rules make it easy for anyone to join).

Unless your organisation is clearly excluded from charitable status, it is safest to work on the assumption (at least for accounting purposes) that it is a charity, until proven otherwise. This means producing accounts to comply with charity law and, in England and Wales, the trustees must apply for the charity to be registered unless it is clearly excepted or exempt (see 'Charitable status', page 13).

However, it is illegal to claim to be a registered charity unless your organisation is actually registered with the appropriate regulator (Charity Commission, OSCR or CCNI).

Furthermore, you will not qualify for charity tax concessions unless your charitable status is clearly established. There is no half-way house on this question – a non-charitable voluntary organisation is treated as a business for tax purposes. If its only income is from grants and donations it is unlikely to incur tax except on investment income, but if it has any trading activities that make a profit (such as journal subscriptions or selling tickets for an event) the committee must make a corporation tax return to **HMRC** and must expect to pay tax. There are certain concessions in relation to 'mutual trading', but if you run a voluntary organisation that plans to rely on this, you should certainly seek advice from an accountant with experience in the tax affairs of clubs and associations.

As a charity treasurer or finance officer, you do not need to be an expert on charitable status, but you do need to understand the basic framework for your organisation's status, and you must certainly be aware of its charitable objects as stated in the governing document. (See 'Further reading' for sources of further information.)

Legal forms

Charities can have one of a number of legal structures; once you have a copy of your governing document it should be clear which structure applies. See 'Legal structures' opposite, which shows most of the main structures.

Until 2013 the vast majority of new charities were established using one of the first three structures in the table, but the charitable incorporated organisation (CIO) form is now by far the most popular structure for new charities. However, some charities have other structures not shown in this table – this is particularly the case with long-established organisations.

To form a new charity, a **charitable trust** is the simplest structure: all that is needed is for someone (the **settlor**) to make an initial donation and by means of a **trust deed** the objects are defined and initial trustees appointed. Many grant-making charities use this structure.

For a more democratic structure, with members electing a committee to act as trustees, the **charitable association** is the easiest model. Essentially, a group of people with common interests agree to associate themselves together, and agree to a constitution or set of rules that determines the criteria for membership and the procedures for electing the committee. A wide range of local community-based charities and service-providing organisations use this structure. But it is vital to keep proper records, to distinguish between ordinary members of the association (who have the right to vote at the annual general meeting) and members of the committee (who have day-to-day control of funds and are thus the trustees of the charity).

Legal structures

Legal form	Governing document	Usual internal term for trustees
Charitable trust	Trust deed (or a will, or a Scheme created by the Charity Commission)	Trustees
Charitable association	Constitution	Committee
Charitable company (company limited by guarantee: CLG)	Articles of association	Directors or board members
Charitable incorporated organisation (CIO)	Constitution	Trustees
Community benefit society (CBS or bencom: established for the benefit of the community)	Rules	Committee
Charities established by Royal Charter (for example, Scouts/Guides and certain professional bodies)	Charter	Council
Charities established by Act of Parliament (for example most Church of England bodies)	Act of Parliament (or regulations made under the Act)	Various terms

A **charitable company** is created by establishing an NFP company (a company limited by guarantee – CLG) under company law and then applying for the company to be registered as a charity. A company has the advantage of being a legally separate 'incorporated' entity: this means, for example, that if the charity needs to purchase freehold property it can be registered in the name of the charity, rather than in the names of individual **holding trustees**. Also, if the charity enters into a **contract** that goes wrong, and the charity finds itself being sued, the rules of limited liability apply, i.e. the charity's own resources could be lost in a court action, but the trustees could not be sued personally for breach of contract. In **unincorporated charities**, such as trusts and associations, if something goes wrong, the trustees could, in theory, be personally liable.

However, the protections of limited liability apply only to charitable companies if the directors/trustees have complied with all the requirements of company law. This gives a vast range of legal responsibilities over and above the requirements of charity law so, for example, unless you know what is meant in company law by 'derivative claims' and how to avoid them, limited liability may not offer as much protection as expected. Also, limited liability is only relevant in contract law; if, for example, you misuse restricted funds (see chapter 3), this is a breach of trust. Further, many risks can be mitigated in all types of charities by appropriate insurance: for example, charities giving advice certainly need professional indemnity insurance. Allowing the whole charity to collapse because of one disgruntled person taking legal action is hardly a good strategy in the first place: limited liability might protect the trustees, but staff would lose their jobs and beneficiaries would lose out. Finally, it has to be said that it is very rare for charity trustees acting in good faith to find themselves facing legal action; the bad publicity that would arise from suing a group of volunteers would put most people off.

A CIO overcomes most of the disadvantages of the first three forms. A CIO is governed purely by charity law and is created simply by being registered with the Charity Commission but it is an incorporated body with limited liability – thus giving most of the benefits of the charitable company without all the additional requirements of company law. In Scotland, the legislation allows for a similar structure, registered by OSCR, known as a **Scottish charitable incorporated organisation (SCIO)** and CIOs will in due course be possible in Northern Ireland through registration with CCNI. Since 2011, when SCIO registrations began, and from 2013, when it became possible to register CIOs in England and Wales, a high proportion of new charities are being formed as CIOs and a number of existing charities are converting to become CIOs. (For more on CIOs –

and on comparison with other structures – see my book *Charitable Incorporated Organisations* also published in this series. This book also has much more on the legal definition of charity and on non-charitable structures such as CICs and cooperatives.)

Even though the CIO form is proving very popular, and some existing charities are converting, there is no requirement to convert. Many charities use the existing structures and these are likely to continue to be used for some time. There are also a few situations where the older structures may work better – for example, where a charity needs to borrow money which cannot be secured as a mortgage on property, some lenders may prefer to deal with a charitable company rather than a CIO because of the ability to register charges against a company at Companies House – and some people establishing new grant-making charities may prefer a charitable trust if they do not wish to reveal details of grants made in the charity's accounts. But these are quite specialised situations.

Key abbreviations for NFP structures

Take care with the abbreviations:

CIO   Charitable incorporated organisation – a CIO is *always* a charity.

CIC   Community interest company (social enterprise) – a CIC is *never* a charity.

CLG   Company limited by guarantee. A CLG *may* be a charity. Most CLGs are NFP organisations but they do not have to be charities. A CLG that is a charity is described as a charitable company.

CBS   Community benefit society (an incorporated society with community aims) – also known as a 'bencom'. Many CBSs are charities, but this is not essential.

As a treasurer or finance officer, you need to be clear about the structure for which you are accounting. If your organisation is a charitable company, your accounting procedures must comply with company law as well as charity law; a number of differences are highlighted in the following chapters. But a CIO is *not* a company and the normal accounting rules apply for charities that are not companies.

Incorporation of existing charities

Sometimes a charity which is established as a charitable trust or association wishes to convert to an **incorporated charity** – i.e. to become a charitable company or a CIO. This is sometimes described loosely as 'incorporating the charity' but in law an unincorporated body cannot take on a new legal form. In practice, what happens is that a *new* charity is formed (a charitable company or a CIO) and then the *old* charity is wound up and all the assets transferred to the new organisation.

This has important accounting implications: the old and new charities are separate organisations, with separate charity registration numbers, and in the year of the change two separate sets of published accounts are needed (unless the old organisation can be wound up exactly on the last day of its accounting year). A treasurer handling such a conversion thus needs to keep completely separate books for the old and new organisations.

Subsidiary groups

Another vital issue on the legal structure, which is often overlooked, is to be clear on the boundaries of your organisation: as the treasurer, you need some control over *all* the finances of the charity that are in any way managed by your trustees. If you have several funds or projects, your accounts must reflect them all. Furthermore, many charities have groups that run their own finances, but which see themselves as part of the main charity. For example, a community association may run an older people's support group and may have an arts and drama club meeting on its premises. As the treasurer, you must be clear whether each such group is:

- legally part of your charity – if so, its work is under the control of the charity's trustees and its finances must be included in the published accounts of the charity; or
- an independent organisation simply using your premises – if so, it must not attempt to use your charity registration number and if its income is more than £5,000 (England and Wales) it will normally need to be registered as a charity in its own right.

This is also important when charities hand out funds to local groups. If you give money to independent groups, there must be a clear point when the grant ceases to be in the funds of your charity and control passes to the separate group. But if the main charity passes money to a group which is still legally part of that charity, your accounts will simply show a transfer between funds: no money has gone out of the charity as a whole.

A few charities also have separately constituted subsidiary organisations that are under their direct control, for example **trading subsidiary companies** (see chapter 11). In this case, the subsidiary has to prepare its own accounts, but they may then need to be included ('consolidated') into the accounts of the main charity (see 'Charities with subsidiaries' on page 118). If this applies you will need help from an accountant or **independent examiner** with experience of group accounts.

Charitable status

As explained above, many different organisations can be charities and not all charities are registered. There are currently six main forms of charitable status recognised in the UK.

- **Exempt charities** (England and Wales): a small number of bodies listed in Schedule 3 of the Charities Act 2011. They are mainly large national bodies whose charitable activities are regulated by a body other than the Charity Commission (for example, universities and major museums). Much of the Charities Act 2011 does not apply to exempt charities, but the Charities Statement of Recommended Practice (SORP) (see chapter 2) is still the normal basis for presenting the accounts, unless a more specialised SORP applies.

- **Excepted charities** (England and Wales): these are excepted from registration under section 30 of the Charities Act 2011 but they are still subject to other aspects of the Act, including the accounting rules. For example, charities whose annual income is £5,000 or less are excepted from registration. As a result of the changes made by the Charities Act 2006, the category of excepted charities is being greatly reduced and the majority of charities that were previously excepted (for example, places of worship, Scout and Guide groups and armed forces charities) will be required to register as charities in the normal way. However, this is being introduced gradually: at present only the formerly excepted charities with an income of more than £100,000 are required to register, then gradually over the years this limit will be reduced. This will also apply to formerly exempt charities such as CBSs.

- **Registered charities** in England and Wales: all other charities in England and Wales must be registered by the Charity Commission, and are given a registered charity number. This status must appear on many documents, including cheques, invoices, receipts and bills.

- **Scottish charities:** these are registered by OSCR and are given a Scottish charity number, beginning with 'SC'. It should be noted that charity registration is compulsory in Scotland – there is no £5,000 lower limit as in England and Wales. If a Scottish organisation chooses not to register, it is illegal for it to call itself a charity on any literature or documents.

- **Northern Irish charities** recognised by HMRC (**deemed list**): until 2013 all decisions on charitable status in Northern Ireland were made by HMRC and at the time of writing, a wide range of charities in

Northern Ireland remain in this category until they are registered with CCNI. Such organisations can describe themselves as 'recognised charities' (or, more accurately 'recognised as a charity for tax purposes') but must not use the term 'registered charity'. However, organisations on this list are deemed to be charities and CCNI can still exercise authority in the event of concerns – their status is thus similar to excepted charities in England and Wales.

- **Registered charities in Northern Ireland:** these are registered by CCNI and given a Northern Irish charity number beginning with 'NIC'. It should be noted that there is no lower limit for charity registration in Northern Ireland and no exceptions from registration for churches or other religious bodies. New charities formed in Northern Ireland since December 2013 must apply for registration with CCNI before they can seek tax recognition by HMRC. Northern Irish charities that were recognised by HMRC before then are required to register with CCNI when called forward to do so. By 2016, more than 5,000 existing charities had successfully registered with CCNI, though a number remain on the 'deemed list' to apply in due course.

So it is vital to appreciate that charitable status is not an optional 'badge'. Even in England and Wales, it is compulsory under the Charities Act 2011 for the trustees of a charitable organisation to apply for registration unless it is clearly exempted or excepted (and they are committing a breach of duty if they fail to do so). It follows that, once all the legislation is fully in force, any voluntary organisation in the UK will need to apply for charitable recognition unless:

(a) its aims fall clearly outside the headings of charitable purposes; or

(b) it clearly would not meet the test of public benefit; or

(c) it operates purely in England and Wales and has an income of £5,000 or less.

In the case of a CIO, the organisation only comes into being once it is registered with the Charity Commission (or CCNI, or OSCR in the case of an SCIO). So a CIO is a registered charity from the outset (and so there is no minimum income requirement for registration of a CIO). In this respect, CIOs are different from all the other legal forms – in other cases there is always a period between the organisation being formed and its formal recognition as a charity.

In the case of a charitable company, the registration as a CLG (with Companies House) and charity registration (with the Charity Commission, or OSCR, or CCNI) are completely separate; the charity must report each year to both regulators.

UK-wide issues

All six forms of charitable status mean that the organisation is a charity for the purpose of the law. Moreover, in terms of tax law, all UK charities have essentially the same tax concessions, as tax law is for most purposes determined UK-wide.

Since 2015 there have been a few small differences in Scotland – in particular the replacement of stamp duty with the Scottish Land and Buildings Transaction Tax, but even under this tax the charity exemptions extend to charities established outside Scotland. Further Scottish devolution may create additional tax differences, but charity law is already devolved, so it is unlikely that there will be any significant changes to charitable status.

However, there are some possible complications because of differences between tax law and charity law. Charitable status for UK tax purposes is determined by the English definition of charity and hence it is possible in theory that a Scottish charity could be registered with OSCR but fall outside the tax definition of a charity. Since 2010 there has also been a tax law requirement for charities to be managed by 'fit and proper persons'. But the definitions across the UK are so close (and, if anything, the Scottish and Northern Irish definitions are slightly tighter than they are in England and Wales) that, in practice, there is little risk of a well-run charity anywhere in the UK failing the tax definition of a charity.

If a charity's work spreads across several countries of the UK, its location for charity law is normally determined by the wording of its governing document, or if this is not specific, by the location of the majority of the trustees.

One important new development in recent years is that many UK-wide charities are now subject to **dual regulation**. This means that if a charity established under the law of England and Wales has regular activities in Scotland then, under the Charities and Trustee Investment (Scotland) Act 2005, it will need to be registered with OSCR *as well as* being registered with the Charity Commission. If this applies, the charity must account to OSCR as well as to the Charity Commission. Its accounts must then comply with the Scottish charity accounting rules, as well as the rules for England and Wales. In most respects the Scottish rules are tighter, so, if you are a treasurer or finance officer of a dual-registered charity, in general you should *follow the guidance for Scottish charities* throughout this book, even if only a small part of the charity's work is in Scotland.

If a charity simply fundraises in Scotland (for example, if you have members or supporters in Scotland, but do not have any regular use of premises in Scotland) registration with OSCR is not required, but all your literature must make clear the country where you are established. So, for example, if you are making use of this rule, rather than just putting 'Registered charity number xxxxxx' on your literature, take care to put 'Registered charity in England and Wales number xxxxxx'.

Note that there is no converse requirement: charities established under Scottish law and registered with OSCR do not have to register with the Charity Commission in order to operate in England or Wales.

The rules are slightly lighter in Northern Ireland – an external charity operating in Northern Ireland does not have to be registered on the main CCNI register but instead on a simpler register – known as the **section 167 register**, though this is not expected to start until at least 2018. But eventually, a UK-wide charity formed under English law will need to be registered with the Charity Commission, and with OSCR, and on the section 167 register with CCNI – and will have to make returns to all three regulators.

The Charity Commission, OSCR and CCNI

In England and Wales, much of the regulation of charities and many of the requirements for charity accounting – such as the Directions to Independent Examiners – are handled through the Charity Commission for England and Wales. (Note that this book refers to the Charity Commission for England and Wales as the 'Charity Commission' unless otherwise stated.) The Commission has various powers and duties as defined by the Charities Act 2011. It is a government department, but independent of direct day-to-day government control. All registered charities have to complete an annual form for the Commission, and the Commission has extensive powers to intervene to protect charitable funds where abuse appears to be taking place. OSCR has many similar powers in Scotland, and likewise CCNI in Northern Ireland. It is worth noting that the powers of the Charity Commission increased considerably as a result of the Charities (Protection and Social Investment) Act 2016. In particular, the Commission can now issue official warnings to charities, and can take extensive action if it considers trustees are acting improperly – even, in extreme cases, winding up a charity and transferring its assets to another charity.

Some charity treasurers mistakenly feel their task is largely about keeping the Charity Commission happy. This is misleading – the Commission's requirements are only one small part of a treasurer's role – as a charity exists for its beneficiaries, not for the Commission! But as a charity treasurer, you will in most cases need to ensure that your accounts are sent to the Commission each year (and/or to OSCR/CCNI) and you will probably be responsible for completing much of the annual return. However, you will also find the **charity regulators** are a helpful source of information and guidance, particularly in terms of their websites and publications – see 'Further reading' for more details.

If you are a treasurer of an excepted charity in England and Wales – which currently includes many places of worship with an income of less than £100,000 – you do not normally have to send accounts to the Charity Commission every year. But your charity is still subject to the Charities Act accounting provisions and almost all the Commission's guidance materials are just as relevant as for registered charities. The Charity Commission has the same powers to take action if it believes that charitable funds are at risk.

2 Accounts at different levels: the legal requirements

When someone asks to look at your accounts, this can have a number of meanings. The term 'accounts' can cover everything from the detailed books and records to the final published accounts, and anything in-between.

Levels of detail

For most charities, accounts will work at three levels of detail.

Accounting levels

Concept   *Official term*

THE BOOKS   **Accounting records**
Record of all transactions.
Must show the financial position of the charity at any time and be kept for six years. Must be seen by the charity's auditor or independent examiner – otherwise for internal use only.

INTERIM REPORTS   **Management accounts**
Typically reports for trustees or key members of staff to monitor progress and take financial decisions. Will not usually show individual transactions, but generally summarise figures for a period of less than a year. May show actuals against budgets and possibly future projections. For internal use only.

PUBLISHED YEAR END ACCOUNTS   **Financial statements**
Show financial position of whole charity.   **or annual accounts**
                                                                    or just **the accounts**
All charities, no matter how small, must produce published accounts, which must be approved by the trustees. The published accounts must include a report by an auditor or independent examiner (unless the charity's income is under £25,000 in England and Wales). The annual accounts should always be circulated with the annual report. They are a public document – anyone can ask for a copy.

The accounts start with the basic books of the charity, where every **transaction** – every receipt, payment or other entry – is recorded individually. The formal term for these is your **accounting records**. As a treasurer or finance officer, you must ensure books are kept up to date with all the relevant entries – chapter 5 explores ways of handling the bookkeeping. The books are the starting point for all other financial analysis.

This is a fundamental difference between charity accounting and personal accounting. With your personal household accounts you can, if you choose, just look at your bank balance and count the cash in your purse or wallet without ever recording the actual income and expenditure. In fact, even some self-employed business people manage to work with minimal records (although this can make it hard to justify profit figures to HMRC). But in a charity, the trustees are handling other people's money and you have both a legal and a moral obligation to keep detailed records of the income as it comes in, and exactly how it is spent.

However, if you have more than about 20 or 30 transactions, it is difficult for anyone to get an idea of how the charity is doing just by looking at the books. You need some way of summarising the records into a form that will be meaningful for taking decisions. Such internal summaries of the books are called **management accounts**. Normally they will show the total income under headings such as 'donations, sales, bank interest', and the expenditure under headings such as 'salaries, premises, printing' and so on, rather than listing every transaction. If you have several funds or projects (see chapter 3) the management accounts will also be broken down by fund. Where budgets have been agreed, management accounts are often presented showing actual figures compared with budgets (see chapter 9).

One of the important tasks of the treasurer or finance officer is to produce regular management accounts for the trustees. In a small charity this may be just a one-page summary, but regular meaningful financial information is essential for decision-making.

The third form of accounts is the final year end published accounts – the **annual accounts** (see chapter 7). One of the conditions of charitable status is that your organisation must, once a year, make available a full set of accounts reporting the income and expenditure for the year, the balances at year end, and the different funds involved. The annual accounts should normally be accompanied by the **trustees' annual report** (see chapter 7) – so the full document is usually called the **annual report and accounts**.

If your organisation is a registered charity in England and Wales then (except for those with an income of £25,000 or less) the annual report and accounts must be sent to the Charity Commission. (For CIOs, there is no lower limit.) Likewise, if the charity is registered in Scotland the accounts must be sent to OSCR and similarly if the charity is registered with CCNI in Northern Ireland. Charitable companies must *also* file an annual report and accounts and annual return at Companies House (for which there is a fee).

But, more importantly, copies of the annual report and accounts must be made available to *anyone* on request. You can make a small charge to cover copying and postage if necessary, although in practice many charities wish to be as open as possible and publish their annual report and accounts on their website. But even if you do not do this, for charities registered with the Charity Commission with an income of more than £25,000, accounts are available from the Commission's website (most charities nowadays file the accounts electronically as a PDF, or if you submit a paper copy it will be scanned by the Commission). Different formats of accounts apply to different sizes of charity, but even a tiny charity with an income of only £100 a year must still produce published accounts – there is no such thing as a secret charity, whatever its size.

The time limit for filing accounts is generally nine months after the year end (this is the time limit for charities registered with OSCR and for charitable companies). For a charity with a 31 March year end, and allowing for Christmas holidays, this means that in practice you need to submit your accounts no later than about 15 December. However, charities registered *only* with the Charity Commission or CCNI can take up to ten months. But an organised charity should be able to submit accounts well before these deadlines: funders will often check the relevant regulator's website (Charity Commission, OSCR or CCNI), and delays in filing accounts can easily affect future support.

The books and management accounts will normally be the responsibility of the treasurer and any staff with a finance role. As a treasurer or finance officer, you may have the task of *drafting* the final accounts, but *approving* the published accounts is one of the key actions of the trustees as a whole in taking responsibility for the affairs of the charity.

The legal framework and the SORP

Charity accounts are governed extensively by law, as summarised in the following box. In most respects, the rules on charity accounting are more extensive than those for commercial accounts: this is because charities are entrusted with other people's money and have a duty to use those funds for public benefit. Charity accounting requirements have changed enormously since the early 1990s, and have also changed further in each year from 2005 to 2016; even many professional accountants, if they are not charity specialists, may be unaware of the full implications.

The basis of the law on charity accounting

England and Wales

- Charities Act 2011 (Part 8)
- Charities (Accounts and Reports) Regulations 2008*
- Charities SORP (see below)
- Charity Commission's directions and guidance (in some areas these have the force of law, especially the Directions to Independent Examiners)

*An update to the 2008 Regulations was due to take effect from 1 January 2015, but this had still not been issued by the end of 2016, so at the time of writing the 2008 Regulations still apply – see next page.

Scotland

- Charities and Trustee Investment (Scotland) Act 2005
- Charities Accounts (Scotland) Regulations 2006 (as amended)
- Charities SORP (see below)
- Guidance from OSCR may also be helpful (but it does not have the force of law)

Northern Ireland

- Charities Act (Northern Ireland) 2008
- The Charities (Accounts and Reports) Regulations (Northern Ireland) 2015
- Charities SORP (see below)
- CCNI Directions and Guidance

The Charities SORP

- Statement of Recommended Practice on Accounting and Reporting by Charities. This is published by the Charity Commission/OSCR with approval by the Financial Reporting Council. Various versions of the SORP apply at different dates – see the text opposite and chapter 7 for more details. The SORP applies throughout the UK and to all charities, including charitable companies.

(See 'Further reading' for sources of these documents.)

In England and Wales, most current charity law comes from the Charities Act 2011 which, either directly or by regulations, gives considerable detail on what a charity must do in terms of accounting. In Scotland, the 2005 Act includes a general power to make rules on charity accounting, but all the specifics are in the Charities Accounts (Scotland) Regulations 2006.

In Northern Ireland the 2008 Act has many similarities to England and Wales with some requirements in the Act itself and other issues left to regulations. In 2014 CCNI used its powers to make interim reporting requirements, followed by full accounting and reporting regulations under the 2008 Act which took effect for financial years starting from 1 January 2016. However, these requirements are only compulsory for registered charities in Northern Ireland and, as explained in chapter 1, not all Northern Irish charities are yet registered with CCNI. But in the meantime, all charities in Northern Ireland are strongly recommended to follow this framework – indeed it is likely that funders will expect charities which are not yet registered to meet the same **accounting standards** as those that apply to organisations which are on the CCNI register.

For charitable companies, the legal framework for accounts depends on the Companies Act 2006, rather than the legislation shown in the box on the previous page, but company accounts must follow relevant accounting standards and the Charities SORP is an essential standard where the company is a charity.

In all parts of the UK, a major addition to the regulations comes from the **Statement of Recommended Practice on Accounting and Reporting by Charities**, usually abbreviated to the 'Charities SORP' or just 'SORP' – often with the relevant year to refer to the latest version, for example 'SORP 2005' or 'SORP 2015'. In practice, people often talk about the whole regime as the SORP, as in the question 'Are your accounts SORP-compliant?'.

There were two versions of SORP 2015, the 'FRSSE SORP' which was for medium-sized charities whose underlying accounting principles are based on the *Financial Reporting Standard for Smaller Entities* and the **FRS102 SORP** which is for charities following the full Financial Reporting Standard 102 as their basis for financial reporting. The FRSSE SORP was slightly simpler and could be applied by most charities with incomes of up to £6.5 million. However, the FRSSE itself is no longer available as an accounting standard and so the FRSSE SORP has been phased out (but see the appendix on page 193 if you are concerned with financial years that began before 2016). For years starting from 1 January 2016 onwards, the only current SORP is the FRS102 SORP (as amended by *SORP Update Bulletin No 1* issued in early 2016). This book therefore focuses on the FRS102 SORP as updated – at least in terms of its use by smaller and medium-sized charities.

Nevertheless, for non-company charities (trusts, associations or CIOs) in England and Wales, as noted in the box on page 22, new regulations under the Charities Act 2011 for SORP 2015 had still not been made two years later. The 2008 Regulations, which remain in force, refer to SORP 2005 – even though it is an out-of-date standard! So some charities in England and Wales are keeping to SORP 2005 as in the Regulations. For more on this crucial choice see 'Which SORP to use?' in chapter 7 (page 108). (There is also more on the changing SORPs and the interaction with accounting standards in chapter 10 and in the appendix on page 193.)

You might ask: does a charity have to follow the SORP as the title of the SORP includes the word 'recommended'? Can you ignore the SORP if you wish? In fact it is compulsory in many respects, except for smaller charities producing **receipts and payments** (R&P) accounts (see 'Accruals or receipts and payments?', page 30). This is for several reasons. Firstly, any accounts designed to give a **true and fair view** (see page 96) should comply with relevant accounting standards. (For example, with charitable companies, the true and fair view is a requirement of the Companies Act 2006 and with other charities it is a requirement of the accounting regulations.) Secondly, in England and Wales, the Charity Commission has stated that 'charities preparing accruals accounts should follow the accounting requirements set out in the applicable statement of recommended practice (SORP)'[1] and in theory the Commission could use its powers to institute inquiries if they do not. Thirdly, the various sets of accounting regulations mentioned above include extensive references to the SORP so, in practice, a large proportion of the SORP is actually made into law. Furthermore, for charities following the SORP, the regulations require that any departures from the SORP must be disclosed by specific notes to the accounts. Finally, most funders nowadays expect SORP-compliant accounts, at least for charities with an income of more than £250,000 (and sometimes below this).

So, except for small charities just using R&P accounts, you ignore the SORP at your peril – and in fact, even for R&P accounting, some points in the SORP (particularly on the trustees' annual report) can still be very helpful.

Thus, in each regime the rules are based on a combination of primary legislation (Acts of Parliament), secondary legislation (regulations issued as statutory instruments) and other standards such as the SORP. But although charity treasurers need an overview of the rules, this book is not attempting to cover the full detail (for more information see 'Further reading').

In some charities there may be additional rules imposed by parent bodies. For example, many national charities with independent local branches require certain information to be shown in the branch accounts as a condition of belonging to the national body or to comply with other legislation, for example the Church Accounting Regulations in the Church of England.[2] But such rules are always additional to the main regime; they cannot override the SORP or relax rules required by law.

What does the law require?

Referring back to the three levels of accounts, in relation to the *books*, the law requires that all charities must keep proper accounting records 'sufficient to show and explain ... at any time, with reasonable accuracy, the financial position of the charity'[3], including records of their receipts, payments, **assets** and **liabilities**. They must also be sufficient to allow the production of proper accounts at year end.

It follows that what is sometimes called 'shoebox accounting', where the treasurer or bookkeeper throws everything in a box and hopes someone else will sort it out at year end, is not only unwise, it is actually illegal. With a shoebox approach there will be many times when the financial position cannot be ascertained.

The law also requires that the records must be kept for six years from the end of the year concerned. If there are changes of treasurer, be sure that the last six years' books and papers are passed on and not destroyed. Also remember that the full records include the bills and vouchers and donation records – not just the entries in the books.

However, the law does not prescribe how the books are to be kept. You are free to use any method of bookkeeping, manual or computerised, that will enable the charity to comply with the overall requirements. With computer systems, ensure you have full printouts at year end. Although some organisations dispense with paper records, for a small charity it is risky to rely on six-year-old computer backups, given the rate of change of hardware and software.

Remember, too, that the full accounting records may be divided between several sets of books or computer systems. If you have staff, your payroll records are part of the books of the charity. If you have people giving individual donations – for example, under a Gift Aid scheme (see chapter 12) – it is unlikely that your main books will show every separate gift, particularly where donors are giving weekly or monthly, so your fundraising records must also be retained. (The need for donor confidentiality does not replace the need for proper records.)

At the second level, the **management accounts**, there are no specific legal requirements. The trustees have a duty to manage the charity properly and, except in a tiny organisation, this will mean monitoring the finances more than once a year, so some kind of interim financial reports are essential (see chapter 9). However, it is for the trustees of each charity to decide what is appropriate.

Most of the law on charity accounting relates to the final level, the published **annual accounts** – references in law to the 'accounts' of a charity mean the published year end accounts. Much of the Regulations and SORP are concerned with the final accounts; chapter 7 outlines some of the steps involved. However, the rules sensibly recognise that a small local charity cannot be expected to produce the same sort of annual accounts as a large national organisation, so the regime has a series of thresholds.

The thresholds

Much of the charity accounting regime is determined by the total income of the charity. For smaller charities, the regime is not particularly onerous; as a charity grows in income, the rules become more demanding. But it is vital to appreciate that all charities, no matter how small, are affected by some rules: occasionally one hears people saying, 'I don't need to bother about the Charities Act because our income is under £100,000' – unfortunately this is a serious misunderstanding.

Table 2.1 shows the main accounting requirements for financial years starting from 2016 onwards for charities in England and Wales (see the appendix to this book for earlier years). Note that there are different rules for charities with assets of more than £3.26 million – though smaller charities are unlikely to be affected by this unless you have a very valuable building or a large investment portfolio. Table 2.2 gives the details for charities registered in Scotland, and table 2.3 shows the rules for Northern Ireland. Note that in each case charitable companies have an additional requirement: they cannot use R&P accounts even if the income is very small. But remember that CIOs and SCIOs (see 'Legal forms', page 8) are *not* companies, so the rules for non-company charities apply. (Note that if a charity is dual-registered – with the Charity Commission and with OSCR – the Scottish rules are generally stricter so these should be followed even if the charity is based in England or Wales. However, external charities operating in Northern Ireland do not face additional rules on the charity's overall accounts – see 'UK-wide issues', page 15.)

In the tables, each level shows the *additional* requirements at that income level; the requirements at the lower levels also apply. The thresholds are based on the total income of the charity for the year, considering all funds and projects together (even if some keep their own books). Under the latest changes, it is no longer necessary to consider expenditure thresholds, or figures from prior years. However, some of the details in the tables only start from 2016 – if you are dealing with earlier years, see the appendix on page 193 for a summary of the differences.

Note that thresholds may change from time to time: be sure to keep up to date with relevant announcements.

Table 2.1 Minimum accounting requirements for charities subject to the law of England and Wales

Income of charity	Minimum requirements for charities with no more than £3.26 million assets	Minimum requirements where charity has over £3.26 million assets
All charities	• Must keep proper accounting records (retained for six years). • Must produce an annual report and accounts: the accounts can be on an R&P basis (*except for charitable companies* which must use the accruals basis and SORP format whatever the level of income). • Must provide accounts to the Charity Commission if requested and to members of the public on request.	
> £5,000	• Must apply to become a registered charity (unless exempt or excepted) – but all CIOs are registered. • If registered, must complete the Charity Commission's annual database update.	
> £25,000	• Accounts must be independently examined (see chapter 8). • Annual report and accounts must be sent to the Charity Commission and the charity must complete the Charity Commission's annual return (for CIOs this applies even for those with an income of under £25,000).	
> £250,000	• Full accruals accounting required following FRS102 SORP. • Presentation of accounts must comply with Regulations – with statement of financial activities (SOFA), balance sheet and notes (SORP format) – but simplified SOFA headings are permitted. • Independent examiner must be professionally qualified.	• Full accruals accounting required following FRS102 SORP. • Presentation of accounts must comply with Regulations – with SOFA, balance sheet and notes (SORP format) – full SORP compliance required including use of functional headings on the SOFA and statement of cash flows. • Full audit required.
> £500,000	• Full SORP compliance required, including use of functional headings on the SOFA and statement of cash flows.	
> £1 million	• Full audit required.	

See the text for explanation of terms used in this table. The table applies to financial years starting on or after 1 January 2016 – see the appendix on page 193 for earlier years. It assumes a non-company charity subject to the SORP has elected to use the 'true and fair override' (see page 109) to follow the FRS102 SORP 2015 but slightly simpler arrangements apply if the trustees opt to keep to SORP 2005 as in the Regulations.

Table 2.2   Minimum accounting requirements for charities registered in Scotland

Income of charity	Minimum requirements for charities with no more than £3.26 million assets	Minimum requirements where charity has over £3.26 million assets
All charities	• Must apply to OSCR to be registered if making any claim to charitable status in Scotland. • Must keep proper accounting records (retained for six years). • Must produce an annual report and accounts: the accounts can be on an R&P basis, but the detailed Scottish regulations for R&P accounts must be followed (*except for charitable companies* which must use the accruals basis and SORP format whatever the level of income). • Accounts must be independently examined (see chapter 8). • Must submit accounts to OSCR and provide to members of the public on request.	
≥ £250,000	• Accruals accounting required following FRS102 SORP. • Presentation of accounts must comply with Regulations – with SOFA, balance sheet and notes (SORP format) – but simplified SOFA headings are permitted. • Independent examiner must be professionally qualified (this also applies to charities with an income of less than £250,000 if the accounts are on an accruals basis).	• Full accruals accounting required following FRS102 SORP. • Presentation of accounts must comply with Regulations – with SOFA, balance sheet and notes (SORP format). • Full audit required. • Full SORP compliance required including use of functional headings on the SOFA and statement of cash flows.
≥ £500,000	• Full audit required. • Full SORP compliance required including use of functional headings on the SOFA and statement of cash flows.	

See the text for explanation of terms used in this table. The table applies to accounting years starting on or after 1 January 2016 – see the appendix on page 193 for earlier years.

The requirements in this table apply to all charities registered with OSCR even if based outside Scotland – see UK-wide issues in chapter 1.

Table 2.3 Minimum accounting requirements for charities registered in Northern Ireland

Income of charity	Minimum requirements regardless of assets[1]
All charities	• Must apply to CCNI to be registered (however, existing charities can wait until called forward to apply). • Must keep proper accounting records (retained for six years). • Must produce an annual report and accounts: the accounts can be on an R&P basis (*except for charitable companies* which must use the accruals basis and SORP format whatever the level of income). • Accounts must be independently examined (see chapter 8). • Must submit accounts to CCNI and to members of the public on request.
> £250,000	• Accruals accounting required following SORP. • Presentation of accounts must comply with Regulations – with SOFA, balance sheet and notes (SORP format) – but simplified SOFA headings are permitted. • Independent examiner must be professionally qualified.
> £500,000	• Full audit required. • Full SORP compliance required including use of functional headings on the SOFA and statement of cash flows.

See the text for explanation of terms used in this table.

[1] *For charities registered in Northern Ireland, the accounting requirements are not affected by the level of the charity's assets.*

The requirements in this table apply to financial years beginning 1 January 2016 onwards – see the appendix on page 193 for earlier years.

This table only applies to charities registered in Northern Ireland. Eventually, charities based elsewhere but operating in Northern Ireland will be included on a separate section 167 register with CCNI – these will have different accounting requirements (see UK-wide issues in chapter 1).

Note that these are *minimum* requirements at each level. A charity is free to do more if it wishes. For example, a charity with an income of around £90,000 that is bidding for a grant which would take it over £250,000 may find that producing full SORP-compliant accounts even at the current income level helps to demonstrate that it has the professionalism to expand.

The main difference for charitable companies is that there is no provision for R&P accounts; accruals accounts (see overleaf) must be produced no matter how small the income. However, annual reports and accounts for companies must also comply with company law, which in some cases includes additional requirements beyond the normal requirements of the SORP (the SORP includes a section on this issue).

Note that, in Scotland and Northern Ireland, some of the thresholds are lower – in particular even the smallest charities, with an income of less than £25,000, must have their accounts independently examined and must submit them to OSCR or CCNI as appropriate.

Accruals or receipts and payments?

In terms of producing the accounts, the biggest difference is whether to prepare them on an R&P basis or on an accruals basis. For charities that are not companies (including CIOs), the R&P basis is allowed throughout the UK for those with an income of up to £250,000; above this (and for charitable companies whatever their income) accruals accounts are compulsory.

It is vital to note that whether you use R&P or **accruals accounting**, the law has requirements about the presentation of the accounts. For example, even if the income of the charity is within the income range where R&P accounts are allowed, you must produce either:

- R&P accounts complying with the Charities Act; or
- accruals accounts complying with the Act, Regulations and SORP.

In either case, there are two main reports: one showing what has come into and gone out of the charity over the year (often described as a 'movements' report), and another showing what is in hand at year end (often described as a 'snapshot' report). The basic requirements are described below – see chapter 7 for further details.

Receipts and payments accounting

(a) **R&P account** (broken down by funds).
(b) **Statement of assets and liabilities (SOAL)** (or a **statement of balances** if following the Scottish rules).
(c) **Notes to the accounts** are also needed in Scotland (in England/Wales and Northern Ireland, notes are not legally required with R&P accounts, except in certain cases with CIOs, although they can be very helpful).

Accruals accounting

(a) **Statement of financial activities (SOFA)**.
(b) **Balance sheet**.
(c) **Statement of cash flows** (required for charities with an income of more than £500,000 following the FRS102 SORP).
(d) Notes to the accounts.

The SOFA was invented specifically for charity accounting: it is basically an income and expenditure account divided into columns for the different types of funds. (The funds are explained in chapter 3; an example SOFA is shown on page 112.) Once people get used to the SOFA they usually find it very helpful in getting a picture of a whole charity. The layout of a charity's SOFA, balance sheet and the various information needed in the notes are covered in some detail in the Regulations and SORP.

With R&P accounts, the rules are less detailed: in general, provided that the different funds are clearly separated, the presentation of the year's receipts and payments is quite flexible (although the rules are more specific in Scotland). But even though you do not have to do a full balance sheet with R&P accounts, the charity must be able to produce a list of its assets (things the charity has – for example, money in the bank or items of equipment) and liabilities at year end (such as unpaid bills): hence the need for the SOAL.

Accountants often regard R&P accounting and accruals accounting as distinct worlds, but in a charity many normal transactions, such as receiving a donation or paying wages, will be treated the same in either case. The main differences relate to **debtors**, **creditors** and **fixed assets**.

For example, suppose your charity rents out rooms to other organisations and had raised a substantial bill for room hire that has not been paid by the year end of 31 March 2017 – this would constitute a debtor in the year end accounts. With R&P accounts, you would simply list the debtor on your SOAL in the 2016/17 accounts, but you would not actually record a receipt until the following year (2017/18), when you were paid.

But with accruals accounts, you would say, 'This rent was income earned by the charity in the year 2016/17, and it should thus be included as part of the charity's income on the SOFA for that year' (balanced by a debtor on the balance sheet – because at that stage the money is not in the bank). Then in 2017/18, when the room rents are paid, you would just make a transfer from debtors to bank – you would not show any new income, as the income had already been recorded in 2016/17 (or, to use accountants' language, the income was **recognised** in the earlier year).

If your charity has incurred significant expenses during the year that have not been paid at year end, you would record a year end creditor on the same lines, using the R&P or accruals approach, as relevant.

Tangible fixed assets are items expected to last several years, for example buildings, computers or vehicles. With R&P accounting, you would record the whole cost of such an item at the time of purchase (and list it on the SOAL for as long as it was kept). But with accruals accounting, you would show the item on the balance sheet and then *depreciate* it over several years. So on each year's SOFA, only that year's **depreciation** appears as expenditure, and the cost is thus spread over the expected life of the item.

The idea with accruals accounting is that the accounts are more likely to show a true and fair view of the income that has *accrued* to the charity for the year and of the expenses incurred in running the charity. Occasionally, if there are few debtors, creditors or fixed assets, the figures will be almost the same, whether you use R&P or accruals accounts. But R&P accounts can sometimes show huge fluctuations from year to year: for example, if a grant was paid just before year end one year and just after year end in the following year, or if one year included the purchase of a large fixed asset. Obviously accruals accounting means a little more work, but it allows much more meaningful comparisons to be made from year to year.

If your income is more than £250,000 (or if your charity is a company) you have no choice and you must use accruals accounts, with the SORP format for your final accounts (SOFA and so on).

Below this limit you have a choice between the R&P or accruals basis, but it is best to be consistent for a number of years. Remember the choice affects both:

• how you record certain transactions (where debtors, creditors or fixed assets are involved); and
• the format in which the final accounts are presented.

However, you must use one approach or the other – it is not possible to choose R&P accounts but then, for example, to include some depreciation in the R&P account. Depreciation is a concept which only applies to accruals accounts, so if you want to include depreciation in the figures, the whole accounts must be on an accruals basis and in SORP format.

Issues of accruals accounting are considered further in chapter 10.

3 Charitable funds

If you were keeping the accounts of a business, apart from certain special professions, you would have just one **fund**: the profit and loss account. All sales income goes into, and all business expenses are charged to, the profit and loss account. Larger businesses may choose to divide the profit and loss into departments, each with their own cost codes, so they can measure the profitability of each area, but this is purely a matter of internal management. At the end of the year, the profits are added together because they all belong to the same owners or shareholders.

In a charity, matters can be very different. Most charities start with one fund, usually called the **general fund**, which receives donations and from which the expenses of the charity are paid. The report of this fund forms an income and expenditure account (or a receipts and payments (R&P) account if you are using R&P accounting). At the level of management accounts, the income and expenditure account in an NFP organisation is equivalent to the profit and loss account in a business.

But it is likely that, before long, the charity will have a special appeal (say, for building renovations) or will want to launch a new project, and will start to seek funding specifically for that work.

If this is successful, and grants or donations are received specifically for the new project, then of course the relationship of trust (explained in chapter 1) means that the trustees must ensure the money is only spent on the purposes for which it was given. This requires careful bookkeeping, because clearly the new project needs its own income and expenditure account, separate from that of the general fund, otherwise there is no way of tracking whether money received for the new project is really spent on the purposes intended.

The new project thus needs to be treated as a separate fund in the accounts – a **restricted fund** – because there are restrictions on how it can be used. If money given for the new roof appeal were spent on the charity's general running costs, those who had given to the appeal (whether individuals or large grant-makers) would, rightly, be concerned; they could ask for their money back, and the trustees would be guilty of a breach of trust.

Sooner or later, other special projects and appeals will come along, each of which needs its own restricted fund if it is supported by grants or donations given specifically for that purpose. Even very straightforward local organisations will often have two or three funds; large charities can sometimes find themselves managing hundreds of funds.

What is a fund?

A fund is essentially a pot of money or resources held for specific purposes.

As explained, most charities will have a general fund which can be used for any purpose so long as it is within the charity's overall objects – this is known as an **unrestricted fund**, i.e. there are no external restrictions on it (apart from the requirement that all funds of the charity must be used to support the charity's objects).

Restricted funds are pots of money or resources where there is some external condition on how the fund can be used. The condition could arise in one of two ways:

- from the way you asked for the money in the first place (as in 'Please give to our new roof appeal'); or
- from a condition imposed by a funder or donor (as in 'This grant must only be used for the salary of the outreach worker').

Many people use some measure of **fund accounting** for their personal household finances: if you put aside money into different jars (or different bank accounts) labelled 'holiday money' or 'children's clothes', you are in fact doing fund accounting. In this case, the funds would be classed as **designated funds**, because you have decided to designate each jar for a certain purpose; however, you could in principle raid your holiday fund for another purpose if there was something more urgent. Designated funds, like general funds, are part of the general class of unrestricted funds. But, on the other hand, if someone else has made a condition – for example, if your aunt gave you a cheque for your birthday and said, 'I want you to spend this on some nice new clothes' – then it would be a restricted fund; spending it on something else would be a breach of trust between you and your aunt.

Quite often charities will want to set aside some money from general funds into a designated fund – for example, many charities with buildings to maintain have a 'repairs fund' and every year make a transfer into it from the general fund. Then, when a major repair arises, hopefully there will be enough in the repairs fund to cover the cost, even though it may be more than they could afford in a single year.

The difference between a designated fund and a restricted fund depends on how the fund came to be set up. If it was an internal decision by the charity trustees to set aside the money, it is a designated fund. If necessary, your trustees could decide that the money was more urgently needed for something else. But if the money was externally given on specific conditions, you cannot use it for something else without getting permission from the donor(s) or funder(s) concerned.

This has implications for fundraising – see chapter 12. Obviously people will often give more generously if they know their money will be used for a specific purpose and some funders, such as the National Lottery distributors, will generally only support specific projects, so their grants are almost always restricted (except perhaps with a start-up grant for a new organisation). But if you allow fundraisers to offer a slightly different project to every supporter, it can become almost impossible to track all the separate funds involved.

There is a further type of fund only found in certain charities, known as an **endowment fund**. This is even more restricted. In the past, these were often just called 'capital funds' but sometimes charities have restricted grants for capital purchases, so it is clearer to use the term 'endowment fund'. Endowment funds arise when someone gives money to the charity and says, 'I want you to invest this, and use the income for certain purposes, but you mustn't spend the capital'. Many grant-making charities derive most of their resources from endowment funds set up by someone who wanted to create a long-term resource that could continue making grants long after their death. But sometimes charities will appeal specifically for an endowment fund: for example, charities raising money for specialist medical equipment often have to raise an endowment fund to provide for the running costs of the equipment.

In such cases, the income of the endowment fund – for example, interest or share dividends – is posted to another fund (either restricted or unrestricted) so that the income can be spent on the required purpose. But the value of the endowment fund itself can go up or down if the assets in the fund (e.g. shares) change in value over the year.

Endowment funds are further divided into **permanent endowments** and **expendable endowments**. Permanent endowment means just that – the capital value of the fund cannot be spent at all (except by following special procedures in charity law, which generally need the consent of the Charity Commission, OSCR or CCNI). However, an expendable endowment is normally kept as a capital fund, but can be spent if the trustees specifically resolve to do so.

Figure 3.1 shows the different types of funds in the way that they are classified by the SORP. Strictly speaking, a normal restricted fund where the income can be spent (within the terms of the restriction) should be called a **restricted income fund**.

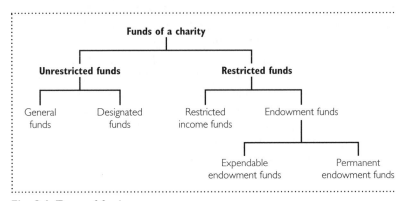

Fig. 3.1 Types of fund

The status of a fund depends on how it came to the charity in the first place. For example, if the charity received a legacy in someone's will which specified that it was to be invested to make grants for a specific purpose, the legacy itself is clearly intended to be invested, not spent, and would thus be classed as a permanent endowment. But it is common nowadays if a donor sets up a new grant-making charity to specify that the initial large gift used to establish the foundation is to be held as an expendable endowment: this gives flexibility to the trustees. Because it is an endowment they are under no obligation to spend the funds quickly – they can invest them for the longer term. But if they decide one year to make grants which come to more than the investment income, they could resolve to spend part of the expendable endowment itself.

Care is needed in the wording of appeals – not all capital appeals lead to capital/endowment funds. If you invite donations for capital items which will only have a limited life (for example, to buy vehicles or computers for operational use) the fund will eventually be fully spent once the purchases have been depreciated to nil – so this would be a restricted income fund. But if you are appealing to buy a permanent asset such as a freehold building to be used by the charity in perpetuity, the funds received – and subsequently invested in the building – would usually be creating a permanent endowment. (These sort of issues are worth discussing in advance with your **independent examiner** or **auditor** – see chapter 8.)

With R&P accounting, the balance of a fund is just the money in the fund. But with accruals accounting, any fund can comprise a mixture of money and/or other assets and liabilities. The balance of a fund could, for example, be made up entirely from the value of a building, or a debt due from a third party. However, even with R&P accounting, the statement of assets and liabilities (SOAL) should indicate which assets belong to which funds.

Multi-fund accounting

The need to account for a number of separate funds is probably the biggest issue that distinguishes charity accounting from business accounting.

You may find, for example, that you need many more categories for income and expenditure than you initially thought. It is no good having just one income category for donations: you need to distinguish general (unrestricted) donations, donations for the new roof fund, donations for the outreach fund and so on. On the expenditure side, if you have staff working on different projects with separate funders, it is no good having one expenditure category for salaries: you need to distinguish general fund salary costs, outreach salary costs and so on. In practice, every income or expenditure category needs to be clearly labelled with the fund to which it relates.

Provided that your books are structured in this way (see 'Analysed cashbook (multiple funds)' on page 60), it is not too difficult to draw out the relevant figures and produce a separate income and expenditure account for each fund, showing what has come in and what has gone out purely on that fund. You may need this for reporting to funders, but it is also vital so that your trustees can monitor each fund separately. Sometimes a charity will find itself relatively well-off in cash terms, but if nearly all the money relates to restricted funds, the position in the general fund may be very tight.

Some charities try to avoid proper fund accounting during the year and leave it to an accountant to sort out at year end. But this can be disastrous: you can easily find you have been spending money that a fund does not have. At the end of the day, if money given for restricted funds has been spent on other purposes, your trustees will have committed a breach of trust. A number of charities have collapsed because the lack of fund accounting meant that no one realised until too late that the general fund was negative and all the cash related to restricted funds.

However, one crucial issue for fund accounting is that a restricted fund will generally continue for more than one accounting year: money given for the new roof or the new outreach worker may not be spent until the next year or later. In that case, in your books you need to be able to work out at year end the balance on the restricted fund (i.e. the income for that fund, less the expenses already incurred) and carry it forward as a restricted 'pot' of resources into next year's accounts. This is clearly very different from the situation described at the start of this chapter, for departments of a business, where all the profits would come together at year end.

Most conventional training for bookkeepers assumes that there will be a single brought forward figure for 'reserves' at the start of an accounting year, but clearly in a charity with more than one fund, you need a *separate figure for each fund* for the balance brought forward at the start of the year. (We will look at the implications of this in chapter 5.) When producing an income and expenditure account for a fund, it needs to show not just the income and expenditure for the year, but also the balance brought into the fund at the start of the year (unless it is a new fund). Similarly, if the project has to continue the following year, you may need the fund to show a substantial balance carried forward at year end, and this needs to be considered when budgeting.

Do we need separate bank accounts?

Many people think fund accounting is easily solved by having a separate bank account for each fund. Sometimes funders seem to imply this, by saying they want their grant held in a separate account, but they usually just mean a separate fund.

However, as you will have seen from the explanation above, provided that your books are properly labelled to show the income and expenditure for each fund, and provided you have a separate 'balance forward' figure for each fund at year end, you do not need separate bank accounts to keep track of different funds. This is the same whether the accounts are on an R&P or an accruals basis.

In some cases a very small organisation with limited bookkeeping skills may find separate bank accounts helpful. But once you have more than a couple of funds it can become totally unmanageable. If you have reasonable sums in hand at any one time you will probably want a deposit account as well as a current account – this means two bank accounts for each fund. Then, if you need petty cash, you will have to apply the same principle and have a separate petty cash tin for each fund.

It can soon get to the point that a charity with just 8 funds will have money held in 24 places. Ensuring that payments are made from the right account becomes a nightmare. If a bill arrives that needs to be split between more than one fund, you will have to arrange payments from multiple bank accounts. Once a payment is inadvertently made from the wrong account, getting everything sorted out is much worse than managing with one bank account in the first place.

Also, particularly when interest rates are low, you will normally find you can get more bank interest if you have one deposit or investment account and just keep enough money in a current account for the short-term requirements of the charity as a whole. (See chapters 4 and 12 for more on managing investments and investment income.)

Similarly, where you need petty cash, one cash tin is fine, so long as all petty cash expenses are clearly marked to show the fund to which they relate (and from a security point of view this is much more manageable).

Transfers between funds

Fund accounting sometimes requires a special transaction in the books – an **inter-fund transfer**. Clearly this is unique to charity accounting, so you will not find it in normal bookkeeping textbooks.

An inter-fund transfer arises when money or resources need to be transferred from one fund to another. You might feel that this goes against the principles of fund accounting, and certainly such transfers cannot be made on a whim, but there are several situations where such transfers are needed.

We have already considered the case of transferring money from a general fund to a designated fund (for example, a fund for long-term repairs); this is a simple example of an inter-fund transfer. However, sometimes trustees will want to transfer funds from the general fund to a restricted fund where a new project is being partly funded by an external grant, but where the charity has agreed to support it partly from general funds.

Trustees cannot, however, restrict money artificially. It is fine to make a funds transfer from unrestricted funds into a restricted fund if it is essential to prevent the restricted fund going into deficit. But if trustees simply wish to put funds aside for a specific purpose, the transfer will be made to a designated fund, *not* to a restricted fund.

However, transfers can sometimes be made from a restricted fund to a general fund, if the funder has agreed. For example, the costs of a new project may include a management fee to cover the general overheads of the charity in running the project (for more details see 'Managing core costs: apportioning overheads and full cost recovery', page 50). If it was clearly agreed with the funder that part of the grant would be spent on these management costs, a transfer of the management fee can be made from the restricted fund to the general fund. (An alternative is to split all costs between funds in the first place, but where funding for a project includes a provision for general overheads, a funds transfer is usually clearer.) Likewise, a decision by trustees to 'spend' resources in an expendable endowment fund should normally be recorded as a funds transfer from the endowment fund to the general fund.

If the different funds are held in the same bank account, a funds transfer is just a 'paper' entry. However, it is, of course, a very important entry, and should only be made if specifically agreed by the trustees. In the books, a funds transfer is, in effect, expenditure from one fund which becomes income to another fund – but of course there is no income or expenditure by the charity as a whole.

The importance of this is shown in the year end accounts, where transfers between funds must appear as a separate line on the SOFA (if you are doing accruals accounting), so they are not confused with external income or expenditure (see figure 7.2, pages 112–113).

4 Financial management and sources of income

In a charity, managing the money is much more than just a matter of good bookkeeping: it is central to the charity's work. In fact, unless you are clear about the sources of your income and how decisions are made about its use, the day-to-day bookkeeping can be quite meaningless. In a charity, the role of financial management has many features specific to the sector.

Financial responsibility

In a charity, the overall financial responsibility rests with the trustees as a whole. However, in practice, one of the hardest skills for a charity treasurer or finance worker is to enable the trustees to exercise this responsibility effectively so that they take all major financial decisions on an informed basis.

As noted in chapter 2, the trustees have a legal duty to ensure that proper accounting records are kept, but clearly it is impracticable for all trustees to be involved in all the day-to-day financial transactions of recording receipts, paying bills and salaries and so on. This must be delegated in some manner.

There are several ways of doing this. It is usual for one of the trustees to be designated as the **treasurer** of the organisation; within the trustees as a whole he or she will then take particular responsibility for financial issues. Sometimes the term 'honorary treasurer' is used to make it clear that it is a voluntary role. This role can operate in three ways.

- In many small local charities, the treasurer does all the bookkeeping, payment of salaries, liaison with the bank and similar tasks. He or she is personally responsible for producing the year end accounts (or for arranging for this to be done by the auditor or independent examiner) and often handles much correspondence on financial issues, for example arranging insurance.
- In slightly larger charities, a member of staff may be employed (often part-time) to act as a bookkeeper, or there could be an administrator whose duties include bookkeeping. The usual arrangement is that the treasurer determines the broad financial procedures and the

categories used in the books (see chapter 5), while the bookkeeper handles the detailed work.

In this case, the day-to-day financial procedures are shared between the treasurer and bookkeeper; for example, the treasurer might indicate the type of management report required for the trustees' meeting, but the bookkeeper might produce it.

- In medium-sized and larger charities, it is impossible for a voluntary treasurer to have any more than a broad overview of the financial arrangements. In such cases the paid managers of the organisation are expected to manage the financial affairs, and simply consult the trustees on major financial decisions. There will usually be a senior member of staff with a job title of finance officer or manager or, in organisations operating on a national scale, finance director.

In organisations working on this model, the treasurer's role is less operational, as the finance officer will usually attend trustees' meetings and present reports directly. The treasurer will meet with the finance officer from time to time to discuss financial policy, propose formal resolutions of a financial nature at trustees' meetings, and liaise with the auditors on issues at trustee level. But usually such treasurers have limited day-to-day involvement.

The first model has the advantage of simplicity, but as an organisation grows it can become dragged down by too much dependence on a voluntary treasurer. For example, the key member of staff – the manager – may have no financial information if all books are kept at the treasurer's home, and there may be considerable delays in raising cheques.

However, once a paid bookkeeper is appointed, the relationship between the treasurer and bookkeeper is crucial: the bookkeeper needs the direction of the treasurer on financial procedures; equally, the treasurer needs information from the bookkeeper in order to report to the trustees. This all has to be handled with sensitivity and, if there is a paid manager, the treasurer needs to take care not to treat the bookkeeper as one of his or her own staff.

In the third model the relationship of knowledge may be the other way round. Even a treasurer who is a professional in the accounting or banking world is unlikely to have as much knowledge and experience of charity finance as a full-time charity finance director. The latter may be attending conferences on charity finance and meeting with others in organisations such as the Charity Finance Group. Certainly the treasurer will not have the detailed financial knowledge of the organisation concerned. In such cases, the accountant or finance director may have to take on a gentle educational role, apprising the treasurer of major financial issues affecting the charity.

When it works well, this can be a fruitful relationship, especially if the treasurer takes the lead on difficult issues that would otherwise make the finance officer unpopular. The treasurer of a charity must normally also take the lead on the issue of proposing the remuneration of senior staff.

However, whatever the size of the charity, it is vital that the treasurer and finance staff accept that they are ultimately the servants of the trustees as a whole. Far too many small charities end up with the treasurer alone deciding what can or cannot be afforded. Finance officers can sometimes make the same mistake. It is the responsibility of treasurers or finance officers to advise the trustees, and to give them sufficient information on which to make an informed decision. But financial decisions, like all decisions, must ultimately be made by the trustees as a whole.

Managing the income and expenditure

Most financial management comes down to decisions about income or expenditure, though, as we saw in the last chapter, where a charity has several funds, you need to look at each fund individually.

In general, you might think the key task would be to maximise the income and minimise the expenditure. But in an organisation where you are not seeking to make a profit the task is more complex. Of course you want to avoid wasted expenditure – especially as the charity will usually be spending other people's money – but you are not seeking to get the expenditure as low as possible in order to maximise a profit. Most charities have to spend money in order to advance their charitable objects, so cutting down on worthwhile expenditure actually reduces the charity's effectiveness.

However, it is vital to consider both sides of the income and expenditure account. Where a charity is struggling to make ends meet, there are always two choices – to cut the expenses or increase the income – but often people only consider one or the other. Often the best course is to do some of each.

On the other hand, if the charity (or a certain fund) is doing well and achieving higher income or lower expenses than expected, financial management involves being creative in identifying new areas of expenditure, so that the objects can be further advanced. If you cannot do this, your reserves will just grow (see 'Cash flow and reserves', page 53), perhaps to levels that will bring the charity into criticism. In extreme cases, where income is increasing and there are few ways to spend it, the trustees may need to get the charity's objects changed (though any change to a charity's objects needs the consent of the appropriate regulator – the Charity Commission, OSCR or CCNI).

However, on a day-to-day basis, managing expenditure in a charity is not particularly different to any other organisation – setting sensible budgets and monitoring expenses against them is usually the best approach (see chapter 9 for more on management accounts). But the management of income in a charity can involve several issues unique to this sector.

Fundraising

What a charity is able to do to advance its objects is usually constrained by the income that it can generate. It follows that attracting sufficient income is a key role of all charity trustees – this is what is meant by **charity fundraising**. Curiously, many charities use the term 'fundraising' only to refer to certain types of income generation and some, especially religious charities, object to the word completely. But the term simply means the process of raising or securing sufficient funds to support the work of the charity. So whether you are asking for committed gifts, applying for grants, selling goods or services or maximising investment income, fundraising is all about raising the resources to support the charity's aims.

Some charities will have another trustee who coordinates the fundraising, quite separate from the treasurer, and where staff are employed there may be a paid fundraiser separate from the finance officer. But treasurers and finance officers need to understand the financial implications of different sources of income. (The links between accounting and fundraising are considered further in chapter 12.)

Sources of income

Fundamentally, there are three main ways in which a charity can get income:
- donations;
- trading;
- investment.

Donated income

Any money or other resources given to a charity count as **donated income**. As explained in earlier chapters, this ability to attract gifts – often for nothing in return – is at the heart of what it means to be a charity.

Donated income includes any of the following:

- coins or notes placed in a collecting box or collecting plate;
- a gift from an individual by cheque, standing order, direct debit or credit card;
- a gift from an individual deducted through their payroll;
- a grant or donation from a charitable trust;
- a grant or donation from a company (provided that it is not seeking anything in return);
- a grant from a local authority or public sector funder (provided that it is genuinely a grant – see below);
- a legacy to the charity in someone's will.

In the case of individual donations to charity, there are very attractive tax rules for direct gifts, payroll gifts and legacies, and with proper understanding of these, a charity can often increase the value of donations considerably. Some charities make extensive use of Gift Aid (see chapter 12), for example, but many others are missing out.

Some grants and donations will be for unrestricted funds; others will be tied to specific projects or activities, and thus need to be allocated to restricted funds (or occasionally to a capital/endowment fund if it was a capital appeal). (See chapter 3 for an explanation of these terms.)

When money is *given* to a charity, the relationship is one of trust. If the money is misused, the trustees could be guilty of a breach of trust and might have to reimburse the funder. Normally there is no contractual relationship. Even if you have a public sector funder that makes a grant with ten pages of conditions on how it is to be used, it is still a grant to a (very) restricted fund. The funder is not purchasing anything from the charity (if it wants that, it will need a **contract** – see 'Trading income' overleaf).

Some funders like to describe their funding agreements as **service level agreements** (SLAs). You sometimes need to read the small print to work out whether an SLA is actually a grant or a contract, but most are in fact grants (restricted not just in terms of purpose, but also to a certain service level that must be achieved). The SORP describes grants linked to SLAs as **performance-related grants**.

Trading income

The second main source of income is **trading income** – charging for goods or services. When charities get income in this way they are working more like ordinary businesses, but there are still many differences. Charities which derive significant amounts of income from trading often like to describe themselves as social enterprises (see chapter 1 for more on this) – but it is still charitable income and the accounts must follow charity law.

Many people think there is some rule preventing charities from trading, but, although there are certain limits and tax implications (see chapter 11), trading income is a normal source of income in many charities.

Trading income can include any of the following:
- an educational charity charging **fees** for places on courses;
- a housing charity charging rents to tenants;
- a charity selling books or publications (where the content is related to the charity's objects);
- a religious charity charging fees for weddings or funerals;
- a counselling charity charging fees for counselling sessions (where a definite charge is made, rather than just asking for a donation);
- a membership charity charging membership fees (where the member gets a definite benefit under the charity's objects – if there is no benefit, the member's subscription is just a donation);
- a health or disability charity charging fees under a contract with the public sector for providing services to people with certain medical conditions.

These would all be referred to as **primary purpose trading**, because what the charity is supplying is directly related to its objects.

For some charities, primary purpose trading is the main source of income. If a funder wants your charity to do work under a contract (rather than a grant) this is a contractual relationship, and the income is trading income. The funder has become a customer, purchasing services, and if the charity fails to deliver the services properly it could be liable for breach of contract. So before entering into major contracts, charities should always review the terms carefully and seek legal advice if in doubt. It is especially important that staff should not be allowed to sign major contracts without approval by the trustees, as a contract may impose long-term obligations.

Trading income also includes:
- selling tickets for a fundraising event;
- selling mugs, T-shirts, cards or souvenirs to raise money;

- selling raffle tickets (this is not a pure donation, because the purchaser may win a prize);
- providing advertising or sponsorship opportunities in return for payment by companies (where they gain substantial publicity);
- selling second-hand goods in a charity shop or jumble sale;
- selling the charity's services in a way that is outside its objects: for example, providing places on courses to people who are outside the charity's beneficiaries, or renting out rooms to commercial organisations.

These activities are classed as **trading for fundraising purposes** – because what you are supplying is not part of the charity's objects; the reason for the activity is simply to raise funds.

In deciding whether an activity is primary purpose trading or trading for fundraising purposes, the key question to ask is: 'Is the purchaser buying a benefit which is part of the charity's objects to provide?' (e.g. an educational charity selling training); or: 'Is the purchaser buying something unrelated to the charity's objects?' (e.g. a souvenir mug or T-shirt). But whenever you are making a charge for something, remember that you are *trading* – you can only treat income as a donation if the donor gets nothing significant in return (in the case of Gift Aid donations there are specific rules on maximum levels of benefit to donors – see chapter 12).

There are few restrictions on primary purpose trading by charities, although VAT sometimes has to be considered. But there are strict limits on trading for fundraising purposes, and above this the charity could be liable for tax (see chapter 11). Activities such as selling raffle (lottery) tickets or selling alcohol also have other legal controls.

In terms of the accounts, primary purpose trading income will normally be posted to unrestricted funds. This can sometimes make a contract more attractive than a grant. You may wish to use a designated fund to keep track of a certain contract-funded project, but the charity's obligation is simply to supply the goods or services contracted. If you are able to do this at less than the price agreed, any profit or surplus can be retained by the charity to support the development of services. This is quite different from the trust relationship that applies with grants, where unspent funds may have to be returned. (If you have funders that object to this, and want you to treat their contract as a restricted fund with any surplus being returned to them, ask whether they expect that arrangement with other purchases – for example, their stationery suppliers.)

While a surplus on trading income may be attractive, remember that if you have under-costed the work and cannot negotiate an increase in the fee, the charity may still be legally obliged to carry out the work, and you may end up subsidising it from other unrestricted income.

Trading income for fundraising purposes will also usually go to unrestricted funds, unless you specifically asked people to buy tickets or support an event on the basis that the proceeds would be used to support a certain project.

Investment income

Investment income includes any of the following:
- interest on deposits or other investments;
- dividends on shares;
- rents on investment properties (where a charity holds property specifically for investment purposes – very rare in small charities).

For many smaller charities the only investment income will be small amounts of bank interest. But for some charities, where there are substantial endowments, investments may be the main source of income; this is the case for many grant-making charities.

Charities are entitled to a number of tax concessions on investment income: for example, interest is untaxed regardless of the amount, and there is no capital gains tax to pay when **investments** increase in value.

Investment income should normally be allocated to the fund to which the investments belong. In theory, this means that where several funds are held in the same bank account, any bank interest should be split between the different funds on a reasonable basis. However, with normal restricted projects, where the funder expects that the money will be spent fairly soon after receipt, few funders will be that prescriptive, and many charities are thus able to allocate all bank interest to the general fund. Nevertheless, some funders may insist that you seek their permission to take this approach – read the small print of grant agreements. But if you have a long-term appeal such as a building fund, where substantial amounts are raised perhaps a year or more before they can be spent, donors have a right to expect that interest on their donations will be added to the fund concerned.

Managing different forms of income

As explained, the trustees have a duty to maximise the income of the charity in order to further its objects and the treasurer or finance officer will usually play a part in implementing this.

With donated income the key issue is an effective fundraising strategy. Some charities accept donations passively, but if the work of your charity is worthwhile, you have an obligation to ask people to support it. With grant income, the charity usually needs to be proactive in applying for grants, and to plan well ahead where grant income has a finite life.

With **primary purpose trading** the key issue is usually how to price the goods or services you are supplying, and then how to market the service. Since the trade is seeking to advance the charity's objects, you will usually be aiming to break even rather than to make a profit on the activity: generally, keeping the price down will enable you to reach more people. But remember that, unlike business trading, with a charity the customer (the funder) is often quite different from the client or beneficiary who will be using your service. Setting appropriate prices when making bids is critical (see 'Managing core costs' overleaf).

However, if you are offering something that will be paid for directly by your beneficiaries, you may deliberately want to price the service below the cost price, and subsidise it using other income. In particular, high fees which mean that a charity's services can only in practice be used by relatively affluent service users may mean that the charity is in breach of the **public benefit requirement**, which is fundamental to the definition of charity (see chapter 1, page 6 for more on this). Trustees must consider the guidance on public benefit from the Charity Commission (or OSCR, or CCNI as applicable) in all their decisions – though charging is only one aspect of this. Those who are poor must never be excluded from the benefits of a charity's work – even if the aims of the charity are unrelated to poverty. Even if beneficiaries do not normally pay their own fees but are funded by a public sector body (for example) that funding may only cover certain specific clients nominated by the funder, and the trustees should consider the implications for other beneficiaries. For instance, some charities raise funds specifically to allow them to support those who have no recourse to public funds.

With trading for fundraising purposes, again, pricing and marketing are key issues, but this time the aim is usually to set the price as high as possible (but without putting people off). There is no point in running a fundraising activity that simply breaks even! If people are giving voluntary time to help run an event, the charity needs to make a substantial return to justify their time and effort.

Management of investment income is sometimes just a case of choosing the best account in which to deposit funds, but for charities with large funds to manage, the management of investments may take up a good part of the time at trustees' meetings. Since the Trustee Act 2000, trustees have much more flexibility in managing investments, but where significant sums are involved they have an obligation to seek professional advice (see chapter 12 for more on this). In such cases, you need to determine an investment policy, which must be stated in the charity's annual report (see chapter 7).

In the case of an endowment fund, the terms of the endowment will normally require that income is allocated to some other fund. (If the income went back into the endowment fund, the fund would just keep growing and would never be spent on the charity's objects – accounting in this way has prompted Charity Commission's investigations.) But with shares and similar investments, take care to distinguish investment income (such as dividends) from capital growth – the latter will remain in the capital fund.

If this is problematic – for example, if the endowment investments are giving too much capital growth and not enough income, or vice versa – provisions under the Charities Act 2011 implemented from 2013 allow trustees of a charity in England and Wales with permanent endowment (see page 35) to apply a **total return** approach where capital growth and investment income are considered together. However, the rules on this are quite complex – a balance has to be made between the release of funds to spend on charitable activity in the current year, and growing the endowment so it is not eroded by inflation in the long term. Regulations require additional information to be disclosed in the trustees' annual report to explain the calculations used which go beyond the scope of this book. Any charity considering this will need to consult the Charity Commission's guidance, and will usually need advice from their auditor, independent examiner or a charity investment specialist.

Managing core costs: apportioning overheads and full cost recovery

Much of the financial management will deal with each fund individually; as explained, you cannot use income to a restricted fund to subsidise deficits elsewhere.

But the relative outcome of each fund is often determined by how overheads (such as the running costs of the charity's premises) are apportioned between funds, or how much you can negotiate in management fees or other contributions to overheads in order to permit transfers from restricted to unrestricted funds.

It is vital to appreciate that, when taking on a new project (for example, involving a new worker), the costs are much more than that person's salary costs and direct project expenses. For example:

- the new person will take up some of the manager's time in supervision;

- he or she will occupy part of your premises (even if the premises are already there, the running costs will usually increase);
- the new worker may need to use the charity's existing equipment (computers, photocopier or possibly vehicles), giving higher maintenance costs;
- the new project will generate additional transactions in your accounts, which may require extra hours for your bookkeeper;
- the extra complexity of the charity's affairs may require additional trustees' meetings;
- the extra income may take the charity over a threshold for its final accounts and thus require extra accountancy fees at year end (see the thresholds in chapter 2);
- if the project finishes and you cannot offer the person other work, you may have to meet redundancy costs;
- the process of bidding for the funds in the first place may have taken up the time of a coordinator or fundraiser.

Different funders have different policies on meeting such costs, and as a treasurer or finance officer you need to be aware of these. Some charities find that they can *only* secure project funding and, unless you can agree a reasonable contribution to overheads from your funders, you may find that you have no unrestricted funds at all. In a number of charities, the unrestricted funds – which provide the all-important reserves (see 'Cash flow and reserves' on page 53) – come almost entirely from funds transfers from restricted funds which arise from management fees or overhead contributions from specific projects.

This is more of an issue with grant-funded projects than contract-funded work because, as explained above, primary purpose trading income is normally allocated to unrestricted funds in the first place (restricted funds usually only arise with projects funded by grants or donations). But when deciding on the price to charge for a contract-funded project – when the charity is preparing to bid for the work – it is vital to set a price which is sufficient to cover the appropriate share of overheads.

Some funders dislike the terms 'management fee' or 'overheads' but are nevertheless willing to pay for a proportion of a manager's time or premises costs as an expense of a project. But obviously your overheads must be reasonable – public sector funders have to consider 'value for money'[4] and a charity seeking to recover the full costs for a well-paid senior manager purely from the overheads of a couple of small projects may find that funders are unsympathetic.

Managing such issues is sometimes described as **full cost recovery**. The government has indicated that when public sector bodies purchase services from a charity, they should generally be prepared to pay the *full costs* of the activity, including an appropriate share of overheads. However, full cost recovery can sometimes be hard to achieve in practice, as public sector funders are often short of resources, and charities are sometimes presented with the stark choice of doing work at less than full cost, or not doing it at all.

But it is also dangerous to assume that there is a clearly defined full cost to any activity. What you consider to be the full costs will depend on how you apportion overheads. It is very easy for a treasurer or finance officer to make some projects look much more attractive than others depending on the criteria used to apportion costs. While you don't want to overload trustees with too many options, a good treasurer will make clear the assumptions used in overhead calculations and will make sure they are generally agreed. Also, if a charity has (say) four similarly sized projects which contribute equally to the overheads but loses funding for one of them, the costs of the remaining projects will appear to increase if the overheads are now split three ways rather than four ways. So all overhead calculations involve a measure of estimation.

Getting an acceptable price for work can sometimes be a challenge: charities seeking to fund their work through contract income need to be actively involved in the commissioning and procurement agenda of the relevant funding bodies. In particular, if you can get dimensions of social impact and community involvement built into the commissioning process, you are less likely to be undercut by commercial providers at the tendering stage. However, good financial management requires being clear about the minimum acceptable price. Charity treasurers need to be actively involved in such bidding decisions: in some charities even a £20 cheque needs the treasurer's signature, but staff are allowed to make major funding bids without any sign-off by the trustees, and under-costed bids end up costing the charity tens of thousands of pounds.

Of course, it is sometimes worth taking on a project where the funding does not cover the full costs if it is sufficiently crucial to the charity's aims, and the overheads are adequately covered from other sources. Sometimes a charity will specifically seek donated funds to subsidise the price of a service, especially where the beneficiaries are paying for the service themselves (see page 49 regarding public benefit). But in other cases, setting prices too low could mean the charity is subsidising an external non-charitable commissioning body. Charity treasurers and finance officers need to be in the lead to ensure that any funding bids are priced appropriately – unless the trustees have clearly agreed to subsidise a project from other income. Sometimes a key task of the treasurer is to support the charity in saying 'no' to a project when funding is insufficient and the core costs will not be sufficiently covered, even if it seems attractive in other ways.

Cash flow and reserves

In any organisation, it is not enough just to balance income and expenditure, it is also necessary to ensure that there is sufficient money in hand at any one time to meet immediate expenses. Otherwise a charity, like any other organisation, can become insolvent.

Given the uncertainty of much charity income, this management of cash flow often requires more care than in other organisations.

In practice, the difficulties are usually greatest with trading income and with charities whose donated income is subject to major seasonal fluctuations (such as Christmas appeals). In most cases, donated income can be received before the money has to be spent and grants are often paid quarterly or half-yearly in advance. However, some grant programmes are only paid in arrears, i.e. the charity has to incur the expenditure and then claim reimbursement (this is particularly the case with certain forms of European funding). There can also be acute problems if a grant is paid late – some public sector funders are well known for this.

Projects funded by trading income (or grant income paid in arrears) often require expenditure on salaries or materials before the work can be invoiced, and there may also be a delay of a month or more awaiting payment of the charity's invoice. It is vital to plan for this (see chapter 9 on preparing a cash flow forecast).

Issues of cash flow lead naturally to considering the appropriate level of **reserves** for a charity – the amount available in general unrestricted funds. (If you are doing accruals accounting, and if the balance of your general fund includes fixed assets, you need to deduct these from the fund balance to get the reserves figure.)

The Charity Commission has had to remind charities from time to time that accumulating money is not itself a charitable purpose. Generally, a charity is expected to spend its income on advancing its objects, unless there is a specific reason for keeping it. There is no problem in retaining money if there is a clear development plan, for example to acquire a new building in a few years' time. But retaining large amounts towards general running costs is not acceptable; this is seen as putting the needs of future (unknown) beneficiaries ahead of current (known) beneficiaries.

There is also a problem that some grant-makers will refuse to help charities with significant reserves; this can encourage inappropriate expenditure prior to year end, just to bring the reserves down to a more acceptable level.

Different charities will need different levels of reserves: a small grant-making charity that only makes one-off grants (i.e. no long-term obligations) may be able to manage with almost no reserves. On the other hand, a service-providing charity running a number of complex projects with uncertain income streams will usually need running costs amounting to at least three months' average expenditure. Where the income is seasonal, or where long-term commitments are made (for example, in a charity funding medical research) much higher reserves may be needed.

It is a legal requirement that charity trustees must state their **reserves policy** in their annual report. This should cover what the trustees feel is a reasonable level of reserves for the charity, how the actual reserves compare with this, and what steps the trustees will be taking to get reserves to a sensible level. This applies even to smaller charities where the year end accounts are on a receipts and payments (R&P) basis. Usually the policy is expressed in terms of months of expenditure, for example:

> The trustees have set a policy of maintaining unrestricted reserves equivalent to six months' expenditure. At present, the reserves amount to just under four months' expenditure and the trustees will therefore be seeking to increase this in the coming year.

To calculate the reserves in terms of months the calculation is as follows:

$$\text{Number of months' reserves} = \frac{\text{Current reserves}}{\text{Annual expenditure}} \times 12$$

Where the reserves are unacceptably low, it may be necessary for a few years to budget for general fund income to be more than expenditure, until reserves have reached a sensible level, but you need to get supporters to understand the need for this. Conversely, some charities have realised over the years that their reserves have become unnecessarily high and are now spending them by increasing their activities, so that for a few years their expenditure will be more than their income.

5 Bookkeeping principles

Some people think that bookkeeping is the heart of a treasurer's work and might be surprised to see just one chapter devoted to this. But bookkeeping cannot be done in isolation; you need an appreciation of the issues discussed in the earlier chapters in order to decide where in the books to allocate particular transactions. You also need to consider what will be needed for management accounts (see chapter 9) and final accounts (chapter 7) in order to decide what categories to use in your books.

Who does what?

Effective bookkeeping depends just as much on the human interactions in the process as on the books themselves. Once the charity reaches the size where day-to-day bookkeeping is done by a member of staff rather than the treasurer, communication between the treasurer, bookkeeper and manager is vital to the task.

Bookkeeping is not just a mechanical exercise: decisions have to be made about what to post where; sometimes a cost has to be apportioned between more than one fund; you need to know if some incoming money is actually a debtor from last year and so on. Also, new categories and even new funds will need to be added to the books from time to time, such as when the charity receives a grant or donation for a new purpose.

So employing a bookkeeper for just half a day a week, for example, is often not very successful. Such bookkeepers may never really gain sufficient knowledge of the charity to make informed decisions, so they either make assumptions (which often have to be corrected at year end, involving a lot of extra time and cost) or, to do the job properly, they have to ask so many questions that you feel it would be quicker to keep the books yourself. The same problem arises with treasurers who are frequently absent from trustees' meetings.

Also, bear in mind that much of the time of treasurers and bookkeepers is taken up with paying bills, banking receipts, chasing outstanding payments and a whole host of related issues. Actually 'posting transactions' (putting entries in the books) rarely accounts for more than perhaps a quarter of the total time.

In practice, operating any bookkeeping system, whether manual or computerised, can be split into three levels:

1   Devising the basic structure of the accounts: drawing up the layout and allocating columns with manual books, or defining a chart of accounts (the list of account headings) in a computer system.
2   Posting entries in the books on a day-to-day basis (together with day-to-day checks such as bank reconciliation – see chapter 6).
3   Closing off the books at the end of an accounting period, working out total figures for each category, and transferring these into appropriate reports for use by others. A very small charity can do this just once a year, but larger charities will usually want monthly or quarterly accounting periods.

Where roles are separated between a treasurer and bookkeeper, the treasurer needs to be involved in levels 1 and 3, but level 2 is usually handled by the bookkeeper alone, except where problems and queries arise. However, an experienced finance officer may handle all three levels, only consulting the treasurer where policy decisions are required.

Format of the books

Clearly, any bookkeeping system must keep a record of all financial transactions affecting the charity. Without a list of individual receipts and payments it is impossible to establish monthly or yearly figures with any certainty.

The simple cashbook

The simplest form of books is just a list of transactions, often described as a **cashbook**, and is usually split into columns for receipts and payments (as shown in figure 5.1).

Date	Cheque no.	Details	Receipts	Payments
3 Jan	000271	Rent		250.00
21 Feb	000272	Wages to administrator		83.33
27 Feb	Paid in	Grant from council	2,000.00	
12 Mar	000273	Singh & Co. – printing		678.00
19 Mar	Paid in	Cash – proceeds of concert	43.90	
21 Mar	000274	Wages to administrator		83.33

Fig. 5.1 Simple cashbook: transaction list

Certainly this format keeps a record of transactions. However, it is worth noting that, with systems of this kind, what you write in the 'details' or 'comment' column is vital in order to know at a later date what the transaction was about. A slight improvement, to ensure that you know why each transaction was entered, is to have two narrative columns, as shown in figure 5.2 – one for the name of the payee or funder and one explaining the purpose or reason for the receipt or payment.

Date	Cheque no.	Payee/donor	Purpose	Receipts	Payments
3 Jan	000271	ABC Properties	Rent		250.00
21 Feb	000272	R. Jones	Admin wages		83.33
27 Feb	Paid in	Midsham Council	Annual grant	2,000.00	
12 Mar	000273	Singh & Co.	Printing		678.00
19 Mar	Paid in	Cash	Concert proceeds	43.90	
21 Mar	000274	R. Jones	Admin wages		83.33

Fig. 5.2 Simple cashbook with name and reason

You can draw up this type of layout in any kind of book or on plain paper, though nowadays most people will keep such records on a computer, typically using a spreadsheet application. However, care is needed with spreadsheets, not least because details can easily be changed retrospectively. Also, remember that the records must be kept for six prior years – you need to be very organised with backups if relying on electronic records alone: for most treasurers and finance officers, the discipline of producing regular printouts from a spreadsheet is vital (you could save the spreadsheet as a PDF if you really don't want paper copies, but if so it's still vital to make backups onto different media).

In practice, however, a spreadsheet used just to keep data in rows and columns with little further analysis offers few advantages over manual books, and for some charities, if the accounts are not complex enough to need a computer-based accounting system, the permanent nature of manual books can outweigh the apparent attractiveness of spreadsheets. Stationery shops sell a wide range of books already set out in suitable columns. (A book also has the advantage over separate sheets in that pages are unlikely to get lost, and there is less risk of fraud from someone taking out pages and changing them.) However, auditors and independent examiners may prefer a charity to use spreadsheets, if they are in good order, rather than manual books, as it is much quicker to check totals or to search for particular amounts.

But although this method of presentation provides a record of transactions, it cannot be said to be a full bookkeeping system, until we look at the issue of **balancing off** the books and adding in whatever funds were in hand at the start of the accounting period.

There are various ways of balancing off or closing off the books at the end of a period. In general, you will want to total the payments and receipts and subtract the payments from the receipts to determine the surplus for the period. You then need to add on the funds in hand at the start of the period in order to know the balance in hand to carry forward to the next period. Figure 5.3 provides an example.

Date	Cheque no.	Payee/donor	Purpose	Receipts	Payments
31 Dec	Balance carried forward			373.45	
3 Jan	000271	ABC Properties	Rent		250.00
21 Feb	000272	R. Jones	Admin wages		83.33
27 Feb	Paid in	Midsham Council	Annual grant	2,000.00	
12 Mar	000273	Singh & Co.	Printing		678.00
19 Mar	Paid in	Cash	Concert proceeds	43.90	
21 Mar	000274	R. Jones	Admin wages		83.33
31 Mar	Totals for quarter			2,043.90	1,094.66
	Subtract payments			−1,094.66	
	Net surplus for quarter (receipts less payments)			949.24	
	Add on balance brought forward at 31 Dec			373.45	
31 Mar	Balance carried forward			1,322.69	

Fig. 5.3 An example of closing off the books

Now that the books have been totalled and closed off, from this simple cashbook you have the figures to produce some helpful management accounts for the quarter for the trustees.

Books like this are quite adequate for a very small charity where everything is done through one bank account and where there are no more than perhaps 30 or so transactions a year. But if you had several hundred transactions, this format would be quite limiting because it does not show in any overall manner from where the income and expenditure has come. Going through a list of more than 100 entries, looking at the purpose of each in order to produce sensible year end accounts, would be a great deal of work.

Analysed cashbook (single fund)

An easy but very useful improvement on the simple cashbook is an analysed cashbook as shown in figure 5.4. Rather than just having single columns for 'receipts' and 'payments' you have a number of columns in which the receipts and payments are analysed. Whenever you post an entry, you take care to write it in the correct column. Most manual bookkeeping systems are based on the use of one or more analysed cashbooks.

Date	Cheque no.	Payee/donor	Purpose	Balance forward	Receipts		Payments		
					Grants	Fundraising	Premises	Wages	Print/stationery
31 Dec		Balance carried forward		373.45					
3 Jan	000271	ABC Properties	Rent				250.00		
21 Feb	000272	R. Jones	Admin wages					83.33	
27 Feb	Paid in	Midsham Council	Annual grant		2,000.00				
12 Mar	000273	Singh & Co.	Printing						678.00
19 Mar	Paid in	Cash	Concert			43.90			
21 Mar	000274	R. Jones	Admin wages					83.33	
31 Mar		Totals for quarter for each category		373.45	2,000.00	43.90	250.00	166.66	678.00
		Total receipts and payments				2,043.90			1,094.66
		Subtract payments from receipts				−1,094.66			
		Net surplus for quarter		949.24		949.24			
31 Mar		Balance carried forward		1,322.69					

Fig. 5.4 Example analysed cashbook (single fund)

However, even with just two columns of receipts and three columns of payments it can be difficult to show them on a single page, and in reality most charities will need many more categories of income and expenditure. Some people combine the 'Balance forward' column with another column, but it is clearer if you can keep it separate. Of course with a spreadsheet you can have many more columns than on a handwritten page, but even so a spreadsheet which requires lots of horizontal scrolling, and which cannot be printed except by reducing everything to 5pt font size is not a very effective means of keeping charity records!

The best way of creating more space is to keep two separate cashbooks: one for receipts (see figure 5.5) and one for payments (see figure 5.6). Both the receipts book and the payments book must, of course, be closed off at the same date.

For those who are happy with manual records, it is possible to buy books with around 16 columns, across a double page spread. Some columns will be used for dates, descriptions and cheque numbers, so it is usually possible to have up to about 12 columns for financial analysis. With separate books for receipts and payments, this will give you around 12 income categories and 12 expenditure categories. This can be a very reliable means of long-term record keeping in a charity if a computer-based accounting package cannot be justified.

However, one advantage of the simple cashbook and analysed cashbooks above is that it is quite easy, if you wish, to add an extra column for the running bank balance (in the example in figure 5.4, you could use the balance forward column). Once you keep receipts and payments on separate pages, you will find this more difficult. But this is not necessarily a problem if you can keep the bank balance somewhere else, such as a running balance on cheque stubs.

Analysed cashbook (multiple funds)

In many charities the bookkeeping must also distinguish separate funds. This means considerably more columns because, as explained in chapter 3, you must be able to distinguish receipts and payments for each fund. However, if you have no more than two or three funds, and if you do not need too many categories for each, you can still work with two analysed cashbooks (manual or as spreadsheets) – one for receipts and one for payments.

In such cases, remember that you need a separate balance forward for *each* fund – this is usually shown in the receipts book.

RECEIPTS BOOK

Date	Receipt ref.	From	Purpose	GENERAL FUND				OUTREACH FUND		
				Balance forward	Grants	Fund-raising	Interest	Balance forward	Grants	Participation fees
31 Dec		Balances carried forward		373.45				0.00		
14 Jan	Deposit	Midsham Trust	Outreach grant						800.00	
27 Feb	DC	Midsham Council	General grant		2,000.00					
3 Mar	Deposit	Cash	Concert			43.9				
19 Mar	Deposit	Cash	Outing							24.00
30 Mar	Int	Midwest Bank	Interest Jan–Mar				3.27			
31 Mar		Totals for quarter for each category		373.45	2,000.00	43.90	3.27	0.00	800.00	24.00
		Total receipts for each fund					2,047.17			824.00
		Subtract payments (from PAYMENTS book)					-1,109.66			-591.21
		Net surplus for quarter for each fund		937.51			937.51	232.79		232.79
31 Mar		Balances carried forward		1,310.96				232.79		

Fig. 5.5 Example receipts book with two funds

PAYMENTS BOOK

Date	Cheque no.	Payee	Purpose	GENERAL FUND				OUTREACH FUND		
				Premises	Wages	Print/ stationery	Trustees	Wages	Travel	Activities
3 Jan	000271	ABC Properties	Rent	250.00						
21 Feb	000272	R. Jones	Admin wages		83.33					
21 Feb	000273	J. Smiley	Outreach wages					230.00		
27 Feb	000274	K. Patel	Travel expenses				15.00			
3 Mar	000275	K. Patel	Outreach travel						49.84	
12 Mar	000276	Singh & Co.	Printing × 2			678.00				
17 Mar	DD	ABC Hire	Play equipment hire							52.00
21 Mar	000277	R. Jones	Admin wages		83.33					
21 Mar	000278	J. Smiley	Outreach wages					230.00		29.37
31 Mar			Totals for quarter for each category	250.00	166.66	678.00	15.00	460.00	49.84	81.37
			Total payments for each fund				1,109.66			591.21
1 Apr			(Start of payments for next quarter)							

Fig. 5.6 Example payments book with two funds

Cashbooks for each fund

If you have more than two or three funds, or if you find you need the whole page width or screen width to cover all the categories for just one fund, the only solution is to keep separate books for each fund.

Many charities do this, but great care is needed with a transaction that is split across funds. In figure 5.6 the printers Singh & Co. have clearly invoiced two printing jobs together – one relating to the General Fund and the other to Outreach – and a single cheque number 000276 has been written for £730 to cover this. But the cost is split into separate columns: £678 to 'General Fund: Print/stationery' and £52 to 'Outreach: Activities'. On a single page, it is fairly easy to read across the line, but with separate books, extensive cross-referencing is needed in such cases.

This shows the limits of single-entry bookkeeping, and if you have split transactions arising regularly double-entry bookkeeping (see page 65) is recommended.

Multiple bank accounts and petty cash

The examples above assume that all receipts and payments go into a single bank account. This certainly keeps things simple, because your books do not need to show where a receipt is paid into, or on which account a cheque is written. If you can bank all receipts as soon as they arrive and make all payments by cheque or electronic transfer, it is much easier than keeping temporary amounts in petty cash.

Deposit accounts

Many charities will need a deposit or investment account of some kind, but provided that this is only used for transfers to and from the current account, it does not add any great complication. Normal receipts and payments will go via the current account, so the main cashbook is unaffected.

It is helpful to keep a separate note of the running balance of the deposit account, with details of transfers in and out (just as you will, hopefully, keep a running balance for the current account – either in the books or in straightforward cases using chequebook stubs). But if you are keeping accounts broken down by fund (as required for charities), rather than broken down by bank account, transfers to or from the deposit account do *not* appear in the payments or receipts. You are simply transferring the assets of the charity from one account to another, but the charity has not actually received any new funds or paid anything out.

When you receive interest on the deposit account, remember that you need to post this in the books as a receipt, and it is easiest if the bank will agree to pay deposit account interest into the current account. If not, remember that deposit account interest needs recording both in the receipts book and in your record of deposit account movements.

Handling multiple cheque accounts and petty cash

If you sometimes pay large receipts directly into the deposit account, or if you have more than one account from which payments can be made, your books need to be more elaborate. This is also the case if you keep money in the form of petty cash or use petty cash to make payments.

The best way to treat petty cash is just like another bank account. So when you draw money from the bank for petty cash, remember that no money is going out of the charity even though you are making a bank withdrawal: it is just like transferring assets between current and deposit accounts. It is only when you spend petty cash that you have payments to enter in the payments book.

Some people make the mistake of simply adding an extra column to the payments book for 'Petty cash drawn', but of course this does not explain the *purpose* of the expenditure and, in any case, not all the petty cash drawn will necessarily be spent. At year end, if all the petty cash expenses have been lumped into one column, a lot of work is needed to go through petty cash books and break down the expenditure: it is much better to do this during the year as petty cash is spent. Also, with a bank account you can rely on the bank to keep certain records, but with petty cash it is all down to you. So, as well as your normal books, it is vital to have a system of petty cash vouchers or a petty cash book where cash expenses are immediately noted. From time to time (perhaps once a month) you can transfer the total petty cash expenses into the main payments book, split into columns as required.

If you take in cash receipts (for example from collections, events or charity shops) it is usually best to bank the receipts gross, and deal with petty cash expenses separately. If you start reimbursing expenses out of cash received it needs very thorough bookkeeping to keep track of what is happening and to satisfy your auditor or examiner.

Many people think petty cash accounting is simple, but in fact it makes life a lot more complicated. It needs considerably more skills to keep accounts correctly in an organisation where petty cash is widely used. It is much easier if small expenses can be met personally by staff or trustees and then reimbursed promptly by cheque or bank transfer. Provided that you devise a proper expense claim form for such cases, this is much easier to trace.

To handle receipts and payments made directly from petty cash, or where there is more than one bank account, you need an extra column in your payments and receipts books to show which account has been used in each case. But it then becomes much harder to reconcile your receipts and payments to your bank accounts. To be sure your figures are correct, you really need to keep a running balance for *each* bank account and *each* petty cash account (and be sure to check regularly that the figure in your book for the petty cash balance agrees to the physical amount in the box).

Once you do this, you are effectively posting every transaction into two places in your books (or 'ledgers' as they are sometimes called) – to the receipts or payments ledger and to the bank or petty cash ledger (you need a separate bank/petty cash ledger for each bank account and each pot of petty cash). This is called **double-entry bookkeeping**.

Double-entry bookkeeping

The bookkeeping systems shown in the previous illustrations are all single-entry systems, where each amount is written in one place only. But professional bookkeepers (and computer-based accounting systems) will normally use double-entry bookkeeping, where everything is written in two places.

Double-entry bookkeeping involves more work, but it has the advantage that it can cope even with very complex systems, and its internal checks help to detect errors. Even if you have seven bank accounts, three petty cash accounts, fifteen funds with forty or more income and expenditure categories in each fund, reliable manual books can be kept on a double-entry basis.

The concept of double-entry bookkeeping relies on having a number of ledgers, each with two columns, called 'debits' and 'credits'. Even if your double-entry bookkeeping is done automatically by a computer-based system it helps to understand the principles in this way. So rather than trying to have vast numbers of columns across the page, you keep each account as a separate ledger. These can be done in a book with two columns per page (plus space for dates and comments) and a separate page for each ledger. (Note that with fund accounting, you cannot have just one ledger for a fund: you need a separate ledger for each income category and each expenditure category of the fund.)

Any transaction always involves at least two postings – a debit to one account and a credit to another account. (In a split case, you could have two or more credits adding up to a single debit or vice versa, but the debits and credits must always balance.)

Here are some simple examples of double-entry transactions:

£2,000 General Fund grant received and paid into bank
    Debit: Bank £2,000
    Credit: General Fund grant income £2,000

£730 Printing bill paid (split between two funds)
    Credit: Bank £730
    Debit: General Fund printing/stationery £678
    Debit: Outreach Fund activities £52

£150 Petty cash drawn (cheque written for cash)
    Credit: Bank £150
    Debit: Petty cash £150

People sometimes query why you debit the bank when receiving money and credit it when paying out: this is the opposite to what you see on bank statements. But the whole concept of **debits and credits** relates to the notion of debtors and creditors (see chapter 10), and if two people enter into a transaction one person's debtor is another person's creditor. Banks have traditionally produced statements in terms of *their* books – not yours – although many banks now use headings like 'money in' and 'money out' on their customer statements and online systems, rather than debits and credits.

So if you deposit money at the bank, from the bank's point of view it is not their money – it is money they owe to you – so in their books the amount is a creditor, and they show the entry as a credit. But in your books, the bank has money which belongs to you – to you the bank is a debtor. In your books, paying money into the bank is increasing the bank's debts to you, so you post it as a debit. (Think about it in a dark room for a few minutes!)

The same applies with normal commercial transactions. If A sells something to B on an invoice (which is not yet paid), the amount due is a debtor in A's books, but in B's books the amount payable is a creditor. (This is taking us into accruals accounting – see chapter 10. But even with R&P accounting, double-entry bookkeeping is very useful if you have several funds or several bank accounts.)

Any double-entry system allows you to do a very useful check called a **trial balance**. This means adding up the net balance on every ledger (debits less credits or vice versa) and putting them down as a list. Because the debits and credits have to balance for every transaction, it follows that total debits and total credits should be the same across all the accounts. If you find that they are not, you must have misposted a double entry somewhere.

To run a proper double entry system manually, you can in principle post everything directly to the two ledgers concerned. But because of the risk of posting one half of a double entry and then getting distracted before you have done the second half, it is often best to write everything in a simple cashbook first, and then post from there into the ledgers.

In a book of this length there is no space to explain all the details of double-entry bookkeeping, but nowadays very few charities (or businesses) do full double-entry bookkeeping on a manual basis. Most computer-based accounting systems work internally on a double-entry basis (with the guarantee that the debits and credits balance). Also, at year end, your auditor or examiner may ask you to post adjustments in your accounts, which they will usually give to you as a list of debits and credits (special transactions of this kind are often called **journals**). So, while few treasurers and administrators are experts in double-entry bookkeeping, it is useful to have a general appreciation of how it works.

Manual books or computers?

Although it is possible to keep even quite complex books on a manual basis, few charities will opt for a system of multiple manual books when IT systems are readily available.

There are three levels of using IT in charity accounting:
* spreadsheets;
* general-purpose accounting systems;
* charity-specific accounting systems.

Spreadsheets

As mentioned, spreadsheet applications, such as Microsoft Excel, Corel Quattro Pro or OpenOffice Calc, offer an obvious way to keep what are effectively manual books on a computer-based system.

But spreadsheets have some serious disadvantages if you are trying to set up a complete bookkeeping system. When you open a spreadsheet you have access to all the cells at once, and even in a modest charity with (say) 50 income and expenditure categories (over a number of funds) and 500 transactions a year, your spreadsheet will have 25,000 cells. The size makes it cumbersome and hard to manage, with a great risk of putting entries in the wrong cell. Moreover, unlike manual books – where corrections are easily spotted if you write the books in ink – there is nothing in a spreadsheet to stop someone changing something entered earlier in the year, so it is easy to wipe out earlier entries that have been checked and balanced.

Also, many people who use spreadsheets for bookkeeping are just keeping a single-entry analysed cashbook – often there is no corresponding record of running balances on bank accounts, petty cash, etc., so there is often no means of doing bank reconciliation from the spreadsheet figures.

If you are an expert spreadsheet user some of these issues can be overcome, but this may almost mean writing your own accounting system in spreadsheet macros (in fact some accounting systems run essentially as applications within Excel, but this is very different to using a spreadsheet of your own devising). Except in the simplest charities, the use of spreadsheets as the sole means of bookkeeping can be very risky.

The real value of spreadsheets is not for bookkeeping, but for financial analysis, management accounts, budgeting for new projects and the like. They can also allow you to take figures from your accounts and present them in attractive graphical ways. Many accounting systems allow you to export figures to a spreadsheet for this purpose.

General-purpose accounting systems

If you wish to keep reliable books of account, an accounting system is much better than a spreadsheet. Computer-based accounting packages allow you, firstly, to define the individual accounts (or ledgers) into which you want your accounts broken down, and then to post transactions using simple methods of input. Because of this, they can maintain an **audit trail** – a list of transactions and where they were allocated – and most such systems use double-entry bookkeeping (although, except for journal transactions, you do not usually have to know about debits and credits).

The audit trail means that it is possible to trace with certainty how the final figures are reached. Moreover, you can be certain when posting an entry that it will only affect the accounts intended. You can usually have as many accounts as you wish (or if there is a limit it is very large) – you are not limited to the columns on a page.

Accounting systems do not necessarily save time in terms of recording transactions in the first place: it takes about as long to enter a transaction in a computer-based accounting system as it does to write it in a book. But the major benefit is that a computer-based accounting system can produce a wide range of reports automatically from the transactions entered. You can usually print a profit and loss account or balance sheet within a few seconds, and you can do this at any time. With manual books it is very difficult to produce reports except when the books are periodically balanced off and even with spreadsheets considerable skill is needed to present bookkeeping totals as a readable report.

Of course, any computer-based application needs time to learn, and care is needed in setting up a sensible chart of accounts in the first place (you may need training to help with this). There is also the risk that if your computer fails, you could lose the whole year's accounts, so it is vital to take regular backups of the files. But this is, in fact, a great advantage of computer systems; the data can quickly and easily be backed up when needed, and the backups can then be taken off site so you could still recover the data even in the event of a fire or flood. Some charities are using cloud-based software where all information is held on the web, which gives the advantage of being able to access your records from anywhere you have Internet access – but of course you need to be confident of the long-term security of data held on the cloud: in most cases it still makes sense to keep local backups.

Compared with manual books or spreadsheets, computer-based accounting systems thus offer several advantages:

- much better financial information and reports available at any time;
- ability to handle many more categories than are (easily) possible with manual books;
- a huge time saving at end of quarter and end of year;
- a reliable audit trail (no risk of imbalanced double entries, for example);
- convenient and robust means to make security backups.

With larger and more complex general-purpose accounting systems, it may be possible to define your own reports to help make them more charity-specific, but this needs a lot of setting up and you will probably need a fairly sophisticated product.

Charity-specific accounting systems

Most smaller general-purpose accounting systems are based around the idea of small business accounts (or sometimes domestic household accounts). So although they will keep your transactions and post them to ledgers, it may take a lot of work at year end to get the accounts into the form you need, and you may need help from an accountant. In practice, charities using general-purpose accounting systems often rely heavily on downloading information into spreadsheets, and then use some spreadsheet manipulations to get what they need. This requires a lot of skill, both with the accounting system and the spreadsheet.

One of the key issues is usually fund accounting. As explained in chapter 3, this is quite different from departments within a business, because you need a separate balance forward on each fund. It is vital that you can determine the balance of any fund at any time without a lot of work. A number of general-purpose accounting systems do have some means of handling fund accounting – they may not use this term but there may be some other facility (e.g. 'classes') which allows you to divide the accounts into funds, rather just a single profit and loss account – but of course you must have a proper understanding of such features before attempting to define your chart of accounts.

Also, some general-purpose accounting systems have specific add-on modules for charity accounting. This may include the ability to handle fund accounting and facilities such as the ability to produce a SOFA (see chapter 7). If the structure of your accounts is directly linked to the accounting system the process is much easier.

However, there are also some accounting systems designed specifically for the charity sector (different products being aimed at differently sized organisations). At the smaller end, even if your charity only plans to do R&P accounts, a simple accounting system that handles multiple funds using double-entry bookkeeping, with the ability to produce an R&P account for each fund, is far better than relying on spreadsheets. But for organisations with more complex needs, charity-specific systems may be available which can handle multiple levels of coding (e.g. by projects, funds and activities) with project reporting across multiple years, and may even offer facilities such as partially exempt VAT calculations (see chapter 11).

Whether you choose a general-purpose or specialist accounting system, you will be making a considerable investment of time in getting a system set up and working. So it is important to consider what support you will get in the event of problems and queries (sometimes this can cost more than the software). Will you be dealing with people who have any charity-specific understanding if, for example, you need guidance on an inter-fund transfer? Also, if the system has documentation written specifically for charities this can be much easier than trying to set up a system using manuals or help features that assume you are running a business.

Posting interest, direct debits, direct receipts and similar items

Any bookkeeping system, whether manual or computerised, must show *all* financial transactions – including those that happen without your involvement at the time.

You will not necessarily know about every transaction in order to post it immediately when it occurred – for example, things such as bank interest, direct debits and bank charges may not be known until you see a bank statement (either in paper form or by online access to the charity's bank account). Likewise, much income may only come to your attention when you see it on a statement: this includes incoming standing orders from regular donors and many funders prefer to pay charities directly into your account by bank transfer (often called a BACS payment – 'Bankers Automated Clearing Services'). If you are regularly invoicing for work undertaken, many customers will pay your invoices by BACS.

In such cases, wait until you get the statement and then post these items in the books before closing off the accounts. In fact, it is always a good idea to do bank reconciliation before closing the books, so you can correct any erroneous postings (see page 87 for more on bank reconciliation).

If you rely on paper statements, you may need to ask your bank to let you have statements at dates that tie up with your accounting periods when you want to close off your books. (Online banking can ease this problem, but do make sure the security arrangements are adequate – see page 80.)

Bank interest is posted in the books as a normal receipt. Direct debits need entering as normal payments (remember – as we saw on page 66 – that, although a direct debit is a debit in the bank's books, with double-entry bookkeeping it will be a credit in your books). If you have incoming standing orders – perhaps for regular donations – enter them as receipts, though if you have a separate database for fundraising records it is usually best to enter incoming standing orders first in the fundraising system, and then transfer just a weekly or monthly total into the main accounts (rather than recording everything in two places).

Because you may have to wait for a bank statement to post these items, the entries in your books will not necessarily be in precise date order, but the date in the books should always relate to the original transaction (e.g. the date when the cheque was written, or the date the money came into your account – not the date of posting). These entries will not have cheque numbers to show in the books, so use codes such as 'DD' (direct debit), 'DC' (direct credit), 'Auto' (automatic payment), 'Int' (interest), 'SO' (standing order) and so on, to make the entry clear.

Wages and salaries

For many treasurers, the normal entry of receipts and payments is not too difficult, but wages and salaries can present particular problems because of the rules on tax, national insurance (NI) and other deductions. This book does not deal with the general principles of employing staff, but the following points outline some of the main day-to-day accounting issues linked to wages and salaries.

The points below relate to employed staff – if you have freelance (self-employed) workers, they will simply invoice you for their fees and you will pay them like any other bill. But do make sure they are genuinely freelance – there are large penalties for claiming someone is a freelancer if there is really an employer/employee relationship. HMRC's employment status indicator – available at www.tax.service.gov.uk/check-employment-status-for-tax – is a useful check.

Taking on staff

If your charity is taking on staff for the first time it is vital to register with HMRC as an employer and get an employer's PAYE (Pay As You Earn) reference – this can take several weeks, and you cannot operate a payroll system properly until you have this, so it is worth applying as soon as possible. PAYE records always relate to the tax year (6 April to 5 April) which is often different from the charity's accounting year – but this is rarely a problem: the PAYE system is normally separate from the accounts of the charity itself. Plenty of guidance is available both from books (see 'Further reading') and from the HMRC website www.gov.uk/topic/business-tax/paye. Courses are widely available for businesses (including charities) taking on staff for the first time.

Records are also needed to justify the initial basic salary levels – for example, if staff are paid according to the hours worked, the relevant time sheets are needed. When new staff are engaged or if staff are awarded a pay rise, the charity's auditor or examiner will expect to see a properly minuted decision from the trustees recording the pay levels agreed. All employees, of course, must be paid at least at the national minimum wage or national living wage if higher (£7.50 an hour from 1 April 2017 for those aged 25 and over, but the rates are reviewed). They must also receive paid holidays – at least 28 days a year for a full-time worker, and pro-rata for part-time.

PAYE calculations and systems

You cannot post salary payments in your accounts until the basic PAYE calculations have been done. The tasks of a treasurer or finance officer may include operating a PAYE system for the charity. However, PAYE is not particularly charity-specific: apart from the importance of understanding the distinctions between staff and volunteers, PAYE principles are the same for any organisation employing staff.

PAYE calculations have to be done each time wages or salaries are paid. In theory they can be done manually, but since 2013 the vast majority of employers must engage with the HMRC RTI (real-time information) requirements, so that salary and wage payments are communicated immediately to HMRC over the Internet – which enables HMRC to calculate tax credits and other benefits. Hence, any charity employing staff who are paid more than the PAYE threshold will normally use one of the following approaches:

- A small charity with no more than nine employees could use 'HMRC's Basic PAYE Tools' which is a free software application that can be downloaded from their website www.gov.uk/basic-paye-tools. You enter the gross salary and it does the PAYE calculations and provides the RTI data back to HMRC. However, it only carries out the basic calculations: you will still need to generate your own payslips, for example.

- A wide range of commercial payroll software applications are available – some designed for very small employers, and others intended for large organisations with thousands of staff (with prices to match) – although some free-to-use packages are available for those with no more than nine employees. Most systems will produce payslips and a good range of useful reports. Any system needs to comply with the HMRC RTI requirements – the HMRC employer's website lists all systems which HMRC has tested and verified.

- Many charities prefer to contract out their payroll arrangements to a payroll agency – indeed a number of charity infrastructure bodies offer specific payroll services for voluntary organisations. You normally pay a monthly fee for each employee, but this can be simpler than managing the payroll in-house – though, of course, you must still advise the agency of all salary changes, sick pay, hours worked by sessional staff and similar issues, so the time saving compared to operating your own payroll may not be as much as you imagine. Some payroll agencies handle the actual payments to the bank accounts of your employees; others will simply do the calculation and leave the charity to make the payments to the staff and to HMRC.

Whatever the approach, once the PAYE calculations are done, there are generally at least two payments to make – a net payment to the employee and a payment of taxes and NI to HMRC (Collector of Taxes). But the numbers can be quite confusing because there are three separate taxes: the employee's income tax (deducted from his/her salary); the *employee's* NI (also deducted from the salary) and the *employer's* NI, which has to be paid by all employers (including charities) on top of the gross salary due to the employee.

From the 2014/15 tax year, the government introduced an Employment Allowance to help businesses and charities with the cost of employing staff: the effect of this in 2016/17 is that the first £3,000 of *employer's* NI in each tax year is waived. Most PAYE systems will deduct this automatically from the amount you pay to HMRC. If the charity has only a few staff on modest salaries, this may mean that you do not pay any employer's NI at all. For example, in 2016/17 you could have one member of staff earning £29,000, or five staff each earning £12,000, without paying any employer's NI. However, you must still pay the deductions for *employee's* NI and income tax to HMRC as normal.

Pensions – auto enrolment

Also, all employers are being required to provide a workplace pension under the government's **auto enrolment** arrangements to ensure that all employees have access to a pension – both the employer and employee contribute. Unless the employer operates another pension scheme at least as good as the government scheme known as NEST (National Employment Savings Trust) all employees aged between 22 and pension age must be enrolled if they are paid over £10,000 per annum. So, with tax and NI this gives at least five elements to every payroll calculation.

Every employer is given a 'staging date' from which staff must be enrolled starting with the largest employers who have been in the scheme for some time. But, apart from those which only started PAYE schemes in 2012 or later, even very small employers should have staff enrolled by April 2017. Initially the minimum pension contribution is 1% of salary by the employer and employee (2% total) but this will rise to 2% and 3% (total 5%) from April 2018 and then to 3% and 5% (total 8%) from April 2019. However, the employee's element is calculated net of tax, and tax relief is added by NEST, so a 5% employee contribution is made up of a 4% payroll deduction and 1% reclaimed by NEST from the government.

An example salary calculation

Figure 5.7 shows a possible case (with hypothetical numbers). The employee has earned £1,500 salary this month, from which you must deduct income tax (£110 in this example) and employee's NI (£100) and employee's pension (£60). So the actual salary cheque – or the amount paid by bank transfer to the employee's account – is £1,230. You must then pay these deductions to HMRC, together with the £140 of employer's NI on top of the salary. So the total payment to HMRC in this example is £350. In addition, you pay £45 employer's pension contribution, so the total pension payment to NEST is £105. (This example does not take into account the possible reduction in employer's NI through the Employment Allowance – see previous page. It assumes any Employment Allowance has already been used earlier in the tax year.)

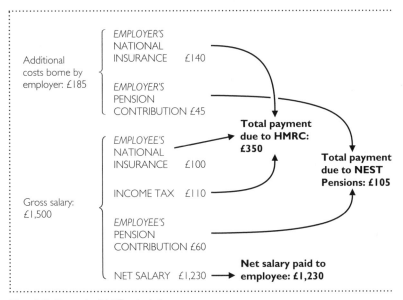

Fig. 5.7 Example PAYE calculations

The three payments – £1,230 to the employee, £350 to HMRC and £105 to NEST – add up to £1,685, which is the total cost of employing the person that month. If these are paid manually by cheque you will need to write three cheques, although in most cases payments will be by bank transfer or direct debit. If you have other deductions such as payroll giving (for donations to charity) or if the employee is making repayments to the Student Loans Agency, similar principles apply and you may then be making four or five payments in all every month.

Other adjustments can arise: in particular, employees may be entitled to statutory sick pay (SSP), statutory maternity pay (SMP), statutory paternity pay (SPP) or statutory adoption pay (SAP). Employers can normally recover 92% of SMP, SPP and SAP from HMRC and for small employers, who pay less than £45,000 a year of employer's NI (which includes all but the largest charities), HMRC will reimburse 103% of the cost. This means you get the full cost back and something towards the administration involved. However, there is no reimbursement of SSP, so if staff are sick, the extra cost has to be treated as an expense met by the charity. If you have employees affected by any of these issues you will almost certainly want to use payroll software to do the calculations.

Posting salary payment in the charity's accounts

It is generally best to post each payment as a separate entry in the books, although if you understand journals it is possible to post an entire month's payroll as a single journal – but be sure to keep a detailed record of how you arrived at the figures, especially if different staff costs are charged to different funds. These computations will form part of the charity's accounting records and will be needed by the auditor or examiner at year end.

Some organisations like to allocate the employer's NI (and any pension contributions paid by the employer) to a different account from the gross salary in order to distinguish 'on costs' (as they are often called) from direct salary. In order to get the correct totals, the example in figure 5.7 would need the following postings (expressed in double-entry format):

£1,230 Net salary cheque
      Credit: Bank £1,230
      Debit: Salary expenditure £1,230

£350 Collector of Taxes cheque
      Credit: Bank £350
      Debit: Salary expenditure £210
      Debit: Employer's NI expenditure £140

£105 NEST Pensions cheque
      Credit: Bank £105
      Debit: Salary expenditure £60
      Debit: Employer's NI pension costs £45

Where salary costs have to be split between two accounts – perhaps because a member of staff is splitting their time between two projects – apportion both the net salary payment and the HMRC payment on the same formula. If you want your books to be linked directly to the format of the SOFA (see chapter 7), you may also need to split salary costs between time spent on charitable activities as opposed to time spent on raising funds. But if you need to do apportionments like this, try to avoid also splitting out the employer's NI, or the whole process could become unmanageable.

If you have several employees you will normally make a single payment to HMRC, to cover the tax and NI for all staff, and likewise a single payment to NEST for the total pension contributions. If you do this, take care to allocate the costs for each employee to the correct expenditure accounts.

The payment to HMRC does not have to be made until the 19th of the following month (22nd if paid electronically), so this can mean that quite a large creditor is outstanding in your accounts at year end.

To show this properly you really need to use accruals accounting (see chapter 10) with the tax amount entered as a creditor. So, in the example above, at the time of doing the payroll you would post:

£350 HMRC amount due
    Credit: Creditor (tax and NI) £350
    Debit: Salary expenditure £210
    Debit: Employer's NI expenditure £140

and then when the payment is made (possibly in the following year) the entry will be:

£350 creditor – payment paid to HMRC
    Credit: Bank £350
    Debit: Creditor (tax and NI) £350

If you do not want to get into this, the simplest way is to pay all the tax and NI to HMRC before the end of the month; you can then use normal payments, as in the example on page 76).

Posting non-bank transactions

The vast majority of transactions in your books will be receipts and payments of some kind, or possibly transfers of money between bank accounts. If you forget to enter any of these you will soon realise when you do a bank reconciliation (see page 87).

Before you close the books at the end of an accounting period, you need some means of checking with others whether any non-bank entries are needed.

A transfer between funds (see page 39) is, in effect, a payment from one fund and a receipt into another fund, but if the funds share the same bank account, no bank entry is involved. Or in double entry terms:

£500 transfer from General Fund to Outreach Fund

Debit: General Fund expenditure 'Transfers *to* other funds' £500

Credit: Outreach Fund income 'Transfers *from* other funds' £500

It is best to post fund transfers to columns or accounts separately from other receipts and payments, so that they can be separated as inter-fund transfers on the SOFA, and are not confused with external receipts or payments.

If you are keeping accruals accounts, you will also need a wide range of other non-bank postings, in order to enter debtors, creditors, depreciation and so on (see chapter 10). With R&P accounts, these do not have to be entered in the monetary books, but you still need to have some means of tracking debtors, creditors and fixed assets – a manual list may be sufficient – so you can include them on the statement of assets and liabilities (SOAL – see chapter 7).

6 Checks and controls

Bookkeeping procedures, as discussed in the previous chapter, are only useful if people are confident about them. A key question for the trustees of any charity (and for its donors, funders, members and others) is: 'Do the books properly record all the income due to the charity and all expenditure as agreed by the trustees?'

To some extent this will be answered at year end by the charity's independent examiner or auditor – see chapter 8. But examiners and auditors rely heavily on the internal controls built into your own systems: if you want your auditors to examine every item of expenditure individually and check whether it has been approved by trustees and posted to the correct fund, you will have to pay an astronomical audit fee. In any case, the trustees have a legal duty to keep proper records, and the examiner or auditor will want assurances from the trustees that they have done so; it is difficult to give such an assurance unless the trustees are confident that proper checks and controls are working.

Moreover, if there are problems in the books, you want to know about them before year end; for example, if a fraud was going on but was not uncovered until after year end, a great deal of money could have been lost. At a lesser level, any treasurer or bookkeeper will make occasional mistakes, and the more these can be picked up through simple checks the better the quality of the financial information obtained from the accounts.

Approval of expenditure

In a tiny charity, every payment might be discussed individually at a trustees' meeting and the cheques written and signed there and then. But most organisations need to delegate decisions for approving day-to-day expenses and writing cheques.

However, these procedures need to be clear and robust, otherwise there is a serious risk of the charity's funds being spent on non-charitable purposes or on costs that are not intended or agreed. Moreover, with multiple funds (see chapter 3) you need to ensure that expenditure is considered separately in relation to each relevant fund, and then posted to the correct fund in the books.

Controls on signing cheques and other payments

A basic requirement now widely accepted in charitable organisations of all sizes is to ensure that all cheques or other payments are authorised by two people – normally two trustees. The Charity Commission expects charities to have such controls, and many funders impose similar conditions on organisations applying for grants.

However, other arrangements are generally acceptable for smaller amounts if the bank will accept formal instructions with different levels of signing. For example, a charity with eight staff and £200,000 income might use the following:

- cheques or other one-off payments of up to £500: one signature required, signatory can be a senior member of staff or a trustee;
- cheques or one-off payments of £500 to £10,000: two signatures, of which at least one signatory must be a trustee;
- cheques of £10,000 and above or any recurring payments (standing orders/direct debits): must be signed by two trustees.

The very largest payments should always require two trustees' signatures – and for the controls to work, the bank must be willing to follow these rules for *all* payments going out of the account, not just cheques. But you must ensure such arrangements are permitted by your governing document; if your constitution or trust deed says 'all payments must be authorised by two trustees', you must keep to this.

Some organisations find it difficult to get two signatories that include at least one trustee, and they try to find ways round it. But provided that you have three or four signatories (on an 'any two out of four' basis), you should usually be able to get cheques signed within a few days, even if they have to go by post between signatories.

Many banks now offer online banking systems whereby electronic payments can be approved remotely by signatories over the Internet. For example, a payment can be raised by a finance officer, which generates an email to the signatories, but the payment will not be released until two separate trustees have each clicked on an appropriate weblink to authorise the transaction and entered a personal password. Such approaches are just as good as requiring dual signatures on cheques.

However, banks sometimes suggest charities operate the sort of online banking arrangements common on personal accounts where a single person can authorise payments with no limit – but trustees should never agree to this on a charity's main account (it may sometimes be justified on a minor account limited to a small balance – see 'Urgent small payments' on page 83). Trustees need to be wary of a finance officer or treasurer who says, 'Could you just sign this form so I can get online access to check statements and so on – it will save so much time' – if the online access will allow the person concerned to authorise payments without a second signatory. (But read-only online access – i.e. where a person can view transactions and statements but cannot initiate payments – is usually fine, so long as passwords are kept confidential.)

Also, great care needs to be taken over Internet security and passwords – most people receive numerous bogus phishing emails pretending to be from banks, and an inexperienced staff member or trustee can easily be fooled.

All payments should, of course, be approved by two *independent* signatories. So, for payments such as reimbursing trustees' expenses, the trustee being paid should not be one of the signatories (unless that specific payment has been discussed by the trustees as a whole).

However, where a charity has separate current and deposit accounts, it is often helpful if the treasurer or finance officer can make transfers between accounts held at the same bank without trustees' approval and without anyone else having to sign. No money is going outside the charity in such cases, and this flexibility can allow the charity to get as much interest as possible on any funds not needed immediately.

Where a charity has **investments**, similar arrangements may be appropriate for small transfers, but the trustees must remain responsible for the investment policy, and hence they should not allow major investment decisions to be made by one person.

The role of the second signatory

Having cheques or electronic payments authorised by two people only offers protection if both signatories give careful thought before signing. For one person to pre-sign cheques before they are completed, or even to sign completed cheques without any real thought, offers no protection at all.

Suppose you are the second trustee authorised to sign cheques and the treasurer presents you with a cheque or electronic payment for countersignature; it is worth asking these questions before signing.

- Is the payment for a definite bill or invoice? If so, be sure you see the bill and check the amount and the payee before signing.
- If the payment is for an item with no invoice, such as wages or salaries, is the amount reasonable? (You need to know salary scales of the staff concerned.) Depending on the deductions, salary payments

tend to be for awkward amounts, but from time to time you should ask to check the PAYE calculations. If there are two payments, one to the employee and one to HMRC, look at the total of the two. If a salary payment is increased because of overtime or a pay rise, make sure you see the paperwork.

- Before signing for standing orders or direct debits, be sure that the trustees have agreed the relevant payment on an ongoing basis. With direct debits, where your supplier can vary the charge, is there a proper procedure to check that the amounts going through the bank are correct?

- With cheques to draw petty cash, always insist on seeing the petty cash records explaining how the previous petty cash was spent. Be very suspicious if someone tells you that extra large amounts of petty cash are needed – what are the reasons, and how will the cash be controlled?

- Does the bill relate to expenditure of a kind that the trustees have approved? Even if the expenditure looks reasonable in principle, does it fall within agreed budgets (see chapter 9)? If not, insist on waiting until the issue can be discussed at a trustees' meeting.

- Even if the expenditure is apparently reasonable, is it appropriate for the fund concerned? For example, an older people's project might have a budget for 'equipment' but if you are asked to authorise a payment to a supplier of children's play equipment you might be suspicious. (Bills should always be marked to show where the cost will be allocated before anyone is asked to authorise payment.)

- Have you already authorised a cheque or payment for the same item? This could be an oversight, but some frauds rely on making payments twice and then diverting the second payment. If there are several co-signatories this needs care – you may want to look back through the chequebook (and with a new chequebook, make sure the cheque numbers run on from the previous one). If authorising electronically, look back through past transactions.

- If it is an electronic payment, check the account number to which payment is being made – does this tie up with the supplier's invoice, or some other authenticated document showing the recipient's bank details? A common means of fraud is to set up what appears to be a legitimate payment, but where the bank details entered are actually a personal account controlled by the fraudster rather than the intended recipient. (This is particularly an issue in grant-making charities. A firm which has supplied goods or services will generally complain if they do not receive payment, but an intended grant recipient may simply assume their application was unsuccessful if they do not receive anything.) Even if there is no fraud, simple errors take a long time to be resolved if a payment is sent to the wrong account.

However, charities need to take care on payments of all kinds – there is no point in having thorough checks on the payment of small bills unless your controls are just as strict for paying salaries. Since many charities pay salaries by BACS the key issue is who is allowed to sign the transfer mandate? In many charities this is the largest single area of expenditure each month so, ideally, two trustees should sign it (following careful checks of the PAYE calculations – see page 73). If this is impossible for timing reasons, and the trustees decide to delegate this to a single trustee, the bank should be given an upper limit. Where a member of staff is basically responsible for his or her own salary computations, regular checks are vital. If, as a treasurer, you do not really understand PAYE and you leave it entirely to a member of staff, the trustees are taking great risks.

Urgent small payments

Where small payments have to be made urgently, petty cash is one solution. An alternative is to open a small bank account, topped up from time to time by transfers from the main account, where cheques or payments up to a small amount can be authorised by just one member of staff. If it is always replenished to a fixed level this is sometimes called an imprest account. The chief control with such an account will be when making transfers from the main account which should always need dual authorisation, just as when drawing petty cash.

Alternatively, the charity may be eligible for a business credit or debit card in the charity's name. Relevant trustees or members of staff are given individual cards linked to a common account to pay for small items of expenditure agreed in principle by the trustees. But the limits on such cards must be very modest (perhaps no more than £250 a month) and the statements need to be checked carefully each month by someone *other* than the cardholders, with a clear procedure for alerting trustees if unauthorised expenditure appears. Even so, the person reviewing the statements should see original receipts, to guard against people making personal purchases using a charity debit or credit card.

Many charities have been victims of serious frauds by treasurers or staff running up personal expenditure on such cards, or even making cash withdrawals, that have remained unchecked for too long. If the treasurer is the person who checks the card statements then he or she should *not* have a card. Also, the issue of any additional cards should always require two signatures.

Purchases and expenditure commitments

Expenditure should not only be controlled at the stage of writing the cheque or authorising the payment. If something has been bought, and the charity has received an invoice from the supplier, it is hard for trustees to refuse to agree payment at that stage. So, care is needed to ensure that members of staff cannot commit the charity to expenditure of any kind unless the trustees have approved it (either in terms of an overall budget for an activity or, with large items, on a one-off basis). Similarly, any new contracts of employment or notification of pay rises to existing staff should require formal trustee approval. If there is clear written guidance on these lines, you would have the possible sanction of disciplinary action if a member of staff deliberately incurred expenditure outside such rules.

Control of income

Many charities have fairly strict controls on expenditure but are quite lax on the income side. There are two main risks to consider:
* the risk of income due to the charity being diverted;
* the risk of accepting income where the obligations are too great in relation to the amount received, so that the net effect is a drain on the charity's funds.

On the first point, charities are particularly vulnerable, especially in terms of donations. A customer who sent a payment to a business but did not receive the items ordered would almost certainly complain, but a donor who hears nothing in response to their donation may simply assume the charity is saving administrative costs by not issuing receipts. A donor who puts money into a cash collection certainly does not expect a receipt. So trustees need to establish systems to reduce the chances of income going astray.

On the second point, it is vital that trustees are involved in approval of all major funding bids – most funders require a trustee's signature on grant applications, but this is not universal. When it comes to tendering for contracts, there is always a risk, if controls are not in place, that a well-meaning member of staff might submit a tender to carry out work at too low a price. Sometimes the first that the trustees hear about such a contract is when they learn of a new 'successful' funding bid which, when examined, is actually committing the charity to significant new expenditure which the trustees have never agreed. This relates to the key issue of apportioning overheads and full cost recovery (see page 50). If a charity is agreeing to undertake new or additional work and sets too low a price, the net result can be as bad as if incoming donations were being put on a bonfire.

So, while very different from expenditure controls, the controls in relation to income are just as important.

For charities whose income consists of a small number of large grants, then as long as the trustees approved the grant applications, the main issue is controlling expenditure. But in charities where much of the income comes from ad hoc donations, there is a huge risk of funds being lost because of donations not being banked into the charity's bank account in the first place.

The risk is greatest with incoming cash. If you have cash collections, for example collections at religious services or community events, try to ensure that the money is within sight of at least two independent people from the moment it is given, until it is counted and signed for. You need some kind of record form, signed by both people at the time the cash is counted. With other kinds of collections – in the street or with static boxes – charities should always use collecting boxes with a seal, and have a clear rule that there must be two people present when the seal is removed and the box opened.

Even incoming cheques present risks. If the charity's name is often abbreviated to initials, it is not that difficult for someone dishonest to alter the payee and pay the cheque into a personal account. More serious cases of fraud have involved dishonest treasurers opening an additional bank account in the charity's name, not known to the other trustees or the auditor, and diverting substantial funds through that account.

Many charities that receive ad hoc donations thus try to arrange for all incoming post to be opened with two people present. This can be difficult in a very small organisation, but if you can only manage one person, try to vary the person, have a strict rule on recording all donations as soon as the post is opened, and make regular spot checks.

Control of income is also about making sure that the charity receives all the income promised. If you have donors or funders making promises of future support, you need a system to check that what is received corresponds (at least) to what was promised – some organisations are very lax about sending reminders. With anyone making a regular gift, it is always worth enquiring if the gifts suddenly stop – the person may still wish to give and it could just be an error by their bank. With major grants that are paid in instalments, the charity normally has to complete a monitoring or claim form to receive the second and subsequent instalments: amazingly, some charities fail to make these claims.

Honesty

Clearly no system of checks can be absolutely secure, particularly in a small organisation, and the first point of control is to ensure that all trustees and all staff involved with the finances of the charity are honest and dependable. With staff, taking up references is important. Similarly, if someone relatively new to an organisation volunteers to become the treasurer, it is worth enquiring about the person's background, and perhaps seeking a reference from any previous charity with which he or she has been involved.

Many charities routinely undertake checks on new trustees under the government's Disclosure and Barring Services (DBS checks – formerly known as CRB checks). However, this is not an absolute requirement unless the charity is working with children or vulnerable adults, and some charities may not be permitted to undertake such checks. In any case, such checks are of no use unless the trustees have a clear policy as to how the results will be considered.

In many organisations honesty is taken for granted, and sometimes treasurers feel threatened if they are asked to have a witness when counting cash or when the second signatory asks questions before signing a cheque. There is an assumption in much of the voluntary sector that honesty is so fundamental to the organisation's beliefs that independent checks are unnecessary.

However, as many organisations know to their cost, even those with the most noble aims are sometimes led astray. Quite apart from the risk of fraud, a second person looking at cheques and receipts reduces the risk of error. Also, even the most honest treasurers sometimes get months behind with their books if no one asks to see them: the charity as a whole needs a means of picking up signs when a treasurer is no longer coping and needs to step down.

Verifying the books

Having proper controls on income and expenditure is the first step, but you then need to be sure that what is recorded in the books corresponds to what has been agreed. Even the most honest person will make occasional errors, and you need the means to identify these and correct them. There have been cases where, either through fraud or incompetence, the books completely fail to reflect the actual monies coming in and out.

Bank reconciliation

One of the most important checks is to do a bank reconciliation every time a bank statement is received. While this does not prove that everything in the books is correct, it does give a strong confirmation that what has been posted to the bank account in the books of the charity corresponds to what has physically gone through the bank.

If you have several bank accounts, you need to do this for each account; and you need to ensure bank statements are received frequently enough so that if there is a discrepancy you have a reasonable chance of finding the cause (normally you will want a monthly statement on your main current account). If the charity does not receive paper statements, the process still needs to be undertaken at least (say) once a month against an online statement (and the online statement needs to be printed, or at least saved as an electronic copy that cannot be easily modified – e.g. as a PDF).

Of course, bank reconciliation is only possible if you are maintaining a bank balance in your books that can be cross-checked. Your own figure could be in a 'bank' column in an analysed cashbook (see chapter 5), or in a separate bank ledger (for example, in a computer system) or, in a very small organisation, the running bank balance could be maintained as a running chequebook balance (provided you also have a cashbook to analyse the purpose of each receipt or payment).

In general, the bank balance in the books will not correspond to the balance on the bank statement because of the issue of uncleared cheques (also known as 'unpresented' cheques). For example, suppose you wrote a cheque for £50 to Jane Smith on 15 January. If she had not paid it into her own account by about 28 January, it will not appear on your bank statement dated 31 January. In your books, you would have deducted the payment on 15 January, when you wrote the cheque, but at 31 January the money is still in the charity's bank account. If this were the only case, the balance on the bank statement would thus be £50 higher than the balance in your books. Uncleared items can also arise with electronic payments if there is a time interval between raising the payment and getting dual online authorisation (see page 80).

There can be similar delays with receipts if they were paid in just before the statement date.

In order to allow for uncleared items, you need a means of marking in your books when each cheque, receipt or any other bank transaction has cleared – many people put a tick against the cheque in their books and on the statement (and computer-based accounting systems often have a means to do this automatically).

You then need to go through the books, noting all uncleared items (which could be in any fund which uses the bank account concerned). Add up the uncleared cheques, and the uncleared receipts if you have any. Remember to include items still uncleared from previous months – in some cases this may mean going back to the previous year's accounts. You can then set down a bank reconciliation calculation (see figure 6.1).

Bank reconciliation – Current account as at 31 January

BALANCE OF ACCOUNT AS ON BANK STATEMENT:			£2,236.75
Less uncleared cheques:			
	000274	15.00	
	000276	678.00	
		693.00	−693.00
Plus uncleared receipts:	None		0
Expected balance in books:			£1,543.75
ACTUAL BALANCE OF BANK ACCOUNT IN BOOKS:			£1,543.75

Fig. 6.1 Bank reconciliation

If the bank statement does not end on the exact date at which you are closing the books, be sure to draw a line on the statement at the relevant date, and use that balance (i.e. not the final balance on the statement).

If the expected balance from the calculation ties up with the actual balance recorded in your books, this is a good confirmation of your bookkeeping. If there is a discrepancy, work out the difference between the two figures, and look for an error of that amount.

The possible causes of bank reconciliation errors must always come down to one or more of the following:

- a payment or receipt entered in the books is marked as cleared, but in fact it has not yet gone through the bank;
- a payment or receipt is marked in the books as not cleared when in fact it has appeared on a bank statement;
- an item on the bank statement has not been entered in the books at all (look especially at interest payments, direct debits, bank charges, transfers between accounts, and incoming and outgoing standing orders);
- an item has been entered in the books twice (and possibly both entries have been marked as cleared when in fact there was only one item on the bank statement);

- an item was entered in the books as a payment but it was actually a receipt (or vice versa) – if so, the discrepancy on reconciliation will be twice the amount of the item (watch too for transfers between current and deposit accounts which have been posted the wrong way round – this has the same effect);
- an item appears in the books and on the bank statement, but the amounts are different, usually due to a clerical error (this takes a lot of time to spot – get someone to call out the statement while you check the books, or vice versa: note that if the discrepancy divides exactly by nine it is likely to be a transposition error, for instance a cheque was written for £23.70 but posted in the books as £27.30: the difference is £3.60, which divides by nine);
- if you have several bank accounts, an item has been posted in the books to the wrong account;
- a calculation error in the running balance in the books, if maintained manually.

The hardest problems to resolve are where there are two or more errors combined, for example a transposition error *and* an item missing, so the total discrepancy does not divide by nine, neither does it tie up with any particular amount entered. But if the reconciliation was correct the previous month, the problem must be something in the books that has changed since then: this is why it is important to do bank reconciliation regularly. Remember that when you mark the books for items that are now cleared, you will often be marking prior months' entries as well as those for the current month. So, in considering what has changed since the previous month, you may be looking at several months' entries.

Other checks on the books

With petty cash, the main check is to count the physical amount of petty cash regularly, to be sure it corresponds with the expected value in the books. If not, is it a clerical error, or has someone been taking petty cash without authority? If the balance in the cash tin is higher than expected – not unknown in charities – it could be because of people putting donations in the tin. It is best to make some other arrangement for cash donations.

With the accounts for the different categories of income and expenditure, physical checks are rarely possible; the main test is one of reasonableness. This is where budgets help enormously. If a given account is heavily over or under budget, is there a good reason, or is it because receipts or payments have been posted correctly as far as the bank account is concerned, but allocated to the wrong income or expenditure category?

With multiple funds, it is particularly important to be certain that all income and expenses are allocated to the correct fund, otherwise restricted funds (see chapter 3) may be used for the wrong purposes. For example, it is not unusual in a charity with multiple projects to find that someone's salary has been charged to the wrong fund for several months. Regular sample checks of this kind by someone other than the treasurer or bookkeeper can help to pick up problems at an early stage.

Subsidiary groups

Many charities have subsidiary groups that handle their own money on a day-to-day basis, but which are legally part of the main charity.

It is important to remember that money under the control of such groups is part of the funds for which the charity trustees are responsible, and at year end these figures must be included with the main accounts in order to produce proper year end accounts for the whole charity. (This is called **consolidation**.)

Make sure that such groups have reasonable controls to prevent money belonging to the charity from going astray, and ensure that charity money is not being held in personal accounts. If such groups have their own bank account, check that proper procedures are followed for cheque signatories and bank reconciliation. To prevent groups harbouring funds that no one knows about, it is important to have a rule that no bank account can be opened by any group without approval by the trustees.

At year end, you may want to give each subsidiary treasurer a form to return to you – see figure 6.2 for an example. These figures can then be posted into the books of the main charity, treating the group as a separate fund and creating an additional bank account or petty cash account in the charity's books for the amounts held by the group. If the main charity provides financial support to the group – line (4) – or if proceeds are transferred from the group to the main charity – line (7) – then, although these are seen as receipts or payments from the perspective of the group, they need to be recorded as inter-fund transfers in the accounts of the charity as a whole, in order to ensure that income or expenditure is not counted twice. Once a group has been operating for more than a year, a crucial but simple check is to be sure that the opening balance of the second year agrees with the closing balance from the previous year.

NAME OF CHARITY

Name of group: ....

Year ending: 31 March ....

(1)	Balance of group at 1 April last year: (Cash in hand + bank if applicable)	£....................
(2)	Receipts from group members:	£....................
(3)	Receipts from external sources:	£.................... (give details)
(4)	Contributions from the main charity:	£....................
(5)	Total receipts	£.................... (2)+(3)+(4)
(6)	Payments by group:	£....................
(7)	Proceeds transferred to main charity:	£....................
(8)	Total payments:	£.................... (6)+(7)
(9)	Balance in hand at year end 31 March: (Cash in hand + bank if applicable)	£....................
(10)	Check calculation:	£.................... (1)+(5)–(8)

If lines (9) and (10) are not equal there is an error in your books – please explain.

I confirm that records have been kept of the above items, which can be made available to the charity's auditor or independent examiner on request.

Signed .... *(group leader)*

Fig. 6.2 A possible form for subsidiary groups to submit to the overall treasurer

7 Final accounts

For many treasurers and finance officers, producing the year end accounts is the most demanding task of the year. But, although you will probably be quite busy in the weeks immediately after year end, if you have been keeping books in good form and maintaining adequate controls, the year end process can be quite rewarding, as you see your work come to fruition and put into a form for digestion by the outside world.

Obviously the work will be considerably less if your books are structured in a way that links closely to the year end accounts. If you are using a computerised accounting system set up in a way that enables you to generate reports in line with the SORP, or for charity-specific receipts and payments (R&P) accounts, the task is simpler still. (But bear in mind that all transactions for the year, including special entries such as inter-fund transfers, must have been posted correctly on your system if you want to rely on reports from the system as a basis for your year end accounts.)

Who are the accounts for?

Although several chapters of this book are concerned with the legal requirements for the accounts, it is important to remember that your final accounts are much more than a document to meet charity law.

Companies in business sometimes produce the briefest possible accounts that comply with the law, in order to avoid disclosing too much to their competitors. But for a charity, the opposite usually applies: your annual accounts are a key means of communication with members, funders and supporters (present and future), and you will often want to include more than the legal minimum. Your accounts may also go to umbrella bodies to which you are affiliated, to Companies House (if your organisation is a charitable company), to HMRC in some cases, and elsewhere. If you are applying for grants, your prospective funders may read your accounts much more closely than the relevant **charity regulator** (Charity Commission, OSCR or CCNI). However, you also want to avoid giving so much detail that readers cannot see the overall picture. To a large extent the legal requirements help in this, by requiring a certain degree of standardisation in the accounts of all charities.

Before preparing a set of accounts for the first time, or before making a major change to the current format, it is worth thinking carefully about all the audiences at whom you are aiming. In principle you could produce different sorts of accounts for different audiences. For example, some larger charities produce full accounts for the Charity Commission and for supporters who want the full detail, and summarised accounts for others. However, for a smaller charity, this is a lot of extra work; the summarised accounts must make clear that they are only a summary, and should preferably include a statement by your auditor or independent examiner that they are not inconsistent with the full accounts. Many charities find that those supporters who want accounts want the full detail, and others are not really interested in accounts at all.

Similarly, a charitable company in England and Wales could, in theory, produce one set of accounts complying with the SORP to send to the Charity Commission, and another set meeting the minimum filing requirements under the Companies Acts to send to Companies House. But in practice, it is much less work to produce one set of accounts that meets the requirements of both charity law and company law.

The full documents

In law, a charity must produce two public documents at year end – the annual report and the annual accounts. Each must be approved and signed by the trustees before they can be circulated, and in most cases the accounts must have an auditor's or independent examiner's report (see chapter 8). They can be printed or copied separately, but anyone requesting the accounts must also be given the annual report and vice versa, so it is usually best to combine them into one document called the 'annual report and accounts'.

As explained in chapter 2, there are two ways of producing the accounts:
- The R&P basis, which is allowed for non-company charities with an income of up to £250,000 (this includes CIOs).
- The accruals basis, following the Charities SORP – this approach can be used by any charity but is compulsory for charities with an income of more than £250,000, and in all cases for charitable companies (regardless of income).

Depending on which basis is used, the final document will comprise the elements as follows.

Presentation of the report and accounts

Charity Annual Report & Accounts – R&P basis	Charity Annual Report & Accounts – accruals/SORP basis
TRUSTEES' ANNUAL REPORT[1] ANNUAL ACCOUNTS comprising: • R&P account • Statement of assets and liabilities (SOAL) (or statement of balances in Scotland) • Notes (if needed – compulsory in Scotland, and for CIOs in England & Wales) REPORT OF THE AUDITOR OR INDEPENDENT EXAMINER[2]	TRUSTEES' ANNUAL REPORT[1] ANNUAL ACCOUNTS comprising: • SOFA • Balance sheet • Statement of cash flows (for larger charities)[3] • Notes to the accounts (always needed) REPORT OF THE AUDITOR OR INDEPENDENT EXAMINER[2]

[1] *The trustees' report is not compulsory for excepted charities in England and Wales (i.e. those excepted from registration with the Charity Commission – see chapter 2. This includes most churches with an income of less than £100,000). However, the link between the accounts and report is so crucial that it is a good idea to prepare a trustees' report even where it is not mandatory.*

[2] *The report of the auditor or independent examiner often appears in front of the accounts (immediately after the trustees' report) so that readers know whether the auditor/independent examiner raised any qualifications before they read the accounts. However, an auditor's or independent examiner's report is not generally required in England and Wales for charities with an income of up to £25,000.*

[3] *Under the SORP 2015 (FRS102), as updated from 2016, a statement of cash flows is needed for charities with an income of more than £500,000.*

Note that these are the only formats permitted by law. Mixtures of R&P and accruals accounting, and other formats from the past, will not generally meet the needs of charity law. (Slightly different rules apply to charitable higher education bodies, registered social landlords and charity investment funds – but these are outside the scope of this book.)

The choice of format — R&P or accruals/SORP

The R&P basis is generally simpler, because the main R&P account only includes details of money received and paid out during the year concerned. You still have to keep track of debtors, creditors and fixed assets but they are just listed on the SOAL. But if the charity has different funds (see chapter 3) the R&P account must still distinguish the individual funds.

However, accruals accounts are generally considered more meaningful, as they show the income which has accrued to the charity over the year – not just the actual cash received. So, for example, on the accruals basis, if the charity has invoiced for work done but has not been paid by year end, this income is included in the year it is billed (not the following year when it is paid) as it is part of the income the charity has earned. On the expenditure side the accounts show the accrued expenses – which may include costs which the charity has incurred for the year, even if they were not paid by year end. With accruals accounts, the cost of major items like fixed assets will be spread over several years, rather than charged in full at the time of purchase. (For more on this distinction, see 'Accruals or receipts and payments?' on page 30. For more on the principles of accruals accounting and specific entries needed in the books, see chapter 10.) If you use the accruals basis, the final accounts must be prepared to comply with the relevant Charities SORP (see chapter 2).

Accruals accounts are much better at comparing the resources of a charity from year to year as they are not affected by the precise timing of payments and receipts – so they are considered to give a **true and fair view** on the financial strength of the charity (rather than just a factual presentation). Moreover, the SORP presentation means that the accounts of different charities can be compared more meaningfully than with R&P accounts.

However, as noted above, the accruals/SORP basis is only compulsory for charities in England, Wales and Scotland with an income of more than £250,000 and for charitable companies – this applies to around 20% of charities in the UK. The remaining 80% of charities have a choice.

Overall there are many more small charities than large charities, and the majority of UK charity accounts are on the R&P basis. Many professional accountants – and some funders – prefer the accruals/SORP basis, but

R&P accounts, if properly prepared, can still be clear and effective. You will also need a less specialised independent examiner with R&P accounts which may save costs – see chapter 8. However, if you are applying to the same funders as larger organisations, having SORP accounts can make the charity look more professional.

In most cases trustees will take the treasurer's recommendation on which approach to use, but it is also a good idea to seek the views of the charity's auditor or independent examiner and to consult with those involved in funding bids. Either way, a trustees' report will almost always be needed alongside the accounts, as explained below.

The rest of this chapter explains the general framework for both the trustees' report and the accounts. But preparing final accounts, particularly accruals accounts in SORP format, involves much more than can be covered in a book of this length. There are plenty of books giving more detailed advice – see 'Further reading'. Figures 7.1 (for R&P accounts) and 7.2 (for SORP accounts) illustrate the formats you will commonly see (but beware of using these examples as models, because they are deliberately quite simple and different information may be needed in other charities).

Contents of the annual report

Because the trustees' annual report normally comes first in the final documents, and because it sets out all the all-important details of the charity's objects and governing document and names of the trustees, it is usually best to start with the annual report before getting into the detail of the annual accounts.

The link between the annual report and the annual accounts is absolutely crucial in enabling someone who does not understand the charity to get a proper understanding (the Charities SORP refers to this on many occasions). Quite often there will be cross-references between them; for example, the annual report of a grant-making charity may refer readers to a note to the accounts for the full list of grants made. A service-providing charity may describe each project in the annual report (explaining which projects are managed as separate funds) and then refer readers to the particular note in the accounts with figures for each fund (see figure 9.2 on page 138 for an example of a report which could well be used for such a note).

The treasurer is usually responsible for arranging the preparation of the annual accounts, but it may be that someone else in the charity – perhaps the secretary or chief officer – will draft the annual report. However, in such cases there needs to be a good deal of liaison, especially if there are cross-references. Liaison is particularly crucial on aspects of the annual report dealing with financial issues, such as comments on funding, the financial performance for the year, the statement of the reserves policy (see chapter 4) and any comments on funds in deficit.

It is not possible in this book to cover the full requirements for annual reports, but the following box gives a summary of the legal requirements. It may fall to you as the treasurer to ensure that the other trustees are aware of these requirements.

The annual report and the accounts must always cover the same financial year. If you are writing a report several months after the year has finished don't report events after year end as though they are part of the year concerned. You may on occasions need to say something like 'After year end the trustees received confirmation of a new £25,000 grant from the XYZ Trust' – that way it is clearly outside the year concerned, and no one will expect to see the grant in the accounts for that year.

Charity annual reports – summary of requirements

Factual section

(a) Official name of the charity (and any working names)

(b) Registered charity number (if registered) and company number (if applicable)

(c) Official address of the charity*

(d) Particulars of the governing document (including date of last amendment)

(e) Description of the objects of the charity (usually this is easily obtained from the constitution or other governing document)

(f) Names* of the charity trustees as at the date of approving the report

(g) Names* of all other trustees who served for any part of the financial year

(h) Any external persons* or bodies entitled to appoint trustees to the charity

(i) Names* of holding trustees at date of approval

(j) Any other holding trustees* during year

*If disclosing trustees' names or an official address would put anyone in personal danger, the charity can apply to the Charity Commission for permission to omit them.[5]

Narrative section (public benefit report)

- Statement that the trustees have considered the Charity Commission's guidance on public benefit
- Charities below the audit threshold:[1] a brief review of the main activities undertaken during the year in terms of public benefit achieved
- Charities over the audit threshold:[1] review of significant activities undertaken during the year in terms of public benefit achieved – including the trustees' aims for the year, progress against the aims, contribution of volunteers and principal funding sources

Policies section

- Policy on level of reserves (see page 53)
- Action being taken on any funds in deficit

Extras needed for charities over the audit threshold [1]

- Organisational structure
- Risk assessment
- Policy on trustee induction and training
- Investment policy and review of investment performance (see page 189)
- Grant-making policy

Approval

This report was approved by the trustees on [date] and is signed on their behalf by . . . . [normally two trustees should sign].

[1] The audit threshold is currently £1 million income in England and Wales (£500,000 in Scotland and Northern Ireland). In some cases an audit may also be needed below this if the charity has £3.26 million or more in assets – see chapters 2 and 8 for further details.

- This is a summary of the rules in England and Wales – for full details see the Charities (Accounts and Reports) Regulations 2008.
- The rules for charities registered in Scotland are very similar – see Schedule 2 of the Charities Accounts (Scotland) Regulations 2006 (as amended) if the accounts are on an R&P basis. With fully accrued accounts, Scottish charities simply need to follow the annual report requirements in the SORP, which – in outline – are as above, although the SORP requires slightly more detail than these Regulations.
- Annual reports under the Charities (Accounts and Reports) Regulations (Northern Ireland) 2015 must cover essentially the same issues as above for R&P accounts, but (as in Scotland) the Regulations require the trustees report to comply with SORP when accruals accounts are produced.

Narratives: public benefit reporting

The most important part of the annual report is the narrative section, which explains what the charity has actually done during the year. In England, Wales and Northern Ireland the law requires trustees to report how the charity has furthered its purposes for the benefit of the public. In other words, the work of the charity must be explained in terms of how it has advanced its objects and the public benefit requirement – see 'What is a charity?' in chapter 1 (page 6) for more on this. So, the annual report should not just contain reports on fundraising events or thanks to individuals; the focus should be on what the charity has done to advance its objects and how people have benefited.

For some charities, such as playgroups working with children, the beneficiaries are obvious, but in other cases you need to identify the beneficiaries before you can meaningfully explain the work in public benefit terms. In a heritage charity the beneficiaries are the people who will use or learn from the building or artefacts you are conserving. In a religious charity, the beneficiaries are people who hear the religious teaching, or those who have the opportunity of worship or spiritual growth. Sometime beneficiaries are worldwide; in other cases they are very local. Whatever the charity's field of work, the report must explain what the charity has done to carry out its objects, who benefits, and how.

It is also a good idea to explain any restrictions on who can benefit to show that they are not excessive – for example, if you charge for your services (see chapter 4, page 49), it is worth explaining your charging approach and any subsidies available. If you are involved in any activities which have significant risks of harm, or making things worse for some people in order to help others, explain why the benefits outweigh these issues.

In making decisions on the work of a charity and who will benefit, trustees in England, Wales and Northern Ireland must by law consider the Charity Commission's (or CCNI's) guidance on the public benefit requirement, and the trustees' report *must* state whether they have considered this guidance (see 'Further reading' for details). There is no formal requirement for public benefit reporting in Scotland, but any explanation of how a charity is carrying out its objects will focus on public benefit issues.

Charitable companies

In the case of a charitable company, it is usual to provide one report that is both the directors' annual report required under company law and the trustees' annual report required under charity law. This dual requirement is sometimes overlooked: a report that only covers the requirements of the Companies Acts is certainly not sufficient. Furthermore, a report that fails to give a proper review of the charity's activities in relation to its objects can be disastrous when applying for funding.

Approval of the report – and supplementary information

The annual report must be a report by the trustees as a whole, and signed on their behalf. Some charities like to produce an attractive document with reports by key individuals, comments by participants or users, photographs and much more. With care on the wording, this can be incorporated into the legal annual report, so long as the whole document is approved and signed by the trustees.

However, if you want to produce an unofficial publication about the work of the charity, it is best to issue this as a completely separate document, and call it an 'annual review' (or something similar) to make it clear that it is *not* the legal annual report. Tell people in such a document how they can obtain the annual report and accounts if they want a copy. (It is generally best to avoid giving figures in an annual review, but if you do it is essential to make clear they are not the full accounts, and to explain how the full report and accounts can be obtained.)

The accounts: who does what?

The term 'preparing the accounts' means taking the information from the books and turning them into a final document which, once approved and signed by the trustees, can be copied and circulated. Nowadays the document is almost always created electronically, so a draft can easily be amended (but in principle, for a very small charity, the document could still be handwritten or typewritten).

Except in the very smallest organisations, your accounts will then be subject to audit or independent examination (see chapter 8). So it is usual to involve your auditor or examiner while the accounts are still in draft. Depending on their complexity and the relative experience in preparing accounts, there are four main ways of sharing the work.

1   *Auditor/examiner appointed only to report*
    In this 'pure audit' model, the charity produces final accounts complying with the regulations and other requirements; these accounts are approved and signed by trustees. They are then submitted to the auditor/ examiner for scrutiny and report.

2   *Auditor/examiner may request amendments and then reports*
    In this approach, the charity produces draft final accounts, including the full notes. These are submitted to the auditor/examiner for provisional approval or to request amendment. The amendments are then incorporated and the accounts signed by the trustees. The auditor/examiner then attaches and signs his or her report.

3   *Auditor/examiner completes accounts and then reports*
    The charity produces the basis of the accounts – perhaps the main
    financial reports from an accounting system and a summary of items
    for the notes. The auditor/examiner then turns these into a full set of
    accounts. These (externally finalised) accounts are presented to the
    charity and signed by the trustees, and the auditor/examiner then
    signs his or her report.

4   *Auditor/examiner produces accounts from scratch and reports on
    them*
    In charities with very limited financial experience, it often happens
    that the charity provides the auditor/examiner purely with the books.
    From these, the auditor/examiner prepares a full set of accounts from
    scratch. These (externally prepared) accounts are considered and then
    signed by the trustees and the auditor/examiner then signs his or her
    report.

Which approach to use?

If possible, approaches 2 or 3 are best. These allow a proper dialogue
between the charity and the auditor or examiner. The main difference
between them is that in approach 2 the charity does the word processing
of the final document and the auditor/examiner requests changes; in
approach 3 it is the other way round.

Although approach 1 can work with very small organisations, the problem
is that if the auditor/examiner is unhappy with anything in the accounts,
there is no alternative but to issue a **qualified** report (i.e. an audit or
examination report that contains qualifications or reservations – see page
124). It can be quite damaging to the charity to have to circulate accounts
with a qualified auditor's/examiner's report. If a small amendment to the
accounts – perhaps adding an extra note – would have solved the problem,
it is much better to be able to incorporate this before final approval by the
trustees.

The main problem with approach 4 is that if someone outside the charity
does almost everything, will your trustees be able to make a sensible
decision about approving the accounts? Remember that in law, producing
the accounts is the responsibility of the charity trustees. It is fine for the
trustees to use an accountant to *help* prepare the accounts, but the
trustees are responsible for the content.

For example, if the books did not properly distinguish a restricted fund
(because the bookkeeper included a special grant with general donations)
there is no way that an accountant could know this unless they are told. If

accounts are prepared showing money in the general fund that should be restricted, it is up to the trustees to spot this when considering approval of the accounts, and ask for the draft to be changed before they sign.

Many charities get into the circular argument of saying, 'These accounts have been prepared by our accountants so they must be correct'. Then the accountant (now acting as auditor/examiner) says, 'Since the accounts were based on the books which I saw and since they have been approved by the trustees, the content must be OK' and each is signing on the basis of an assumption of what the other has done.

The rest of this chapter focuses on the two possible formats for the final accounts:

• R&P accounts; or
• accruals accounts, which have to comply with the SORP.

Final receipts and payments accounts

The Charities Act 2011 says that when a charity opts to produce R&P accounts, the trustees must provide:

• an R&P account (which must distinguish the different funds of the charity); and
• a SOAL.

This also applies for R&P accounts under the Charities Act (Northern Ireland) 2008. In Scotland, the SOAL is replaced by a statement of balances but the idea is very similar; however, the Scottish Regulations are more specific on the different categories needed for receipts and payments.

Receipts and payments account

In England and Wales, and in Northern Ireland, there are no rules in law about how the R&P account is to be laid out, so you are free to break down the receipts and payments into whatever categories you feel would be helpful to your readers. It is normal to include a comparative column for the previous year, which means trying to keep the same categories from year to year. However, to help you set out an R&P account, the Charity Commission publishes some very helpful guidance in its pack CC16 – in fact, if you are happy with the layout it is possible to produce a complete set of R&P accounts by filling in the Commission's forms (which can be downloaded as Excel templates or as PDFs, but be sure to download the guidance notes as well). Similar templates are produced by OSCR and by CCNI for the specific requirements of R&P accounts in Scotland and Northern Ireland (see 'Further reading').

MIDSHAM COMMUNITY ACTION CIO: ACCOUNTS FOR THE

RECEIPTS AND PAYMENTS ACCOUNT I APRIL 2017 TO 31 MARCH 2018

	General Fund	Outreach Fund	Total	Last Year
		——— 2017/18 ———		2016/17
	£	£	£	£
Receipts				
Members Subscriptions	534		534	467
Council Grant	25,000		25,000	10,000
Miscellaneous Donations	429		429	500
Tax Reclaimed on Gift Aid	140		140	0
Christmas Bazaar	1,732		1,732	1,103
Bank Interest	53		53	71
Grant from Midsham Trust		4,000	4,000	0
Participants Activity Fees		713	713	0
TOTAL RECEIPTS	27,888	4,713	32,601	12,141
Payments				
Administrator Salary	1,079		1,079	980
Heat & Light	869		869	934
Rates, Water Rates, Cleaning	403		403	389
Stationery	291		291	321
Publicity Literature	1,781		1,781	783
Postage & Telephone	1,237		1,237	1,089
Purchase of Minibus	18,000		18,000	0
Independent Examiner's Fee	200		200	200
Trustees Travel Expenses	126	50	176	171
Repairs & Maintenance	3,708		3,708	6,981
Outreach Worker Wages		2,760	2,760	0
Outreach Worker Travel Costs		402	402	0
Outreach Activities		1,342	1,342	0
TOTAL PAYMENTS	27,694	4,554	32,248	11,848
NET RECEIPTS LESS PAYMENTS	194	159	353	293
Transfers Between Funds				
Outreach Contribution	−100	100	0	0
Cash Funds Last Year End	373	0	373	80
CASH FUNDS THIS YEAR END	467	259	726	373

Fig. 7.1 Example R&P accounts

R ENDING 31 MARCH 2018 (Receipts and Payments Format)

STATEMENT OF ASSETS AND LIABILITIES AT 31 MAR 2018

31 Mar 17 £		31 Mar 18 £
	Monetary Assets	
	Current Asset Investments	
250	Investment Account – Midwest Bank	690
	Cash at Bank and in Hand	
115	Current Account – Midwest Bank	21
8	Petty Cash	15
123	Total Cash at Bank and in Hand	36
373	TOTAL MONETARY ASSETS	726
	Represented by Funds	
	Unrestricted Funds	
373	General Fund	467
	Restricted Funds	
0	Outreach Project	259
373	TOTAL FUNDS	726
	Non-Monetary Assets and Liabilities	
	Fixed Assets for Charity Use	
120,000	Community Centre	120,000
0	Minibus	18,000
2,000	Furniture and Equipment	1,800
122,000	Total Fixed Assets for Charity Use	139,800
	Debtors	
140	Tax due from HM Revenue & Customs	170
	Creditors Due Within One Year	
−200	Independent Examination Fee Due	−250
121,940	TOTAL NON-MONETARY ASSETS	139,720

These accounts were approved by the Trustees on 24 May 2018 and signed on their behalf by:

K. PATEL – Chairperson
J. CORRIGAN – Treasurer

NOTES TO THE ACCOUNTS
1. These accounts are prepared on a receipts and payments basis, with all revenue and expenses shown on a cash basis. Non-monetary assets and liabilities are shown at estimates of the value at the end of the year.
2. The CIO has two funds: an unrestricted General Fund and an Outreach Project. The latter is a restricted fund supported mainly by a grant from the Midsham Trust, enabling the charity to employ a P/T outreach worker to visit families in two particular wards with high levels of disadvantage. As a condition of the funding application, the charity itself provided £100 towards this project: this is shown as a transfer from General Fund to the Outreach Fund.
3. The CIO had no outstanding guarantees to third parties nor any debts secured on the assets of the CIO.
4. No remuneration was paid to any trustee. Travel expenses totalling £176 were paid to four trustees: £126 of this was from the General Fund, and £50 from the Outreach Project Fund.

Where there are several funds, you can show a completely separate R&P account for each fund – if so, it is more readable if you use a separate page for each fund. But if there are more than about three funds, or if there have been transfers between funds, it may be clearer to show all funds together in a SOFA-type layout as used in accruals accounts (as in the example in figure 7.1), so long as it is clearly labelled as being on an R&P basis – this is the approach used in the CC16 pack. However, if several funds are added together into one column, a note explaining the different funds is clearly needed.

In Scotland the Regulations are more specific on the categories to be used for the R&P accounts; however, OSCR publishes helpful guidance on its website.

Statement of assets and liabilities

The SOAL (or, in Scotland, statement of balances) must list all the assets and liabilities of the charity. It is easiest to divide this into the monetary assets (which will correspond to the balances of funds) and other, non-monetary assets and liabilities such as fixed assets, debtors and creditors. In principle the non-monetary assets could be presented as just a list of items, but if you have estimates of values it is sensible to show them.

Hopefully, as treasurer you will know about any unpaid bills and amounts due to the charity and will thus be able to work out the debtors and creditors, and you will know about new capital items bought during the year. But the fixed assets must include all long-term items owned by the charity (including items acquired or given many years previously) and, if no one has produced one before, you may have to compile a fixed asset list from scratch. Do not forget to include buildings and investments, as well as obvious items of furniture, equipment and vehicles. Also, make sure you know about any loans or other commitments: these will need to appear as liabilities on the SOAL.

From this it is clear that, even with R&P accounting, the task of the treasurer is more than just keeping track of the money: you must know about fixed assets, debtors and creditors even if these do not actually appear in the day-to-day books. But once you have produced the SOAL for one year, the pattern is usually followed in subsequent years, adding new categories if needed.

Notes to the accounts

With R&P accounts, in England, Wales and Northern Ireland there is generally no legal requirement to show notes to the accounts, except in the case of CIOs. In the case of a CIO established in England or Wales, because it is a limited liability body, two specific notes are needed:

1   Particulars of any guarantee given by the CIO (if still in force at year end). For instance, if the CIO has agreed to underwrite the costs of an activity run by another organisation or if underwriting a commitment on behalf of a beneficiary this must be explained.

2   Details of any debt outstanding at year end which is a secured charge on an asset of the CIO. For example, if it has a property with a mortgage outstanding, this must be made clear.

These are not necessarily extra requirements for a CIO, as a well-prepared SOAL for *any* charity using R&P accounts should include these disclosures if applicable. However, if they are omitted, readers may wonder if they have simply been overlooked. So, if the charity is a CIO but neither of these is needed, it is a good idea to add a note on the following lines:

> The trustees confirm, in accordance with the CIO (General) Regulations 2012, that at year end the charity did not have any outstanding guarantees to third parties nor any debts secured on assets of the CIO.

There is no corresponding requirement for SCIOs, but a well-produced statement of balances for a SCIO would cover the same issues.

Even where notes are not required by law, in practice your accounts will be much more meaningful to readers if you include relevant information by way of notes – certainly the Charity Commission's guidance is that the accounts should make clear which funds are restricted and should give details of any payments to trustees (including expenses). The following box lists the notes needed for R&P accounts in Scotland, but charities throughout the UK would be well advised to follow this list (cross-references to the annual report are permitted if relevant details have been given there).

List of notes for receipts and payments accounts

(a) The nature and purpose of each fund, including details of restrictions on specific funds.

(b) Details of grants paid (number, amounts, types of activities supported, and whether the grants were to organisations or to individuals).

(c) Details of any remuneration or fees paid to any trustees or their close relatives or businesses (a nil statement is needed even if there were no such payments).

(d) Total expenses paid to trustees, including the number of trustees involved (or a nil statement if applicable – for example, 'No expenses were paid to any of the trustees during the year').

(e) Other information needed to assist readers to understand the accounts.

Summarised from Schedule 3 Part 2 of the
Charities Accounts (Scotland) Regulations 2006.

Final accruals accounts

Accruals accounts differ from R&P accounts in two fundamental ways:

- The figures will be slightly different because they show accrued income and accrued expenses, not just money received and paid out. Also, debtors, creditors and fixed assets are included in the fund balances.
- The presentation must follow the Charities SORP format. Under the SORP, the accounts must comprise three elements:
  – a SOFA;
  – a balance sheet;
  – notes to the accounts.

From 2016, when following the SORP 2015 (FRS102), charities with an income of more than £500,000 will also need to include a statement of cash flows – see page 114.

Which SORP to use?

The SORP has undergone a number of revisions in recent years, with major changes both from 2015 and from 2016, but for financial years starting on or after 1 January 2016, only one SORP is regarded as 'current': the Charities SORP (FRS102) effective from 1 January 2015 (abbreviated in this book to 'SORP 2015 (FRS102)'). This has been slightly revised from 2016 by the *SORP Update Bulletin 1* (see 'Further reading' for sources of these documents).

The term 'FRS102' refers to the underlying general purpose accounting standard on which the SORP is based: The *Financial Reporting Standard applicable in the UK and Ireland (FRS102)*. See 'The impact of accounting standards' on page 152 for more details. FRS102 is now the main accounting standard for almost all kinds of entities including commercial companies producing accounts that are intended to give a **true and fair view** (as opposed to cash-based R&P accounts). It follows the principles of international financial reporting standards (IFRS). Under the FRS102 approach, the measurement rules for valuing income and assets are somewhat more complex than in the past – they are based on the IFRS concept of **fair value** and this is reflected in the FRS102 SORP. FRS102 also has specific rules about the presentation of investment gains and losses, which means charities using the FRS102 SORP have a slightly different format for the SOFA (compared to earlier SORPs) if they have investment movements.

(If you are dealing with earlier years, see the appendix on page 193 for details. In particular, as mentioned in chapter 2, two new SORPs were issued in 2015 with slight differences but the other version, known as SORP 2015 (FRSSE), cannot be used for financial years which begin on or after 1 January 2016 – it was only valid for accounting years that began at some point in 2015. From 2016, only the SORP 2015 (FRS102) is regarded as current.)

However, there is a complication for non-company charities (e.g. trusts, associations or CIOs) in England and Wales: they must, by law, prepare accounts in accordance with the requirements in the Charities Act 2011, but regulations implementing SORP 2015 had still not been made two years after it was meant to take effect. The Charities (Accounts and Reports) Regulations 2008 remain in force under the 2011 Act, and they refer to SORP 2005 – even though it is an out-of-date standard! So, trustees face a dilemma when deciding how to produce their accounts – whether to stick with SORP 2005 as in the Regulations, or to apply SORP 2015 in order to be sure the accounts give a 'true and fair view' under current standards. The Charity Commission's guidance (in publication CC15d) points out that the Regulations allow the accounts to depart from SORP 2005 where needed to give a true and fair view – this is known as applying a 'true and fair override'. But on the other hand, SORP 2015 (FRS102) itself says (in para 18 of the Introduction) that 'in those jurisdictions where the applicable SORP is specified in regulations [which includes England and Wales], this SORP cannot be adopted until the applicable regulations are made allowing its application'. So, it seems almost impossible for a charity follow the letter of both the Regulations and the latest SORP, and discussion will be needed with the charity's auditor or independent examiner to agree the most appropriate way forward. Either way, the accounts will need to include a note to say which SORP was used and why. (For more on these issues, see 'The impact of accounting standards' on page 152 and see the appendix on page 193 for discussion of which SORP to apply at which date.)

Fortunately, this problem does not apply in Scotland or Northern Ireland where the regulations applicable from 2016 properly refer to the SORP 2015 (FRS102). Likewise, the problem does not affect charitable companies in England and Wales as their accounts are not subject to the 2008 Regulations under the Charities Act 2011 – their accounting framework follows the Companies Act 2006 and they are required to give a true and fair view in accordance with current standards, which would include SORP 2015 (FRS102) where the company is a charity. The remainder of this chapter therefore assumes that the SORP 2015 (FRS102) will be used if the charity is producing accruals accounts.

The SORP rules are quite specific about the principles and layout of the SOFA and balance sheet, and on information that must be given in the notes to the accounts. There are some minor concessions for smaller charities (which the SORP now defines as those with income of £500,000 or less) and in some cases these concessions extend to all charities below the audit threshold (thus including most charities with up to £1 million income in England and Wales). But in general, once a charity issues accruals accounts, even if it is very small, the full SORP presentation and notes must be used.

Statement of financial activities (SOFA)

The SOFA is essentially an income and expenditure account divided into columns for the three types of funds: unrestricted funds (this includes designated funds); restricted income funds; and capital or endowment funds (see chapter 3 for definitions). There is also a column showing the total income and expenditure of all funds, and a comparison column with the overall totals for the last year.

The SOFA can seem complex at first, but once people get used to it, it can prove to be a very helpful way of understanding the income and expenditure of an organisation, without confusing restricted and unrestricted funds, but showing the whole charity on one page. (In fact, the SOFA has become so well accepted as a basis for charity accounting, that the multi-column format is increasingly used even for R&P accounts, as in the example in figure 7.1.) There is a separate line for any transfers between funds, so support from one fund to another is not confused with external income or expenditure – see chapters 3 and 4 for more on this. This line must, of course, total to zero in the 'All funds' column, because the transfers out of one fund must be balanced by transfers into other funds. Sometimes the SOFA has to include a further section for gains and losses where assets are revalued, but this is not shown in the example in figure 7.2.

Within each column there may be several funds added together – for example, the second column could have the totals for ten or more projects supported by restricted funds – but notes to the accounts must give individual balances for each fund (see figure 9.2, page 138 for an example). The notes should also give details of the prior year's figures for each column of the SOFA (you are not required to show these on the SOFA itself, as you would generally need eight columns in all and the SOFA would then be very hard to read).

As well as determining the columns, the SORP rules specify the general headings to be used for income and expenditure, in order to ensure comparability between different charities. These tend to vary slightly with each revision of the SORP – the format in figure 7.2 is based on the SORP 2015 (FRS102).

For full SORP format, the income and expenditure must be broken down on a functional basis, showing how much was spent on particular purposes. So, for example, rather than having a single expenditure line for 'Salaries', salary costs for fundraising come under 'Expenditure on raising funds', while time spent on the main work of the charity appears under 'Expenditure on charitable activities' – and the heading 'Charitable activities' can itself be split if a charity undertakes work in several distinct fields.

In a medium-sized charity, this requirement for functional allocation of expenses on the SOFA may mean splitting the salaries of individual staff –

MIDSHAM COMMUNITY ACTION CIO: ACCOUNTS FOR THE

STATEMENT OF FINANCIAL ACTIVITIES 1 APRIL 2017 TO 31 MARCH 2018

	2017/18				2016/17
	Unrestricted Funds	Restricted Funds	Endowment Funds	Total Funds	Prior Year Funds
	£	£	£	£	£
Income and endowments from:					
Donations and legacies	25,599	4,000		29,599	10,500
Charitable activities	534	713		1,247	467
Other trading activities	1,732			1,732	1,103
Investments	53			53	71
Total	**27,918**	**4,713**	**0**	**32,631**	**12,141**
Expenditure on:					
Raising funds	2,072			2,072	1,104
Charitable activities	12,372	4,554		16,926	10,744
Total	**14,444**	**4,554**	**0**	**18,998**	**11,848**
Net income	**13,474**	**159**	**0**	**13,633**	**293**
Transfers between funds:					
Contribution to Project	(100)	100		0	0
Net movement in funds	**13,374**	**259**	**0**	**13,633**	**293**
Reconciliation of funds:					
Total funds brought forward	2,313	0	120,000	122,313	122020
Total funds carried forward	**15,687**	**259**	**120,000**	**135,946**	**122,313**

The notes on page 3 to 6 form part of these accounts.

NOTES TO THE ACCOUNTS

This example does not show the notes; however, as these are accruals accounts, full notes covering all the issues required by the Regulations and SORP will be needed on the pages after the balance sheet. In a simple charity such as this, the notes might include:

1. Accounting policies.
2. Description of each fund and explanation of inter-fund transfers.
3. Summary of movements on each fund (this would be needed if more than one fund was included in any column of the SOFA – see *figure 9.2 on page 138*)
4. Breakdown of the expenditure on charitable activities.
5. Table of fixed asset movements showing additions, depreciation, etc., for each type of asset.
6. Explanation of debtors (unless fully shown on balance sheet).
7. Explanation of creditors (unless fully shown on balance sheet).
8. Details of staff numbers and salary costs and confirmation that no staff are paid more than £60,000.
9. Explanation of trustees' expenses, and a statement that there were no other transactions with trustees.
10. Note of the independent examiner's fee (and any other services the examiner provided).
11. Details of any grants made to other organisations (or individuals).
12. Confirmation that the charity has no guarantees to third parties.
13. Breakdown of the net assets across the unrestricted and restricted funds.

The notes also need to include last year's comparisons where applicable.

Fig. 7.2 Example accruals accounts

R ENDING 31 MARCH 2018 (Accruals Basis – SORP 2015 (FRS102) Format)

BALANCE SHEET AT 31 MARCH 2018

	31 March 18 £	31 March 17 £
Assets and liabilities		
FIXED ASSETS		
Tangible assets		
Community Centre	120,000	120,000
Furniture & equipment	1,800	2,000
Minibus	13,500	0
Total fixed assets	135,300	122,000
CURRENT ASSETS		
Debtors		
Tax due from HMRC	170	140
Current asset investments		
30 Day Account Midwest Bank	690	250
Cash at bank and in hand		
Current Account – Midwest Bank	21	115
Petty Cash	15	8
Total cash at bank and in hand	36	123
Total current assets	896	513
LIABILITIES		
Creditors due within one year		
Independent Examination fee due	(250)	(200)
NET CURRENT ASSETS	646	313
Total net assets	**135,946**	**122,313**
Represented by funds		
Unrestricted funds		
General Fund	15,687	2,313
Restricted funds		
Outreach Project	259	0
Endowment funds		
Freehold building	120,000	120,000
Total funds	**135,946**	**122,313**

Approved by the Trustees on 24 May 2018 and signed on their behalf by:

K. PATEL – Chairperson
J. CORRIGAN – Treasurer

NOTES TO THE ACCOUNTS
(These will follow on subsequent pages – see box opposite.)

for example, the chief executive may spend 25% of her time on funding bids and meeting donors, with 75% of her time on the operational work of the charity.

If this seems too hard, smaller charities (defined by the SORP as those with an income of up to £500,000) are allowed to use natural classifications of expenditure on the SOFA (for example, 'Salaries', 'Premises', 'Running costs' and 'Depreciation') to simplify things. Likewise smaller charities can use a natural breakdown for the different kinds of income to the charity.

The balance sheet

The balance sheet shows all the charity's assets and liabilities, balanced against the relevant funds. The key thing to appreciate with accruals accounts is that the value of every fixed asset, debtor or creditor is included in the relevant fund (unlike R&P accounts, where the fund balances consist only of money). (See chapter 10 for more on this.)

The top half of the balance sheet is similar to the format used for business accounts, but the bottom half is quite different because all the assets and liabilities belong to the charity. All assets are held either for the general objects of the charity (unrestricted funds), or for certain restricted or endowment purposes.

Like the SOFA, the content and layout of the balance sheet is laid down by the Regulations and SORP. One key requirement under the SORP 2015 (FRS102) is that assets are normally shown at **fair value**. Functional assets may be valued at cost less depreciation but any investments (including property which is held as an investment) must be shown at market value (rather than at their original cost).

The balance sheet must be signed by the trustees to show that they have approved the accounts.

The statement of cash flows (for larger charities)

As well as a SOFA and balance sheet, larger charities (those with more than £500,000 income) preparing accounts under the FRS102 SORP are also required to include a statement of cash flows in the final accounts. Where needed, this usually appears immediately after the SOFA and balance sheet but before the notes – although, as it only applies to larger charities, the statement of cash flows is not covered in detail in this book.

A cash flow statement literally shows movements of money (cash, bank balances and short term deposits) in and out of the charity. At one level it takes figures from the accruals accounts in the SOFA and balance sheet and shows what the results would look like on an R&P basis (although the format is quite different from R&P accounts). It can be helpful to highlight cases where, for example, a charity appears to have a lot of income, but cash flow is very tight.

Module 14 of the FRS102 SORP sets out the requirements for cash flow statements. However, the statement of cash flows only shows monetary movements under very broad headings and it generally just shows cash flows for the charity as a whole without separating the funds. While a cash flow *forecast* is a very important report for managing cash flow issues (see chapter 9) a cash flow *statement* in the final accounts only provides historic information.

For many charities with more than £500,000 income, the statement of cash flows is a major new requirement from 2016. Previously the cash flow statement was only required for charities which fell outside the definition of 'small' in company law (the company law thresholds applied even for non-company charities). In most cases (at current thresholds) that would mean only those charities with more than £10.2 million income. (Non-company charities in England and Wales that are continuing to follow SORP 2005 – see page 23 and the appendix on page 193 – can still use this higher threshold before a cash flow statement is needed.)

Notes to the accounts

Unlike R&P accounts, where (except in Scotland) notes are largely the discretion of the charity concerned, with accruals accounts it is a legal requirement to provide a great deal of additional information in notes to the accounts. All the points shown in the following box must be covered by notes, if there is anything applicable.

Accruals accounts – summary of requirements for notes to the accounts

(a) Adjustments to last year's figures.
(b) Accounting policies and estimation techniques.
(c) Details of any material changes to accounting policies and techniques.
(d) Nature and purpose of each fund following SORP principles (normally provide a table with a line for each fund showing opening balance, income, expenditure, transfers and closing balance (see example in figure 9.2, page 138).
(e) Transactions with related parties (i.e. with trustees and their relatives or businesses) including trustees' expenses paid (if none, must state none).
(f) Total staff costs (split into gross salaries, NI and employer's pension contributions).
(g) Details of individual staff salaries over £60,000 (in £10,000 bands) (if none, must state none).
(h) Details of any incoming resources to capital/endowment funds.
(i) Details of inter-fund transfers affecting restricted funds, with explanations.
(j) Details of any subsidiaries of the charity (including turnover, net profit and details of any audit report).
(k) Details of any guarantees given to third parties.
(l) Loans to the charity (if secured on the charity's property) or loans made by the charity to others.
(m) Explanation of any funds in deficit (in such cases, a note will also be needed in the annual report explaining the trustees' proposed action – see page 99).
(n) Auditor's/independent examiner's remuneration (and fees for any other services provided to the charity by the auditor/examiner).
(o) Grants made – details as specified in the SORP.
(p) Details of any ex gratia payments made.
(q) Breakdown of the SOFA resources expended line 'Charitable activities' – first this should be split into the main separate activities of the charity, and then for each activity give:
   • cost of work undertaken directly by the charity itself;
   • grant-making activity;
   • support costs.
(r) Breakdown of support costs (details as in the SORP).
(s) Analysis of balance sheet figures for fixed assets, debtors, creditors (details as in the SORP).
(t) Analysis of all material movements in fixed asset values – this may be combined with (s) – it is usual to give three separate notes:
   • debtors;
   • creditors;
   • fixed assets – in categories showing additions, disposals, depreciation, revaluations and impairments.
(u) Previous year's figures for all the above except (i), (o) and (t).
(v) Accounting standards used (e.g. SORP 2015 (FRS102)) and details of any major departures.
(w) Reasons for any change of accounting date.
(x) Reasons if any departure from the Regulations had to be made in order for the accounts to give a true and fair view.
(y) Any other information needed to give a true and fair view or to assist the user to understand the accounts.

This is a summary of requirements for charities in England and Wales under the Charities (Accounts and Reports) Regulations 2008.

See also the SORP 2015 (FRS102) for several further notes required which are not in the Regulations: for example, the SORP also requires a breakdown of net assets between funds, details of grant and contract income, and details of fundraising expenditure.

While an appropriate accounting system can help to produce the SOFA, balance sheet and one or two key notes, most of the task of preparing the notes is best done by word processing. Although the rules state what is required in the notes, the charity is free to choose the wording: if you are using a professional accountant to help prepare the accounts, try to ensure that the notes are worded in a language that will make sense to other readers. You can always give more information than the legal minimum if it will help readers understand what the charity is doing. For a very simple charity preparing accruals accounts, the Charity Commission's pack CC17 can be used as a template, but in most cases it is better to set out the accounts from first principles in a suitable layout, including notes as needed for a specific charity.

It usually takes several pages to cover all these issues, so the shortest SORP-compliant accounts tend to be around five pages: the SOFA, balance sheet and three or more pages of notes.

Specialist software is available to help accountants prepare a full set of accounts in SORP format, including all the notes (and a few larger charities use such software themselves). The better products can be very useful in generating smartly presented final accounts that cover the vast majority of the SORP requirements; though such products must, of course, be updated for each new SORP. However, much of the content – for example, explaining the purpose of each fund, or details of grants made – must be drafted individually for each charity: it is not unusual to see such notes missing from charity accounts if they were based on a template from another charity. Even with the best accounts preparation systems, the wording and layout for one charity may not be appropriate for another, so take care to review the draft accounts carefully and ask for notes to be reworded to make them clear to your readers, or to add additional notes if appropriate.

Additional reports

In a few cases, accruals-based charity accounts may need additional financial statements in addition to the SOFA and balance sheet – although these rarely arise for smaller charities.

A charitable company will occasionally need a separate income and expenditure account for the purposes of the Companies Acts. However, this only applies in rare cases (e.g. where a charity has received new endowment funds), where company accounting requires a different treatment from the SORP. Apart from such special cases, the 'All funds' column on the SOFA will usually meet the Companies Act requirements.

Charities with subsidiaries – group accounts

In cases where a charity owns a trading subsidiary company (see chapter 11) or in a few rare cases where one charity is a subsidiary of another, there may be a legal requirement to prepare **group accounts** – accounts based on taking the figures from the charity and its subsidiary (or subsidiaries) together. This has long been a recommendation under the SORP, and enforced by regulations. Currently, group accounts are compulsory in England and Wales where a charity has a subsidiary and the aggregate gross income (see below) is over £1 million (£500,000 in Scotland or Northern Ireland).

In the charity's own accounts, for a charity with a subsidiary, the SOFA will include a single line under 'Income and Endowments' for the profits donated to the charity by the subsidiary. But if group accounts are needed, the entire SOFA and balance sheet usually have to be presented in double columns, with figures for the charity itself and for the group (i.e. the charity plus its subsidiaries).

The threshold at which group accounts become compulsory in each **jurisdiction** is the same as the audit threshold. So in England and Wales, it is based on £1 million **aggregate gross income** across the whole group (i.e. the income of the charity, plus the income of the subsidiaries, but deducting income received by the charity from subsidiaries to prevent double counting). Also, if a group in England, Wales or Northern Ireland exceeds this threshold, the charity will always need an audit (even though the charity's own income could be well within the level where an independent examination would normally be allowed) – see chapter 8 for more on audits and auditors. In Scotland the Regulations refer to 'consolidated accounts' rather than 'group accounts' but the principle is the same.

The details of group accounts are beyond the scope of this book; your auditors should be able to help. The principles are covered in module 24 of SORP 2015.

8 Audit and independent examination

As explained in the previous chapter, your trustees are responsible for producing the annual accounts. They may seek help from an accountant or independent examiner to get them correctly presented to meet requirements but that is simply helping the trustees – it is quite different from the task of scrutinising the accounts from an independent perspective.

Except in the very smallest charities in England and Wales, once the accounts are complete there is a further legal requirement before they can be circulated – they must be subjected to independent scrutiny by someone unconnected with the trustees. This person will provide a report, which must be attached to the accounts. Many people use the term 'audit' to describe this process, but this is slightly misleading because, as we will see, only the largest charities need a full audit.

The independent report is a vital protection for all concerned. Most funders and donors expect any organisations that they support to produce independently scrutinised accounts. It is also a vital issue for the trustees themselves, because inevitably the day-to-day finances have to be delegated. So an independent report on the final accounts enables the trustees to have confidence in the overall position of the charity.

Forms of scrutiny

There are two possible forms of independent scrutiny for the accounts of a charity:
- independent examination;
- full audit.

These two kinds of scrutiny now apply through the UK, although the precise duties and thresholds vary slightly between England/Wales, Scotland and Northern Ireland.

Until 2008, there was a further form of scrutiny – by a 'reporting accountant' on the accounts of a charitable company – but now charitable companies below the audit threshold can have an independent examination in the same way as other charities.

It is vital to know which of these is required, and what sort of person you can approach. Many people talk loosely about 'audited accounts', but the various Charities Acts across the UK draw a clear distinction between audit and independent examination, so it is worth using the terms correctly.

The rules are largely based on the organisation's total income (nowadays only the current year has to be considered) but there are some differences for charities with more than £3.26 million of assets. There are also some important differences between England and Wales, Scotland and Northern Ireland. In England and Wales many charities with an income of up to £1 million can have an independent examination, but in Scotland and Northern Ireland the upper income limit is £500,000. (In Northern Ireland, as explained in chapter 2, the full rules only apply to charities registered with CCNI financial years beginning 1 January 2016 onwards – see the appendix on page 193 for earlier years.)

The different levels of requirements for the presentation of charity accounts are shown in tables 2.1, 2.2 and 2.3, in chapter 2. However, tables 8.1 and 8.2 set out the current minimum requirements in law specifically related to the *scrutiny* of charity accounts. These tables show the requirements for normal charities; slightly different rules apply in England and Wales to NHS charities, and to exempt charities such as academy schools.

Some charities may need more scrutiny than the minimum set out in the tables. For example, although charities in England and Wales are not required under the Charities Act to have an independent examination if their income is £25,000 or below, an independent examination might still be required – by a funder, or by the rules of any umbrella body to which they belong. Similarly, some charities whose income would normally put them clearly in the independent examination band may have a governing document that requires a full audit.

Approval of accounts by trustees only

In England and Wales, for charities with an income of £25,000 or below, generally no independent scrutiny is required, and your trustees can simply approve the accounts themselves. This is intended to keep things simple for many small trusts and local voluntary groups with modest income. This provision even includes CIOs and charitable companies – though remember that with a CIO the accounts must still be sent to the Charity Commission even if the income is under £25,000.

Table 8.1 Minimum requirements for accounts scrutiny – normal charities with modest assets (no more than £3.26 million)*

MINIMUM PERMITTED SCRUTINY OF ACCOUNTS	CHARITIES IN ENGLAND AND WALES (REGISTERED OR EXCEPTED) Income levels:	SCOTTISH CHARITIES (and other charities registered with OSCR wherever based) Income levels:	REGISTERED CHARITIES IN NORTHERN IRELAND Income levels:
Approval of accounts by trustees only	£0 to £25,000	Not permitted	Not permitted
Independent examination by examiner of charity's choice	£25,000 to £250,000	£0 to £250,000 (if R&P accounts)	£0 to £250,000
Independent examination by professionally qualified examiner	£250,000 to £500,000	£250,000 to £500,000 (and below £250,000 if accruals accounts)	£250,000 to £500,000
Full audit	More than £1 million	£500,000 or over	More than £500,000

*This table applies for accounting years ending 31 March 2015 onwards (although the rules for Northern Ireland only take effect from 1 January 2016). The level of assets does not affect charities in Northern Ireland.

It is important to appreciate that there must still be a formal trustees' meeting at which the accounts are approved, and the trustees need to consider what this involves. As the treasurer, you will probably have prepared the accounts and presented them to the trustees, but should they approve them just on your say? This is unwise, because no matter how much they trust you, something could have gone wrong – what if you have simply mistyped a crucial figure? There should still be at least one other trustee, not involved in the day-to-day bookkeeping, who goes back to the original records and considers whether the accounts are correct before recommending their approval to the rest of the trustees.

Table 8.2 Minimum requirements for accounts scrutiny – charities with substantial assets (over £3.26 million)*

MINIMUM PERMITTED SCRUTINY OF ACCOUNTS	CHARITIES IN ENGLAND AND WALES (REGISTERED OR EXCEPTED) **Income levels:**	SCOTTISH CHARITIES (and other charities registered with OSCR wherever based) **Income levels:**	REGISTERED CHARITIES IN NORTHERN IRELAND **Income levels:**
Approval of accounts by trustees only	£0 to £25,000	Not permitted	Not permitted
Independent examination by examiner of charity's choice	£25,000 to £250,000	£0 to £250,000 (if R&P accounts)	£0 to £250,000
Independent examination by professionally qualified examiner	Not applicable	Not applicable	£250,000 to £500,000
Full audit	More than £250,000	£250,000 or over (or below this if accruals accounts)	More than £500,000

*See footnote to table 8.1.

At the level of less than £25,000 most charities will choose to do receipts and payments (R&P) accounts, but remember this is not allowed for charitable companies. So even though the accounts will not need external scrutiny, a charitable company with an income of less than £25,000 must produce proper accounts on an accruals basis complying with the Companies Acts and the Charities SORP. Also, the balance sheet must contain a declaration under the Companies Act 2006 that the company has dispensed with the audit requirement.

However, this option for the trustees of a small charity to approve the accounts without external scrutiny *only* applies in England and Wales. For charities registered in Scotland or Northern Ireland the accounts must at least have an independent examination no matter how small the income.

Independent examination

Until the mid-1990s, many smaller charities had an 'informal audit' whereby someone with modest accounting knowledge was asked to look over the books and sign his or her name at the end of the accounts. But these kind of informal audits were often haphazard, with no indication of what the 'honorary auditor' had actually done. Even with accounts prepared by professional accountants, the accountants' report often said only 'These accounts have been prepared from the books and vouchers presented to us' with no opinion as to their completeness or accuracy.

Independent examination was brought in to replace the informal audits of the past, by providing a scrutiny regime which would give some real certainty without requiring smaller charities to bear the cost of a full audit. In England and Wales, independent examination is now usually appropriate for most charities with an income in the range of £25,000 to £1 million (in Scotland and Northern Ireland there is no lower limit – even a charity with an income of £5 needs an independent examination – and the upper limit is an income of £500,000). The two main differences between independent examination and audit relate to who can act and the nature of the report attached to the accounts.

A wide range of people can potentially be **independent examiners**, though there are important criteria to consider, as explained in 'Selecting an independent examiner' overleaf, and in some cases (see tables 8.1 and 8.2) it is a legal requirement to use a professionally qualified independent examiner. But the task of an independent examiner is much more than just looking at the accounts to check the figures.

In England and Wales the duties are laid down by section 145 of the Charities Act 2011, by the Charities (Accounts and Reports) Regulations 2008, and by the Directions of the Charity Commission on the Carrying Out of an Independent Examination (available in the Commission's publication CC32). Slightly different rules apply in Scotland under the Charities Accounts (Scotland) Regulations 2006, but the principles are similar. Directions for independent examiners in Northern Ireland have been issued by CCNI in publication ARR07 (see 'Further reading'). For Scotland, OSCR has published guidance for independent examiners which is very helpful if not legally binding. No one can validly claim to have carried out an independent examination of a set of charity accounts unless they have followed all these requirements.

An independent examiner's report provides a 'negative assurance'. The examiner's role is to state whether any material matters have come to their attention giving them cause to believe:

1   proper accounting records were not kept; or
2   the accounts do not accord with those records; or
3   the accounts do not comply with requirements of the relevant Charities Act; or
4   there is further information needed for a proper understanding of the accounts.

If the examiner is happy, the report says that no concerns were identified under any of these headings.

This is called an **unqualified report** – in other words, the independent examiner isn't raising any reservations or qualifications regarding the charity's accounts. However, there are times when the examiner cannot say that no matters of concern arose: there could be issues which the trustees cannot resolve such as gaps in the accounting records, or improper use of restricted funds, or problems with the presentation of the accounts. If that happens, the examiner must explain the concerns in his/her report: this is called a **qualified report** (note that this is nothing to do with whether the examiner is professionally qualified). In most cases a qualified report is not a disaster, but it shows readers that issues need to be addressed in the charity's accounting processes.

Research shows that around 1% of independently examined charity accounts actually have some kind of qualified wording.[6] Since 2014, the Charity Commission has been asking charities about this, as part of the annual return process. But many charities are misunderstanding the question and are telling the Commission that their accounts have been qualified by their auditor or independent examiner when this is not the case[7] – thereby causing needless concern to funders and supporters.

However, the examiner's declaration can only be made after following ten stages of Charity Commission's Directions, so it is not simply a case of the examiner saying casually that no problems were spotted. The examiner's report has to cover a number of issues prescribed by the Regulations, so it will usually need a whole page. For most smaller charities an independent examination provides very effective scrutiny which goes much further than the informal audits of the past, but which can be carried out without the need for a registered auditor.

Selecting an independent examiner

Independent examiners come from a wide range of backgrounds, including accountants, bankers, engineers, staff of community accountancy projects and experienced charity treasurers acting as independent examiners to other charities. Some work professionally and thus charge a fee, but this is usually a good deal less than the cost of a full audit; however, many independent examiners, especially those acting for the smallest charities, work on a voluntary basis or charge only a nominal fee.

There are two kinds of independent examiner: an ordinary examiner (described in tables 8.1 and 8.2 as an 'independent examiner of the charity's choice') and a professionally qualified independent examiner.

Ordinary independent examiners

In England, Wales and Northern Ireland, ordinary independent examiners can act for charities with an income of up to £250,000. In Scotland, they can also act for charities with an income of up to the same limit, but only where the accounts are on the R&P basis.

An ordinary independent examiner is defined in law as 'an independent person who is reasonably believed by the charity trustees to have the requisite ability and practical experience to carry out a competent examination of the accounts' (this definition applies throughout the UK).[8]

In such cases, no specific qualification is required, but clearly the person must have a good understanding of accounts, and charity accounts in particular. However, there can be certain concerns about the issues of 'requisite ability' and 'practical experience'. Even among accountants, only a few firms specialise in charities and others can easily be caught out by all the requirements. Where people are acting informally as independent examiners there is wide ignorance of the new regime, for example some informal auditors are doing just as they did in the past but simply putting 'independent examiner' after their name – this is illegal.

The issue of independence is also very important: in the past some informal audits have been carried out by funders, landlords or close relatives of trustees, where there is clearly insufficient independence. It should be noted that an independent examiner must always be an individual: there is no provision for independent examination reports to be signed by a firm.

While there is no legal requirement to have any specific qualification in order to be an independent examiner to smaller charities, guidance from charity regulators stresses the need for trustees to check that a prospective independent examiner really does have the appropriate competence, and a relevant qualification is certainly recommended for charities with an income of more than £100,000.

Professionally qualified independent examiners

For charities with an income of more than £250,000, or in Scotland for a charity of any size where the accounts are on an accruals basis, the accounts must be examined by a professionally qualified independent examiner. This is defined as an independent person who holds one of a number of qualifications listed in the Charities Act 2011 and the equivalent legislation for Scotland and Northern Ireland. The person must be a qualified member of one of the following bodies:

- Institute of Chartered Accountants in England and Wales (ICAEW)
- Institute of Chartered Accountants of Scotland (ICAS)
- Institute of Chartered Accountants in Ireland (ICAI)
- Association of Chartered Certified Accountants (ACCA)
- Association of Authorised Public Accountants (AAPA)
- Association of Accounting Technicians (AAT)
- Association of International Accountants (AIA)
- Chartered Institute of Management Accountants (CIMA)
- Institute of Chartered Secretaries and Administrators (ICSA)
- Chartered Institute of Public Finance or Accountancy (CIPFA)
- Association of Charity Independent Examiners (ACIE)
- Institute of Financial Accountants*
- Certified Public Accountants Association*

(The bodies marked * were recently added to the list: their members are not yet authorised to act as professional independent examiners for Scottish charities, but they may act in England, Wales and Northern Ireland.)

This list includes the six chartered accountancy bodies, several other accountancy bodies, broader professional bodies such as ICSA, and ACIE, which was established specifically to provide advice, training and qualifications for independent examiners. For a charity looking to find an experienced independent examiner, ACIE can provide lists of full members (for contact details see 'Useful addresses').

In the case of ACIE, the rules specify that the person must be a Fellow (holding ACIE's highest qualification – 'FCIE') in order to act for a charity with an income of more than £250,000. However, an ACIE Associate (with the 'ACIE' qualification) is still a full member and can act as a professionally qualified examiner for smaller charities. (But ACIE also has affiliates who are not formally qualified – they can only act as ordinary independent examiners.) Note that most of the other bodies on the list also have specific rules which members must meet before they can act as an independent examiner (for example, they may insist that members hold a practising certificate, and this may apply even to act as an ordinary independent examiner).

It is possible to be a professionally qualified independent examiner but still be a volunteer; of course independently examining the accounts of a charity with an income of more than £250,000 is a demanding process which will take a good deal of time, and only a few people holding the necessary qualifications would be able to do this voluntarily. In general, a charity must expect to pay a fee to an independent examiner, but in most cases this will be less than an audit fee.

Full audit

For a charity with an income of more than £1 million in England and Wales, or more than £500,000 in Scotland or Northern Ireland (or a lower limit if the charity has substantial assets on its balance sheet – see table 8.2), the accounts must be subject to a full audit by a firm of registered auditors. (This is more than just being a qualified accountant – registered auditors must meet specified criteria and are subject to extensive professional monitoring.)

An audit report goes further than an independent examination; an audit report, if satisfactory, states that in the **auditors'** opinion the accounts give a 'true and fair' view of the charity's position. (This is for accruals accounts. In the rare event of a full audit of accounts on an R&P basis, the auditor declares that they are 'properly presented'.)[9] However, as with independent examiners, an auditor will sometimes have to issue a qualified report.

The precise terms of the audit are slightly different depending on whether the charity is a company, but in all cases a charity audit goes a good deal further than a general audit. For example, the Regulations under the Charities Act require the auditor to state whether the accounts have been prepared in accordance with the methods and principles in the Charities SORP.

Selecting an auditor

To find an auditor you will always need to use a firm of accountants who are also registered auditors (although some accountants in practice on their own are recognised as audit firms). The key thing is to find a firm appropriate to your size of organisation with reasonable experience with charities and voluntary organisations.

You can start from local directories, ask for recommendations from other local charities, or approach the relevant professional accountancy bodies (see 'Useful addresses'), most of which offer a referral service for organisations seeking an accountant. They may also be able to give you details of charity specialists in your area.

All UK-registered auditors will be regulated by one of the first four bodies in the list above (ICAEW, ICAS, ICAI or ACCA). Internet searches may also help, and it is worth looking for advertisements in specialist charity-sector magazines. Also, a body such as ACIE has a number of members who are charity auditors but joined ACIE because they specialise in smaller charities and also act as independent examiners.

Either way, you must normally expect to pay proper fees for accountants' time and costs. Some firms have lower rates for charities, but an audit always involves considerable expenses, and with charity accounts now forming a specialist field, free charity audits are nowadays extremely rare. Because of the issues of different funds, all the notes needed to comply with the SORP, and the different sorts of income in the sector, an audit of a charity is typically much more work than a business audit of a company of the same size. In fact, most non-charitable companies are nowadays exempt from the audit requirement unless their turnover is over £10.2 million, so those firms of accountants who continue to provide audit services below this level will often be paying significant fees to maintain their audit registration specifically because of their charity audit work.

Some charities seeking a full audit ask two or three firms to tender, but you must be clear about what you are seeking, what information you will supply, and the timescales involved (remember many groups have a 31 March year end, so charity accountants tend to be very busy in the late spring, summer and early autumn). But do not just choose the cheapest figure – look at whether the firm really has the expertise to understand your charity.

Issuing the accounts to others

Whenever you are asked to send a copy of your accounts (for example, with a funding application), you must always provide:
- the annual report (signed by the trustees);
- the annual accounts (signed by the trustees);
- the independent report on the accounts (signed by the auditor or independent examiner).

Once everything is complete and signed, it is worth getting enough copies made for your trustees, members, funders and others who may need to see the accounts – normally they are photocopied as a single document. A photocopied or printed signature is fine, so long as the name and date of approval are clear. (With increasing concerns about identity fraud, some trustees and independent examiners prefer just to sign the original set of accounts held by the charity, but with a printed signature on all circulated copies; such accounts are accepted by the Charity Commission. However, printed signatures are *not* currently accepted by OSCR – if filing accounts electronically with OSCR, the accounts must contain at least a photocopied signature.)

Remember that, as a charity, your annual report and accounts form a public document, and anyone is entitled to see them (if necessary you can make a small charge to cover photocopying and postage, but you cannot refuse). Normally, an electronic version of your report and accounts will also be available to anyone from the website of the Charity Commission, OSCR or CCNI as applicable (although the Charity Commission and OSCR do not publish accounts for charities with an income of less than £25,000 unless they are CIOs or SCIOs). OSCR and CCNI only started publishing accounts from 2016.

However, the accounts should never be copied to anyone external until you have all three elements – the annual report, the accounts and the independent report – complete and signed (many funders will, quite rightly, reject unsigned accounts or accounts without the independent report, because legally they are no more than draft documents). If your accounts are not complete and you need to send accounts urgently to someone such as a prospective funder or donor, it is much better to send the previous year's accounts – perhaps with a covering letter explaining recent developments – rather than to send incomplete accounts for the current year.

9 Management accounts and budgets

As shown in chapter 2, accounts are not just a legal requirement at year end, they are vital for making day-to-day financial decisions in a charity. So, although the structure of your books needs to relate to the legal requirements, this is hardly their main purpose. In a well-run organisation, the largest use of information from the books is for ongoing financial monitoring and for decisions by trustees throughout the year.

Presenting information internally

Taking information from the books and presenting it in a form for internal decisions is the field of **management accounting**. Management accounting in a charity is also concerned with monitoring figures against budgets, analysing the cost-effectiveness of different approaches and handling issues of cash flow.

In a small charity, few people use the term 'management accounts' – most treasurers just talk about giving a current financial report – but the way you provide such information to the trustees has a huge effect on their ability to take meaningful decisions.

Traditionally, in many small charities you will hear something like the following exchange at trustees' meetings.

Chair: And now we come to the treasurer's report. Joe – can you give us an update on how we are doing?

Treasurer: Many thanks. I'm pleased to say we've got £273.29 in the current account and £1,503.50 in the deposit account, so we're doing quite well – we had over £200 in from the sponsored walk. But we've got some bills coming in next month so we mustn't get complacent, although I hear Sue has managed to get a new grant from a local trust, so that will help.

Sue: Yes, but we need to bear in mind that the new grant is specifically for play equipment.

Chair: Well that's very helpful, I'm sure the treasurer will make a note of that, and thank you once again, Joe, for all you do to keep our finances in such good order.

As a form of management accounting, this is almost useless. Apart from other factors, very few people can take in financial information that is only given verbally. But, more seriously, knowing how much is in the bank is only important if there are tight cash flow issues – a summary of income and expenditure, plus balances on each fund, will often communicate much more, especially if the income and expenditure is shown with actual figures compared with budgets.

Furthermore, as indicated by Sue's comment, this treasurer seems very vague about restricted funds (see chapter 3). As we have seen, fund accounting is not just an issue to sort out at year end to meet the charity accounting rules. It must be possible for the trustees to know at any time the resources available in each fund separately if they are to make proper decisions.

Using budgets

Budgets versus expenditure limits

Budgets are a vital tool in management accounting, but people use the word 'budget' in different ways:

- as an estimated income and expenditure account for next year (as in, 'The budget of the charity was approved last night') – this is the way 'budget' is most often used in management accounts;
- as a target for the level of income or expenditure against a given account heading – one line within a budget statement in the first sense (as in, 'Our budget income from services is £3,000');
- as an agreed level of expenditure that can be incurred by the budget holder without further approval (as in 'I have been given a budget of up to £400 to spend on stationery').

So it is important to be clear with others what you mean. If the trustees approve a budget statement in the first sense it is simply a target – it does not necessarily mean they are giving authority for all the expenditure shown in the budget without further discussion. Also, some people used to public sector budget controls think they have to spend to the limit of a budget before year end. This may occasionally be true with a time-limited restricted fund but normally, in a charity, avoiding unnecessary expenditure means that more resources are left for future work.

Of course, as we saw in chapter 6, the trustees need to give delegated authority for the treasurer or finance officer to pay certain normal bills without individual discussion. Also, for certain costs you may want to give a senior member of staff the authority to spend up to a certain amount per year. But it is best to use a term such as 'authorised expenditure' to cover such policies. For example, the trustees may have agreed a budget statement that gives £750 as the estimated training expenditure in the coming year. However, the policy on incurring training expenses might be quite different, with delegated authority for small amounts, but still needing trustees' approval to spend over £200 on any single training event.

Preparing budget statements

As noted earlier a finance report at a trustees' meeting is of little use if it only gives the bank balances, but even a report of actual income and expenditure does not tell people much unless they have some basis of comparison. You could simply make comparisons with last year, but in a fast-changing organisation this is not always relevant. Comparing actual figures against budgets is usually the best tool.

So, in a well-run charity, towards the end of the financial year the treasurer or finance officer will prepare a draft budget for discussion by trustees, showing for each line of income how much the charity reasonably expects to receive *next year*, and for each line of expenditure an estimate of the costs. A draft budget looks just like an income and expenditure account (or receipts and payments (R&P) account), but the figures are estimates for the future, rather than actual figures from the past. Where there are several funds (see 'Funds in management accounts', page 137) a separate budget statement is needed for each fund.

Some lines on next year's budget will be easy to determine, for example income from a known grant or expenditure on a fixed rent. Other items can be calculated quite accurately, for example salaries linked to specific scales (but with salaries, remember to allow both for inflationary rises *and* for individual staff moving to higher points on a scale, and, where applicable, do not forget the employer's NI and employer's pension contributions on top – see page 74). However, some income lines, such as 'fundraising', can be very hard to predict accurately in a small charity – these uncertainties need to be highlighted.

If you have inter-fund transfers, such as for management fees or contributions to overheads (see chapter 3), remember to include a line in the budget for these. The management fee is certainly an expense of the fund or project, and it will leave other funds in deficit if the transfer is not made. Alternatively, if all overheads are charged directly to each fund, remember to include the share of overheads in the project budget.

On the other hand, a project sometimes has a specific subsidy from another fund, allowing you to show a funds transfer on the income side of the budget.

Many people think that budget statements have to balance, but there are three possibilities:

surplus budget: planned income > planned expenditure
deficit budget: planned income < planned expenditure
balanced budget: planned income = planned expenditure

A surplus budget is essential if you need to build up reserves (see chapter 4). On the other hand, if a project has funds brought forward from the previous year, which are now to be spent, a deficit budget for the coming year is quite normal.

When preparing a draft budget, it is often best to put the estimates together and present the draft to the trustees for discussion, even if there is a large surplus or deficit. If the draft shows an unacceptable deficit, the trustees can then discuss what expenditure to cut, or they can resolve to increase income (thus creating a case for fundraising). If you present a draft budget that balances, they may simply approve it without serious discussion.

Since a budget statement is based on estimates, you need to be clear about any assumptions used. All budget statements can be optimistic or cautious (pessimistic); an optimistic budget assumes good levels of income and modest costs; a cautious budget allows for the highest levels of expenditure that might be needed but only assumes modest income. But if you prepare a pessimistic budget to make the case for more funds, make sure everyone realises the expenditure figures are worst cases and that they do not represent approved levels of expenditure.

Like the accounts themselves, budgets can be prepared on an accruals or an R&P basis (see chapter 2). This makes a big difference when budgeting for capital items. In an accruals-based budget the cost of capital items will be spread over several years with a provision for depreciation each year, but on the R&P basis, the full cost of a capital item is shown in the budget for the year when the purchase is made, with no cost in later years. Alternatively, some charities take fixed asset costs entirely out of normal management accounts and have a separate budget for capital expenditure.

In particular, when drawing up budgets for fundraising bids, many funders dislike seeing a line labelled 'depreciation' and prefer to see capital costs and operating costs listed separately.

Using budgets in management accounts

If a realistic budget statement has been agreed, the best way of presenting interim financial reports is by showing actual figures against budgets, as in figure 9.1. In many cases, computerised accounting systems allow you to enter budget figures, so they can automatically generate reports of actuals against budgets. However, do make sure your reports add on the balance brought forward from last year in order to show the current balance of the fund – this is vital in knowing what is actually available to spend.

Some people like to add a column for the **budget variance** – the difference between the actual figure and the budget figure – this can be given as an amount in pounds either over or under, although many people find it easier to interpret when the variance is given as a percentage. This is calculated as follows:

$$\text{Budget Variance (\%)} = \frac{\text{Actual} - \text{Budget}}{\text{Budget}} \times 100$$

(However, you must then have a non-zero budget amount on every line: if the budget is £0.00 then even if the expenditure is only £0.50, the overspend expressed as a percentage is infinity and any system will give you an error!)

You need to be clear about positive and negative variances: on the income side a positive variance is good; but on the expenditure side you hope for a negative variance (actual expenditure less than budget expenditure).

Adding variances means more columns on reports, so do be sure your trustees will understand this – knowing that 'The budget variance on stationery is −77.5%' may actually confuse people rather than help them.

More elaborate reports can most easily be produced using spreadsheets. In particular remember that your books will be kept to the penny, but budgets and other figures for decision-making are normally easier to follow if rounded to the nearest £1.

You may also want to consider presenting information graphically where it will help trustees to understand the position more easily – many people find pie charts showing where the money has gone easier to understand than figures. Bar charts can be useful when comparing the current year against a prior year.

MIDSHAM COMMUNITY ACTION CIO: GENERAL FUND BUDGET REPORT
Internal Report for Trustees Only   For trustees meeting April 2018

Last Year: Actuals 2016/17 £		Current Year Budget 2017/18 £	Current Year Actual 2017/18 £
	Receipts		
467	Members' Subscriptions	500	534
10,000	Council Grant	25,000	25,000
500	Miscellaneous Donations	400	429
0	Tax Reclaimed on Gift Aid	170	140
1,103	Christmas Bazaar	1,100	1,732
71	Bank Interest	60	53
12,141	TOTAL RECEIPTS	27,230	27,888
	Payments		
980	Administrator's Salary	1,200	1,079
934	Heat & Light	1,000	869
389	Rates, Water Rates, Cleaning	400	403
6,981	Repairs & Maintenance	4,000	3,708
321	Stationery	300	291
783	Publicity Literature	1,000	1,781
1,089	Postage & Telephone	1,100	1,237
0	Purchase of Minibus	18,000	18,000
200	Independent Examiner's Fee	200	200
171	Committee Travel Expenses	200	126
0	Contribution to Outreach Project	0	100
0	Contingency	50	0
11,848	TOTAL PAYMENTS	27,450	27,794
293	SURPLUS (BUDGET: DEFICIT)	−220	94
80	Add: Balance brought forward at 1 April		373
373	Balance carried forward 31 March		467

Notes to trustees:

1. You have seen my reports on these lines at previous meetings showing progress over the year – this is now the year end budget report covering the full 12 months.
2. The left-hand column shows the figures used in our published receipts and payments account for 2016/17. The far-right column shows the actual figures for the year to March 2018 (subject to any adjustments by our independent examiner). The budget column shows the 2017/18 budget figures which we agreed in February 2017.
3. You will recall that we budgeted for a £220 deficit for the year, after allowing for the minibus purchase (supported by the one-off increase in the Council Grant). We felt we could meet a small deficit because we expected to carry forward about £300 (actually £373 in the end) from 2016/17.
4. However, we have actually made a small surplus of £94. The main gains are due to better than expected receipts from the Christmas Bazaar, and lower than expected costs for Administrator's Salary (less overtime than expected) and for Heat & Light and Repairs. But you will see that several expenditure areas were higher than predicted, particularly Publicity Literature. The final cost of the minibus was exactly as per the quotation which we used for the budget. Because of the deal we got, so far we have not yet incurred any running costs for the minibus, but we will need to include these next year.
5. Note that these figures *only* cover the General Fund. I have not presented a report for the Outreach Fund as the project is still at an early stage and we haven't yet set budgets, but you will see we have transferred £100 from the General Fund towards this.

Jane Corrigan – Treasurer 4.4.18

Fig. 9.1 Example of a year end budget report to trustees

Breaking down the income and expenditure

A key issue with budget statements is how much detail to show. For a very simple fund you might need just one income line and one expenditure line. However, for the fund representing the main work of the charity, you may need 10 or more income lines and perhaps up to 30 expenditure lines.

Large organisations sometimes use multi-level budgets with different degrees of summary, but this is rarely needed in a small, local charity. So try to ensure that the full budget for any fund can show income, expenditure and balances on one page (and certainly no more than two) in a normal font size.

Remember that, in order to monitor actual figures against budgets, every line will have to be maintained as a separate category in your books (see chapter 5) so the more categories you create, the more complex the bookkeeping. For example, if you have 9 funds and they each have 30 kinds of expenditure, your books will need 270 expenditure accounts (9 × 30). This is not difficult with a computer system, but great care is needed to ensure that expenditure is posted correctly. Moreover, if everything is budgeted, you will then have 270 separate expenditure budgets to monitor! So try to keep things simple.

Funds in management accounts

As we are starting to see, budget reports are fairly straightforward for a single fund or project. But if a charity has nine funds – say a general fund and eight restricted funds – then the trustees are managing nine different resources. It is almost like running nine organisations. You may need to take time with new trustees to ensure that they appreciate this.

You therefore, ideally, need separate management accounts for each fund. But, although it is possible to produce an income and expenditure report for each fund showing actual figures against budgets, this would mean your management accounts would run to at least as many pages as the number of funds – and people simply will not read them. The opposite extreme to the scenario presented at the start of the chapter – but which can have the same result – is where the treasurer or finance manager overwhelms the trustees with so much financial information that they remain dependent on the treasurer for any understanding. There are cases of larger charities where trustees routinely get a 30-page set of management accounts for each meeting. Occasionally this may be helpful if the trustees want to discuss a certain project in detail and compare it with other projects, but in most cases it is useless.

Some trustees from a commercial background say, 'I can't follow this – I want to see one overall budget' but it simply does not make sense to mix income and expenditure for different funds in a single budget report. Knowing that you are underspent on the salaries budget across the whole charity does not mean you can take on a general administrator if the underspend is mainly due to a specific unfilled post in a restricted fund. Usually the best compromise is to provide:

- a summary report showing the financial position of the whole charity, broken down by funds (but without trying to show budgets);
- detailed income and expenditure budget reports for one or two funds where key decisions are needed (a capable treasurer will consider what is important for a given meeting).

As regards the summary for the whole charity, many organisations find that once trustees are used to the SOFA (see chapter 7) it can be very useful, not just at year end but also as a management report during the year. It shows immediately the split of resources between unrestricted and restricted funds, including the balances brought forward, and the income lines make it easy to distinguish what has come in through grants and donations, through trading and fees, and through investment income.

MIDSHAM COMMUNITY ACTION CIO: FUND MOVEMENTS REPORT 2017/18

BALANCE 01 Apr 17 £	FUND	INCOME £	EXPENSES £	TRANSFERS £	BALANCE 31 Mar 18 £
	UNRESTRICTED FUNDS				
2,313	General Fund	27,918	14,444	(100)	15,687
2,313	Totals for Unrestricted Funds	27,918	14,444	(100)	15,687
	RESTRICTED FUNDS				
0	Outreach Project	4,713	4,554	100	259
0	Play Equipment Fund	5,000	0	0	5,000
39	Midsham Disability Project	143	73	0	109
39	Totals for Restricted Funds	9,856	4,627	100	5,368
	ENDOWMENT FUNDS				
120,000	Community building	0	0	0	120,000
120,000	Totals for Endowment Funds	0	0	0	120,000
122,352	TOTALS FOR ALL FUNDS	37,774	19,071	0	141,055

Note: This report is based on accruals accounting. The fund balances thus include fixed assets and debtors/creditors where applicable.

The figures here do not tie up exactly with the accounts in chapter 7 because two further funds are included in this example.

Fig. 9.2 Example of a report summarising movements on all funds

However, the SOFA lumps all the restricted funds together in one column, which means you may not easily spot an individual restricted fund that is close to being overspent. So another helpful way of presenting a summary of the whole charity is simply to show a line for each fund, as in figure 9.2 (in fact, the Charities SORP requires a note on these lines to be included in year end accounts). This type of report also makes it easy to spot when there are still funds in hand on a project that has finished, so that appropriate decisions can be taken.

Frequency of reports and accounting periods

It is best to link your management accounts into the cycle of trustees' meetings. For example, if your accounting year starts on 1 April and the trustees would like to see quarterly reports on finances, having trustees' meetings in mid-July, mid-October, etc. may work well.

If you have monthly trustees' meetings it is worth asking whether you really need full management accounts every month, or whether bimonthly or quarterly would suffice. Although finance is important, it is not the only issue to discuss. For a small charity, the change in the financial picture during just one month may not be significant except at a time of major crisis.

Once you have established the cycle of reporting, you need to decide whether to divide the year into separate **accounting periods**, or whether year-to-date reports will be best. For example, at the October trustees' meeting when you present figures for the second quarter (July–September) would it be best to show just the last three months' income and expenditure, or would it be more meaningful to show the year so far (April–September)?

To do separate reports for each quarter, you will need to close off your books, or select 'close of period' on your computer system at the end of each quarter. Figures for a single period are most useful with trading income, where you may need to monitor profitability for each period separately, but for general monitoring, year-to-date figures can be more meaningful.

When producing reports for part of the year, you also need to decide whether to show part-year budgets or full-year figures. For example, at the nine-month point (April–December in this case) it can be useful to see whether you are over or under budget based on 9/12 of the full-year budget. Other people prefer to show the full-year budget so it is clear (particularly on income) whether you are close to the full-year target. Another possibility is to show just the last period (October–December) against 3/12 of the budget.

Computerised accounting systems will often give you a huge choice of reports of this kind: it is worth experimenting with the options and then settling on one format that suits your trustees. Moreover, some systems will allow you to enter different budgets for each month – rather than just spreading the annual budget evenly across the year. But it is easy to get bogged down in excessively detailed budgets which are easily thrown off course when circumstances change.

Also, bear in mind that some funders will need you to report on a 12-month cycle that is different from your normal accounting year: this may mean combining period figures from two different accounting years.

Although management accounting reports based on comparisons of actual figures and budgets can be useful, they are often criticised for focusing too much on the past when, arguably, trustees should be focusing more on the future. But in preparing future budgets you will often need to be presenting three years' figures. For example, if it is January 2018 and you are preparing a budget for the year beginning 1 April 2018, you will not yet have the final figures for the current year (2017/18). So you may need to present:

- actual totals for last year (2016/17);
- budgets agreed for the current year (2017/18) – agreed a year ago;
- actual figures for the first nine months of the current year (April–December 2017);
- suggested budget for next year (2018/19).

However, this can mean a lot of numbers and it is rarely possible for a full trustees' meeting to grapple with such detailed figures – such discussions may be better considered by a small group such as a finance committee. There is also a tendency to set future budgets by applying a small percentage change to past budgets, which does not encourage the trustees to think in visionary terms. Some people advocate **zero-based budgeting**, where every budget starts from zero each year and you ask, 'What can we really expect to achieve next year?', starting from first principles.

Cash flow

Thinking about cash flow is a great way to focus on the future. We saw in chapter 4 the importance of cash flow planning for some charities. This is quite separate from normal budgeting, but where cash flow is tight your management accounts may need to include cash flow projections.

A cash flow forecast is usually presented as a table, showing the expected money in and money out each month on a cumulative basis (this must be done on an R&P basis, even if the charity is otherwise doing accruals accounts, because it is the cash in and out that matters). Alternatively, it can help to present the cash flow as a graph.

It is important to distinguish a **cash flow forecast**, which is a key management accounting tool for planning ahead, from a **statement of cash flows** which larger charities must include in their final accounts (see page 114) alongside the SOFA and balance sheet, but which only shows cash flow information from the previous year. Also, the cash flow statement in the final accounts usually just shows total cash flows over a 12-month period, but, for charities where cash is tight, a cash flow forecast needs to use much shorter time periods (quarterly, monthly or even weekly).

A spreadsheet can be helpful in putting together the figures for a cash flow forecast, but you cannot expect to generate this automatically from an accounting system, since your books (whether manual or computerised) will only tell you about the past. Figures from the past may help your projections, but only someone with a good knowledge of the expected future income and expenditure streams and the timings can prepare the forecast.

When doing a cash flow forecast for a new project, the largest negative figure determines how much money you must have in hand from somewhere else to support the cash flow. For example, if the forecast goes to –£10,000 at its lowest point, the charity must not undertake the work unless it can support the project with £10,000 of working cash from elsewhere (preferably more, to allow for contingencies). Also, the trustees must be satisfied that the risks of the project do not jeopardise other funds.

The working cash could come from other funds of the charity, or via a loan (but if the charity considers borrowing, check the charity has powers to borrow in its governing document). Alternatively, when you demonstrate the cash flow problems, you may be able to persuade the funder to pay earlier, particularly if it is keen for you to do the work. HM Treasury guidance to funders of third sector organisations indicates that payment in advance can often be justified as good value for money.

If cash flow is the main issue, your management accounts will want to focus on actual cash received and paid out each month compared with the projected cash flow from the project plan. Frequent trustees' meetings may be vital to monitor this closely and, if problems occur, expenditure may have to be postponed. If there is any chance that the charity may run out of funds completely, take professional advice urgently, or the trustees could find they are acting illegally.

Cash flow planning is usually done in relation to a whole charity, rather than fund by fund, as you will normally have one set of bank accounts for the whole organisation. Charities often rely on higher balances in one area to support projects that are temporarily in deficit, and this is an effective means of cash flow management. However, care must be taken on this: if the project in deficit does not recover, the trustees could find that they have spent restricted funds on a completely unrelated purpose, and so they could be in breach of trust. Also, if such arrangements mean that a restricted fund loses out on interest, there is a case for regarding the arrangement formally as an 'internal loan', where the fund with the cash flow difficulties might make a transfer to reimburse another fund for interest lost.

Supporting a charity through a major cash flow crisis is perhaps one of the ultimate tests for a treasurer or finance officer.

Communicating accounts meaningfully

Producing management accounts has no value unless they are meaningful to the readers. You cannot expect trustees to make informed decisions unless they understand the information they are given.

Pure verbal reports are not much use, but neither is a large pile of papers with numerous figures and few comments. Try to get management accounts circulated before the meeting if possible. At the meeting, talk people through what you have provided (but without commenting on every figure) and encourage questions. With larger meetings, projecting the key figures can help (but not if you go through slides too quickly for people to follow them). It can be useful to have one trustees' meeting each year – perhaps the annual budget-setting meeting – when someone explains the overall structure of the charity's accounts and the purpose of each fund (but try to keep this separate from the meeting where the trustees formally approve the previous year's accounts).

Try to use meaningful names for accounts and funds and carefully consider font sizes, paper colours and other readability issues (and use a consistent format from one meeting to the next). Graphical presentations can help, particularly if trustees are being asked to decide between two options – if you are an experienced spreadsheet user this will not be difficult. If any trustees have disabilities affecting what they can read, you need to take this into account – ask them directly how they would like the information presented.

However, do bear in mind that spending hours each month or quarter reformatting your accounts in spreadsheets can add enormously to the work of the treasurer or finance officer, so be wary of taking on ever-increasing demands that you cannot sustain. If the standard reports from your computer-based accounting system can serve as management accounts, it is obviously much easier.

10 Accruals accounting

As outlined in chapter 2, and explained more fully in chapter 7, once a charity's total income (across all funds) exceeds the relevant threshold, the final accounts must be prepared on an accruals basis and presented in the SORP format. If the charity is a company, the final accounts must be on an accruals basis whatever the income. For charities which are *not* companies (this includes CIOs) accruals accounts are only compulsory once the income reaches £250,000 (from 2016 this limit applies in all three UK jurisdictions: England and Wales, Scotland, and Northern Ireland). However, many charities may want to do SORP accounts at lower levels of income to give a more professional look to the accounts.

For many treasurers and finance staff, the SORP format is not the problem: once you understand the idea of fund accounting, the layout of the SOFA and balance sheet is quite logical. What often needs more thought, if you do not have a formal accounting background, is making the correct postings in the books (or on your computerised accounting system), for items such as debtors, creditors and fixed assets.

Who does what?

If you feel the accruals principles are too much for you, it is possible to keep the books during the year on a receipts and payments (R&P) basis, and then pay an accountant at year end to convert everything to accruals for the final accounts. Accountants are used to working on this basis, and it is probably better to use this option than to try accruals accounting if you do not understand the principles at all.

However, if you do this, it means that your internal management accounts may end up looking very different from your final accounts. For example, you may think a fund had money in hand at year end, but once the accountant has adjusted for a creditor, the fund may be in deficit in the final accounts. On the other hand, a fund might appear fully spent when calculated on an R&P basis, but once a fixed asset purchase is capitalised (see 'Fixed assets', page 150), the fund may look as though very little has been spent.

So, even if you do not feel able to keep your day-to-day books on the accruals basis, it is vital for charity treasurers and finance workers to have at least some understanding of the accruals principles used by your accountant to make these adjustments. Otherwise you may have to ask your trustees to approve accounts you do not understand yourself. Moreover, if you send out accounts that you do not understand, how will you deal with queries from funders?

It follows that if you can get on top of the basic principles of accruals accounting, there is a lot to be said for keeping your books on this basis. All but the smallest computer-based accounting systems are designed to use the principles of accruals accounting. For example, you should be able to post an invoice from a supplier and your subsequent payment of the invoice as two separate events with separate dates. (Between these dates – when the invoice is entered but the payment is not yet made – the invoice is included as a creditor in the balance sheet, but the expenditure has been charged to the fund concerned. We say the expenditure has been **recognised** even though money has not yet gone out of the charity's bank account.) So it is not necessarily difficult.

On the income side, the same concept allows an accounting system to maintain a sales ledger – which is very useful if your charity provides any kind of service under contract and you have to keep track of unpaid invoices you have issued. Also, it is worth noting that if your charity has to register for VAT (see chapter 11), the books *must* be kept on an accruals basis, unless the charity is within the limits to operate the VAT cash accounting system.

Standard bookkeeping texts offer much more on the principles of accruals accounting concepts than we can cover in a short book (see 'Further reading') – in fact, most accounting textbooks do not even mention R&P accounts. However, the rest of this chapter summarises the key issues and gives some examples, and then explains how accruals accounts link with accounting standards.

As explained in chapters 2 and 7, the SORP intended for use for financial years starting in 2016 onwards is the FRS102 SORP 2015 (although some non-company charities in England and Wales are keeping to SORP 2005 until the 2008 Regulations are updated). But all versions of the SORP rely on accruals accounting as the basis. However, the discussion on page 152 illustrates why in a few cases more complex calculations of accrued income or expenses may be needed under FRS102.

Concepts of accruals accounts

The key principle of accruals accounts is that they show the *income due* to the charity (or to a certain fund) during the year and the costs and *expenses incurred*. This is clearly a better way of understanding the charity's resources and demands than simply recording cash in and out. For more on this and some of the differences, see 'Accruals or receipts and payments?' on page 30.

Showing income and expenditure in terms of revenue earned and costs incurred has several important implications.

- *Accruals accounts may need estimates and judgements.* For example, choosing a depreciation policy or deciding whether to include a promised donation as a debtor. These will affect postings in the records and hence the final figures on the SOFA and balance sheet. There are no right and wrong answers: it is a matter of judgement and, depending on the judgements made, different sets of accounts could be produced for the same charity.

  However, if you were to make ludicrous judgements, your auditor or independent examiner would have to give a qualified report. In many cases the SORP gives guidance on such issues – many paragraphs are concerned with the criteria for 'recognising income' (deciding what income should be included), and for 'recognising expenses'.

- *Accruals accounts must give a true and fair view.* This is always the aim when judgements and policies are made. Accounting standards are very important in this respect in setting the principles to be used in such judgements – these include not just the SORP but also more general accounting standards (outlined overleaf). Such judgements ultimately have to be agreed by the trustees, on the basis of trying to ensure that the accounts give a true and fair view of the charity's affairs, but in most cases the trustees will be guided by the recommendations of their treasurer, finance officer or accountant.

  Accountants spend a lot of time studying the phrase 'true and fair', but for the layperson it is best to take the words at face value. For example, if your charity had received a bill for £10,000 just before year end for costs it had incurred during the year, it would hardly be 'fair' to show accounts with £2,500 in hand if, in reality, you would be £7,500 in deficit once this bill was paid. R&P accounts may show a true record of money received and paid out, but they will rarely be 'fair' in the sense of this example.

- *The going concern basis.* Unless stated otherwise, accounts are prepared on the basis that the organisation has sufficient resources to continue. This is crucial for issues such as depreciation of fixed assets (see page 150) – by spreading the cost of a major purchase over several years, you are assuming the organisation will continue to exist for that time.
- *Ten fundamental qualitative characteristics are assumed to apply to the accounts* (unless there is a specific note to the contrary). This list is taken from FRS102, though the explanations are the author's.

  1 *Understandability.* Accounts are not just prepared following a set of rules: they should be understandable to the reader. (This may mean providing more information than the legal minimum.)

  2 *Relevance.* Information included should be relevant to readers. Not everyone will be interested in everything, but accounts should not be cluttered with information that has no value to the user.

  3 *The concept of 'materiality'.* This applies to all figures in the SOFA, balance sheet and notes. It means that you do not have to worry about where to show something if it is too small to be material to readers of the accounts. But care is needed when applying this to charities. For example, an item that is small in relation to the charity as a whole may be material in relation to a certain fund. Even a very small payment to a trustee will almost always be **material** because it could affect the issue of trustees' independence and the public benefit requirement (see chapter 1).

  4 *Reliability.* The information provided in **financial statements** must be reliable and free from deliberate bias or distortion.

  5 *Substance over form.* When in doubt about how to show something, focus on the substance of the transaction – in particular whether it gives an economic benefit to the charity.

  6 *Prudence.* Prudence is used when making estimates in the accounts, so that assets or income are not overstated and liabilities or expenses are not understated. However, the exercise of prudence does not permit deliberate bias to make things look worse than they are – it does not override the other criteria.

7   *Completeness.* To be reliable, the information in the accounts must be complete (within the bounds of materiality and cost).

8   *Comparability/consistency.* Where judgements are made, they should be consistent each year so the accounts can be meaningfully compared over a number of years.

9   *Timeliness.* Accounts should be issued promptly – not delayed so long that the information is out of date.

10 *Balance between benefit and cost.* The charity is not expected to incur enormous costs providing information which will be of limited value to users (though any omissions for this reason must be explained).

Accruals transactions

Although people sometimes imply that accruals and R&P accounting are totally distinct, the vast majority of day-to-day transactions, such as receiving a donation or paying wages, will be entered in the same way in both systems.

Similarly, certain transfers that have no net income or expenditure to the charity will be the same with R&P or accruals accounting. These include transactions for moving money between bank accounts, drawing petty cash and most inter-fund transfers.

Where differences arise, they mainly relate to debtors, creditors and fixed assets. Even with R&P accounts, you need to keep track of these items, in order to include them on the statement of assets and liabilities (SOAL). But the big difference with accruals accounting is that the value of debtors, creditors and fixed assets is directly included in the value of relevant funds. This can give rise to transactions that do not involve movements of money but which affect the balances of funds.

To record these correctly, use of double-entry bookkeeping is strongly recommended (see chapter 5), but if you are using a computer-based accounting system, you can probably make many entries without needing to understand debits and credits. However, to cover all cases, including manual books, we use the format of debits (DR) and credits (CR) in the following examples. If your system includes provision for entry of journals (see page 67), *any* transaction at all can be entered on this basis – though most systems provide considerably easier ways of entering common transactions such as raising an invoice.

Money owed to the charity (debtors)

If there is an increase in the amount of money owed to a charity (the debtors figure), for example if you suddenly hear on 5 December 2017 that someone has died and the charity is entitled to receive a £12,000 legacy, you will need to make an entry in the books to record this income, even though it may be many months before the money is physically received. The transaction to post would be:

5 Dec 2017	DR	Debtors	£12,000
	CR	Donated income	£12,000

This appears as £12,000 income to the fund. The income appears on the SOFA, balanced by the debtors figure on the balance sheet. This is correct: the charity is legally entitled to this money, it is part of your resources and your trustees can decide how to spend it. (But if cash flow is tight, you might want to wait until the money comes in before spending it.)

When the legacy is finally paid over, perhaps not until well into the next accounting year, take care not to record it as new income: you have already *recognised* (see pages 31 and 144 for more on this term) the income. All that happens in the new year is that the debtor is converted to money in the bank:

13 Sep 2018	CR	Debtors	£12,000
	DR	Bank	£12,000

The effect of this is that the bank balance goes up by £12,000 and the debtors figure is reduced by £12,000. The balance of the debtors account is now zero (assuming there are no other debtors). Since the income was recorded previously, the fund balances are unaffected.

Money owed by the charity (creditors)

Creditors are typically unpaid bills at year end. For example, assume that on 23 March 2018 you received a bill for £775 for gas consumed, but this was not paid by your year end of 31 March. Clearly this was part of the expenses of running the charity in the last year and, for a true and fair view, it must be recognised as an expense. You can post this by entering:

23 Mar 2018	CR	Creditors	£775
	DR	Heat/light expenses	£775

(If the gas bill is normally apportioned between funds, there may be several debits to different expenditure accounts.)

The balance of the relevant fund(s) has now gone down by £775 because of this expense. The expenditure appears on the SOFA, and is balanced by the creditors figure on the balance sheet.

In the following year when you pay the bill remember that, although you are making a payment, this is not new expenditure – the expenditure was included last year. You are simply transferring money out of the bank to settle a creditor. So post this as:

| 23 Apr 2018 | DR | Creditors | £775 |
| | CR | Bank | £775 |

The bank balance has gone down and, if this was the only creditor, the creditors balance (which was negative – in credit) is now back to zero. But the fund balances are unchanged in the new year – the expense was recognised last year.

Sometimes you will need to provide for a creditor even though you have not received a bill by year end because you know that the charity has incurred the relevant costs – such entries are often called **accruals**. The most common example is the fee due to your auditor or independent examiner: even though it may not be billed until many months after year end, the expense relates to the year of the accounts concerned. If you are posting all entries yourself and preparing the final SOFA and balance sheet, remember to get confirmation of this figure before you close your books (and remember to include VAT if applicable).

Prepayments and deferred income

The converse can apply where money is paid out in the year *before* the one to which the expenditure applies. For example, you might have to pay a large deposit to hire a venue for an event next year. This is called a **prepayment** and appears as a debtor on the balance sheet.

Conversely, you will sometimes receive income in advance, for example a grant paid early but with a clear condition that it cannot be spent until next year. Although you will have the money in the bank, the charity is not yet legally entitled to it, so it is balanced by a creditor on the balance sheet. The logic is that if the charity closed down at the end of the current year, the money would have to be repaid. You are not entitled to the income until next year. Creditors related to amounts received in advance are often called **deferred income**.

Estimated prepayments and accruals

To make matters harder, **prepayments** and accruals sometimes have to be estimated. For example, if it has been two months since your last gas bill, then at year end you owe a certain amount for gas even though you have not yet been billed: this requires an estimated accrual if the accounts are to allow for the full year's energy bills. Or you may have paid an insurance premium at the end of January for the following 12 months: strictly speaking if you have a 31 March year end, only 2 months of this payment relates to the current year and 10 months is a prepayment towards insurance for the year ahead. For really precise accounting, you need to estimate these figures and post appropriate accruals and prepayments.

At one time accountants placed much effort in calculating and entering such adjustments. But often a lot of work can be saved by applying the principle of materiality – would it affect a reader of the accounts? If you were running a steel works, the accrued energy costs at year end could make a big difference to a company's final accounts, but for the majority of small to medium-sized charities (except, perhaps, those whose main activity is providing accommodation) the effect of such adjustments will be too small to be material. So long as you have paid four quarterly gas bills in the year, small adjustments at the start and end of the year may have little impact on the total picture.

Posting prepayments and accruals can become complex and if you have to enter these you may need help, particularly if estimated amounts then need to be adjusted the following year. But remember they are only needed when the effect is material. Whatever you do, try to follow the principle of consistency from year to year; however, if you realise that the practice in past years was giving a seriously misleading result and thus decide to make a change of **accounting policy**, remember this needs a note of explanation in the final accounts (see line (c) in 'Accruals accounts – summary of requirements for notes to the accounts' on page 116).

Fixed assets

Fixed assets need some thought, but the key thing to bear in mind is that if you are buying furniture, equipment or anything with a life of several years, the cost needs to be spread over several accounting years – this is generally known as 'depreciation'. The depreciation figure in the accounts is a measure of how much fixed assets were 'used up' in the year concerned. (Depreciation is part of the broader issue of **impairment** of fixed assets – see module 12 of the FRS102 SORP 2015.)

For example, if you spend £1,500 on computer equipment and you expect it to last about three years, after which it will be virtually worthless, you will probably want to show £500 of expenditure in the accounts for three successive years. On the balance sheet, the equipment appears under 'Fixed assets' with a value of £1,500 when first bought and the value goes down as the depreciation is charged: so the value will be £1,000 after the first year, £500 after the second year and £0 after the third year. (This is called 'straight-line depreciation' – there are other methods.)

The SORP does not require any specific depreciation policy: it is up to the trustees to make reasonable judgements based on the expected life of assets bought, but try to avoid anything too complex or having too many different rates. However, it is normal to have a **capitalisation limit**, where purchases for less than a certain amount (typically £250 for a small charity) are entered in full when the purchase is made. To depreciate items costing less than the limit, even if they might last several years, will rarely be material.

For everything above the capitalisation limit, you need a **fixed asset register**, where you record the item at the time of purchase (this is also useful for insurance purposes, though, if you are using it for this purpose, do not forget to list the smaller items, too). Then note each year's depreciation when you enter it in the books. Without this, it is almost impossible to enter depreciation correctly for something bought several years ago.

Consider a charity that buys a minibus for £28,000. The key thing to remember when you make the purchase is that, although you have written a cheque for this amount, you are simply converting money in the bank into assets of a different sort. So the entry in the books might be:

| 18 Jan 2018 | CR | Bank | £28,000 |
| | DR | Fixed assets – minibus | £28,000 |

The bank balance has gone down by £28,000 and the fixed assets have gone up by £28,000. As yet there has been no expenditure, and the fund balances are unaffected. If, for example, the minibus is funded by a special grant, the balance of the restricted fund will still show the full £28,000. The only change is that the assets of the fund now comprise a minibus instead of cash in the bank.

It is only when you enter depreciation that the fund goes down. If the minibus is to be depreciated at 25% for the first year, the depreciation at the end of that year will be:

| 31 Mar 2018 | CR | Fixed assets – minibus | £7,000 |
| | DR | Expenses – depreciation | £7,000 |

This does not affect the bank balance, but it does represent real expenditure on the SOFA. (This example assumes the common policy of charging a whole year's depreciation in the first year, regardless of how long the asset has been held.)

The depreciation expense account must be an expenditure category in the fund that is paying for the minibus. If this was a restricted fund specifically for the minibus purchase, the balance of the fund will reduce gradually over the years (rather than immediately after purchase). This is fully in accordance with the SORP, but sometimes needs explaining to those reading the accounts.

Applying the concepts – an exercise

In the light of the principles in this chapter, you may like to look back to the examples in figures 7.1 and 7.2, which show the accounts of the same charity on an R&P basis and accruals basis. Taking into account the items on the SOAL at the start and end of the year, you might like to see if you can work from the R&P accounts in figure 7.1 to get to the SOFA and balance sheet amounts in figure 7.2. Notice the differences in the fund balances.

The impact of accounting standards

The principles of accruals accounting are not just abstract ideas. They have been developed by the accountancy profession over many years, and the relevant principles are nowadays set down in accounting standards.

In order to give a true and fair view, accruals accounts should take account of *all relevant published accounting standards* in terms of the principles and judgements used. Although the Charities SORP provides charity-specific guidance, it is important to note that the SORP is based on more general standards – from time to time you may need to refer to the key underlying standard (FRS102).

Listed companies whose shares are traded on stock markets are required to use IFRS for their accounts. Charities do not have to follow IFRS in full, but under a process known as 'convergence', UK standards have been gradually brought into line with IFRS.

General-purpose UK accounting standards – as opposed to industry-specific SORPs – are issued by the Financial Reporting Council (FRC).

There used to be many different UK financial reporting standards (FRSs) but for financial years from 1 January 2015 the FRC has produced just one general-purpose standard – FRS102 – which is simply called the *Financial Reporting Standard applicable in the UK and Republic of Ireland*. FRS102 is based on the 'IFRS for SMEs' – a simplified version of IFRS applicable to small and medium-sized enterprises (though even the largest UK companies can use this if they are not listed on a stock market).

The latest revisions to the Charities SORP, which led to the SORP 2015 (FRS102 version), were primarily concerned with bringing charity accounting into line with FRS102.

Until 2015, a simpler general-purpose accounting standard known as the FRSSE (Financial Reporting Standard for Smaller Entities) was available, which could be used by most entities with up to £6.5 million income, instead of FRS102 and its predecessors. So, when the Charities SORP was revised from 2015, two versions were issued: the FRS102 SORP and the FRSSE SORP, and only the very largest charities had to use the FRS102 SORP. (See the appendix on page 193 if you are concerned with charity accounts for years before 2016.)

However, the FRSSE was based on older accounting concepts (pre-IFRS) and so the FRC decided to withdraw the FRSSE from 2016 in order to avoid fundamental inconsistencies of differently sized companies and organisations preparing accounts under different principles. Instead, they issued some simplifications to FRS102, known as 'Section 1A'. This change means that the FRSSE SORP *cannot* be used by charities for accounting periods which began from 1 January 2016 or later.

So the only option now for charities preparing accruals accounts is to use the FRS102 SORP 2015 (or possibly to keep to SORP 2005 in the case of non-company charities in England and Wales if they are waiting until the 2008 Regulations are updated – see page 109). However, the SORP Committee issued a SORP Update Bulletin No. 1 in early 2016 (available from www.charitysorp.org) clarifying some of the issues regarding smaller charities and the FRS102 SORP. There could also be further SORP changes in the future (although no major changes are expected before 2019).

One of the key issues of accounting under the principles of FRS102 is that assets and liabilities should normally be shown on the balance sheet at fair value – an estimate of what they would be worth in a free market transaction. This can have important implications for charities, especially for obligations which go more than 12 months ahead. For example, the FRS102 SORP generally requires that multi-year grant commitments are discounted to give a net present value (see the example calculation in table 10.1) as this is the best estimate of the fair value of the commitment. However, this is just one example – when a charity first adopts accruals accounting under the FRS102 SORP a wide range of accounting policies may need to be reviewed in discussion with the charity's auditor or independent examiner.

Table 10.1 Different approaches to accounting for a multi-year grant

Example: In October 2016, a charity receives confirmation of a three-year grant (£100,000/year) to be received in February 2017, 2018, 2019. Although it is income for a restricted fund, it is *not* a performance-related grant. It is a firm commitment and there is no real doubt about receiving the future years' payments.

The charity's accounting year ends on 31 March. How should the income be shown in the 2016/17 accounts?

R&P accounts	Receipts are only shown when grant payments are received. So the 2016/17 accounts just show £100,000 received.
	(The remaining £200,000 should be noted as a debtor on the SOAL at 31.3.2017 as it is money firmly promised to the charity, to be received at a future date.)
	In future years, each instalment appears as a £100,000 receipt (and the debtor on the SOAL goes down).
SORP 2005 basis (assuming discounting to net present value is not material). This approach would also apply under the former FRSSE SORP.	In 2016/17 the charity became entitled to £300,000 of additional income. While it will be paid over several years, the whole of the income was earned in 2016/17. So the full £300,000 is shown as income on the SOFA.
(See paras 110–11 and 323 in SORP 2005 or module 11 of the FRSSE SORP)	Of this, £100,000 has been received, with the rest outstanding, so the balance sheet at 31.3.2017 will show an extra £100,000 in the bank and £200,000 as a debtor.
	No income appears on the SOFA in 2017/18 or later, because the second and third instalments of the grant are just balanced by a reduction in the outstanding debtor.

FRS102 basis

(See module 11 of the FRS102 SORP 2015)

In 2016/17 the charity became entitled to a three-year grant, which is recognised as income as above. However, to establish the fair value of the grant at the point of entitlement, we must consider that amounts due in future years are not worth as much today after allowing for the effects of inflation or borrowing. (The trustees need to decide the charity's typical cost of borrowing and use this as a discount rate.)

If the rate chosen is 4%:

- £100,000 received in the current year is worth £100,000.
- £100,000 to be received in a year's time is only worth £96,000 today.
- £100,000 to be received in two years' time is worth £92,160 today (the discount is calculated like compound interest).

So the total income from this source shown on the SOFA in 2016/17 is £288,160. The balance sheet at 31.3.2017 will show an extra £100,000 in the bank and £188,160 as a debtor for the amounts due in future years.

In a year's time, when the second £100,000 is received, £96,000 of it is a reduction in the level of debt. The other £4,000 is treated as finance income (equivalent to bank interest) so this appears as income on the 2017/18 SOFA. (Further adjustments are needed for the third instalment.)

11 Social enterprise, trading income and taxes

For many years charities have been encouraged to develop their sustainability by finding services that they can *sell*, rather than seeking to fund their work entirely through donated income, and the government is keen for third sector organisations (where appropriate) to provide services under contract to the public sector. In addition, many methods of fundraising ultimately come down to selling something to supporters (e.g. tickets for an event) rather than seeking pure donations.

In each of these situations, the charity is *trading*, as we saw in chapter 4. Such trading activities are often described as social enterprises (see chapter 1, page 2 for more on this term). However, there are big differences in legal and tax terms between social enterprise activities operated by a charity (the subject of this chapter) and non-charitable social enterprises structured as CICs, for example, which are taxed in the same way as normal businesses.

Even if such activities are only a small part of the organisation's total income, any charity treasurer or finance officer needs to understand the accounting implications of trading income – the biggest of which is tax.

Charities and tax

There are many ways in which tax works differently for charities compared with individuals or businesses. Many of the complications relate to trading but there are also special tax rules in other areas (many of them beneficial), which can affect both income and expenditure.

There is a widespread myth that charities are not subject to tax. In fact the situation is much more varied, as shown in 'Major taxes – issues for charities' overleaf.

Charity taxation is a complex field, and in a book of this size we can only highlight a few key issues that treasurers of smaller charities need to keep in mind. In the following major tax examples, it is clear that trading income is the area that most often gives rise to problems. For more guidance see 'Further reading', and bear in mind that the rules and thresholds change slightly each year. Some of the tax reliefs create special opportunities for fundraising – see chapter 12.

Major taxes – issues for charities

Examples

A. No special reliefs for charities:
- Employer's NI
- Insurance premium tax

B. Some reliefs in specific situations:
- VAT (limited concessions for charities – growing slowly)
- Business rates (more extensive concessions)

C. General relief for most charitable work:
- Corporation tax (on primary purpose trading)
- Income tax (on investment income)
- Capital gains tax (on investment gains)
- Inheritance tax (on legacy income)

Understanding different funding channels

We have noted that a funder may potentially support a charity in two completely different ways:
- by making a gift to the charity (a grant or donation); or
- by purchasing services from the charity under a contract.

In the case of funds given to the charity it is usual to speak of a 'donation' if it is from an individual or a 'grant' if it is from an organisation, but the two terms mean the same thing. A grant may, of course, be subject to conditions on its use (sometimes running to many pages), in which case the grant income will certainly need to be allocated to a restricted fund. But ultimately, if a funder is providing resources to a charity without requiring anything in return (other than feedback and monitoring), the income needs to be treated for tax purposes as donated income.

As explained in chapter 4, the contract funding situation is very different – the funder is procuring services from the charity under what is essentially a commercial agreement. If the services are not up to the agreed standard, the funder could potentially sue the charity for breach of contract. But if the charity completes the work in accordance with the agreement, it is entitled to retain any surplus made. See figure 11.1 for more on these differences.

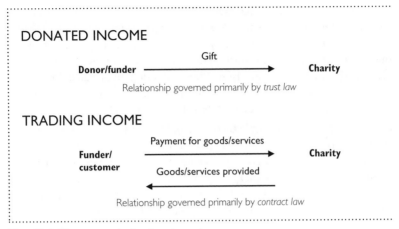

DONATED INCOME

Gift

Donor/funder ————————————————————▶ **Charity**

Relationship governed primarily by *trust law*

TRADING INCOME

Payment for goods/services

Funder/ ————————————————————▶ **Charity**
customer

Goods/services provided

◀————————————————————

Relationship governed primarily by *contract law*

Fig. 11.1 The two main funding channels

Sadly there is much confusion on this issue; in fact, as noted in chapter 4, some funders are unclear themselves. Some SLAs devote pages to the service provision, but when it comes to the section on money it may be so brief that it is not always clear whether a grant or a contract is intended.

This is very dangerous for both parties as it is not clear where the obligations lie and, moreover, there could be huge differences in the VAT position between a grant and a contract. Getting this wrong can seriously jeopardise the financial viability of a charity. Usually the grant/contract distinction will also affect whether the funds are restricted:

Accounting for grant and contract income

TREATMENT OF INCOME	UNRESTRICTED	RESTRICTED
DONATED INCOME	Only general donations can be unrestricted	**Grants for a specific purpose are always restricted**
TRADING INCOME	**Normally unrestricted:** the only obligation is to provide the required goods/services: any surplus/deficit is retained by the charity	Only restricted if customers were promised that any surplus would be used for a specific purpose (e.g. a fundraising event for a specific project)

Ambiguity on funding channels is also contrary to HM Treasury's guidance *Improving Financial Relationships with the Third Sector: Guidance to funders and purchasers* (see 'Further reading'), which states that public sector funders must be clear when working with third sector organisations whether they are seeking to develop an organisation's work (in which case a grant is normally best) or want to procure a service (in which case the funding should be based on a contract).

Part of the task of a charity treasurer should include advising the trustees on the impact of any new funding, and this will normally involve reviewing any funding agreement before the trustees sign it. Where the nature of a funding agreement is ambiguous (or if any other terms of the agreement present serious problems) it is worth insisting that it must be amended before agreeing to sign – even if this means delaying a new project.

Types of trading income

In chapter 4 we explained that trading income means any income to the charity from selling goods or services (as opposed to donated income and investment income). We also saw that there are two distinct types of trading income:

- primary purpose trading – where the goods or services provided are directly part of the charity's objects;
- trading for fundraising purposes – where the goods or services provided are sold simply as a means of raising funds.

See chapter 4 (page 46) for more on these terms and common examples. Most contract funding for the main work of a charity is likely to be primary purpose trading, but there are exceptions. For example, if a charity's objects are to provide relief for older people in a particular district, then a contract for an older persons' support project in that district would clearly be primary purpose trading. But if the charity then extended its services and accepted a contract to support older people from a *different* area, the second contract would be trading for fundraising purposes (even though it involved the same work) because the charity would be receiving fees for work outside its objects. (In such a case the charity might wish to seek approval for a change of objects to widen the area of benefit.)

However, primary purpose trading does not mean that the 'customer' has to be a public sector body. The purchasers may be the service users themselves: this is often the case with housing charities, charities providing fee-based training courses and welfare charities where clients may themselves pay for services under **direct payments** schemes.

Whenever trading income is involved, there are two tax questions to consider:
- Should the charity be charging VAT on what it is selling?
- Is the charity liable to corporation tax if the activity makes a profit?

Charities and VAT

Most businesses, other than the very smallest, are VAT-registered, which means that they have to charge VAT on what they sell, but they can reclaim the VAT on what they buy.

Purchases by the charity

Many people think that charities can also reclaim VAT but in most cases this is not possible because grants, donations and investment income do not count as trading income, and the ability to reclaim VAT only applies when an organisation is trading. So normally, whenever you buy anything, your charity will have to pay the supplier's price including VAT. In the books, few small charities therefore need to show VAT separately, and just enter all expenses at the total value including VAT.

Remember to bear VAT in mind when budgeting. (The examples in this chapter are based on VAT at 20% but always be sure to use the current figure). For example, if you are quoted a price of £1,200 excluding VAT for a new photocopier and you want to apply for a grant to cover the cost, you will need a grant of £1,440. The extra £240 is to cover the 20% VAT you pay to the supplier, but which the supplier passes on to the government. Across the sector, charities pay hundreds of millions of pounds of tax to the government in this way.

There are a few concessions for some items supplied to charities, but they only apply in certain fields such as press advertisements and new buildings. When someone places an advertisement in a newspaper it would normally be subject to 20% VAT, but if the advertisement is placed by a charity, the newspaper company should only charge 0% VAT.

With buildings the rules are complex and, if you are considering major building work, it is important to get professional advice on the VAT position at an early stage. The general principle is that a new charity building (though not an extension or alteration) will be zero-rated for VAT (i.e. VAT will be charged at 0%) if it is used exclusively for 'non-business charitable purposes' – in other words, if the charitable work which takes place in the building is funded entirely by grants, donations or investment income. Once the level of business use exceeds 5% – for example, if more than 5% of the charity's work is funded by fees or contracts – this concession is likely to be lost, and the full 20% VAT will be charged on the construction price. (However, there are various ways of calculating the 5%, such as income, staff count or floor area.)

For charities in a small number of specific fields there are special schemes enabling them to claim VAT refunds even when they would not normally apply. In these cases the charity pays VAT to the supplier but is then entitled to reclaim it, even if it relates to work funded by grants and donations. The largest scheme offers VAT refunds to hospices, air ambulance charities and search and rescue charities and is administered by HMRC themselves as part of normal VAT procedures (see HMRC VAT Notice 1001). There is also a long-standing government grant scheme to refund the VAT on building repairs in the specific case of listed buildings registered as places of worship (the Listed Places of Worship Grant Scheme – see www.lpwscheme.org.uk). Nevertheless, a range of conditions has to be met and it is important to note that this is a grant scheme: it does not affect the basic tax rules for VAT. But these schemes only help charities in the specific fields listed – other charities must pay VAT as normal.

Goods and services sold by the charity

If your charity has any trading income, it is classed as a business for VAT purposes. In certain cases the charity will need to register for VAT, and charge VAT on what it sells. If this applies, you will need to separate out the VAT amounts in your books. Your trustees *must* apply to register for VAT if your total trading income (across all funds and projects) exceeds the VAT-registration level (£83,000 in 2016/17, although the limit increases slightly each year). However, in calculating the total trading income, you can exclude sales which, if you were VAT-registered, would be VAT-exempt (see below).

VAT registration is normally nowadays done online – see www.gov.uk/vat-registration/overview – although as part of the process you must first create a Government Gateway account (unless the charity already has one).

Charities that do have to register for VAT are usually VAT-*partially exempt* (because the grants and donations side is *non-VATable*), which makes the VAT issues more complex than in a normal business. If this is the case, you will need further guidance – beyond the scope of this book – on VAT accounting.

The aim of this section is simply to help you work out if your charity is safely below the VAT threshold. If you conclude that you do not need to register, you can ignore VAT issues in relation to income – but in that case remember to allow for all expenditure at prices including VAT. (If a charity has some trading income, but below the threshold, it is possible to register for VAT voluntarily, but there are few cases where you would gain by doing so. The main examples where voluntary registration is worth considering are where most or all of the sales would be zero-rated, for example if the charity derives substantial income from charity shops selling donated goods, or from sales of books and publications.)

Where an organisation is VAT-registered, it must charge VAT at the appropriate rate on everything sold. In most cases this is bad news. For example, if you sell packs of Christmas cards at £4.00 each, and the charity becomes VAT-registered, you would have to charge your supporters £4.80 (including 20% VAT – 80p – which you would pass on to the government). Alternatively, you could keep the price at £4.00 and absorb the VAT, but selling packs at £4.00 including 20% VAT works out as £3.33 plus 67p VAT, so you would lose 67p on each pack sold. A charity raising thousands of pounds through Christmas cards would be much worse off. (To convert a VAT-inclusive price to the VAT-exclusive amount, divide by 1.20 if VAT is at 20%. In this example £4.00 ÷ 1.20 = £3.3333 = £3.33 to the nearest 1p.)

On the other hand, if you were providing a service to your local authority, or to a normal VAT-registered business, they would not mind if you had to add VAT, because they could reclaim it. So the implications of VAT depend enormously on your customer. Where a charity is doing work for a local authority it is often much better to do it under a contract where the work is subject to VAT, because then you can register for VAT and reclaim the VAT on the things you buy. If the work were grant funded, the charity would not be trading so you could not register for VAT and therefore the VAT you spent on purchases would be irrecoverable. In such a case, doing work under a VATable contract rather than a grant can make funding go further (provided that you feel confident about accounting for a VAT-registered charity).

Irrecoverable VAT – as illustrated in the previous paragraph – is a major problem for charities. On large projects it may be worth consulting a VAT specialist to see if there is any way round the issue – for example, by persuading a funder to convert a grant to a contract, or by altering the balance of the charity's work to affect the calculation of **non-business use** on a new building.

There are currently five categories of income for VAT purposes.

- Most goods and services are subject to standard rate VAT (20%) – this includes everything not in the categories below.
- A few items are subject to a lower VAT rate (5%), including home energy supplies, supplies of energy to charitable non-business premises, renovation of empty houses or flats, children's car seats and contraceptive products.
- Some items are zero-rated for VAT – VAT is charged as normal, but the rate is 0%. Products include books and other publications, children's clothing and cold food. VAT can still be reclaimed on purchases (for example, the paper to print the books, so charities selling publications can often benefit from this). The 0% rate also applies to sales of donated goods (for example, jumble sales and charity shops).
- Some sales are VAT-exempt, which means that you do not have to charge VAT on the sale but you cannot reclaim any corresponding VAT on purchases. VAT-exempt sales do not count towards the turnover in deciding whether you should be VAT-registered. A number of charity services fall into this category, including educational services and welfare services provided by a 'relevant' charity (for definitions, see the publications on VAT under Charities and tax issues in 'Further reading'). Fundraising events exempt from corporation tax are also classed as VAT-exempt (see 'Charities and corporation tax', page 166).
- Some income is classed as non-business income and is therefore outside the scope of VAT. This includes grants, donations and investment income.

The above list is only a very general summary – the full lists of zero-rated and VAT-exempt items take up many pages of legislation. Also, make sure you understand the crucial distinction between activities which are zero-rated and those which are VAT-exempt. Zero-rated sales are everyone's first choice in a charity: you do not have to add VAT to the sale price, but you can reclaim any VAT on related purchases. VAT-exempt sales are not so attractive – you do not have to add VAT to the sale price, but any VAT on the corresponding purchases will be irrecoverable.

Should our charity be VAT-registered?

If your charity's total income is more than £83,000 (2016/17 figure), work out how much of this is trading income. This means being very clear whether funding agreements are grants or contracts (see 'Understanding different funding channels', page 158). Then deduct items that would be

VAT-exempt (see above). If the total comes to more than about £70,000 you will need to watch the position carefully. If it goes over the threshold for any 12-month period (not necessarily your accounting year) you must register for VAT within a month.

Note that *all* trading income – both primary purpose trading and trading for fundraising – counts for the VAT threshold.

Here are four examples.

- *Charity A* has a total income of £72,000. This is below the VAT threshold so, however the income is made up, it does not have to register.
- *Charity B* has a total income of £120,000, but £55,000 of this is from grants and donations. The remaining £65,000 is below the VAT threshold, so even if all of this was potentially VATable it does not have to register.
- *Charity C* is an educational organisation. Its total income is £120,000, of which £92,000 comes from course fees. Although this is trading income above the VAT threshold, the course fees would be VAT-exempt, so it does not have to register.
- *Charity D* has a total income of £120,000, of which £25,000 is from grants, donations and investments. The other £95,000 is trading income – half from publications sales and half from contracts for advice and consultancy services. All of the trading income is VATable (either zero-rated or standard-rated VAT) and, as it totals more than £83,000, it must register immediately.

If you do this calculation and realise that your charity went over the VAT threshold some time ago, but you never registered, then a retrospective registration will be needed. In other words, on the form VAT1, where you give the date from which the charity needs to be registered, this may be several years in the past. This can give rise to complex issues such as the need to re-invoice past work or, if this is not possible, previous income may have to be treated as VAT inclusive – which is a very expensive mistake.

For example, if for the last three years the charity had £85,000 of income from a home repairs service but had not registered for VAT, this £255,000 would be treated as a VAT-inclusive amount and £42,500 would have to be paid over to HMRC (less any VAT reclaimed on purchases). You would also have to submit retrospective VAT returns and the charity would be liable for VAT penalties unless the trustees could persuade HMRC they had a *reasonable excuse* for not realising the position at the time. So you would almost certainly need specialist help.

However, in some cases, charities making a retrospective registration where they are able to re-invoice work (e.g. to a local authority) have found they are able to reclaim substantial VAT on past expenditure which more than covers the cost of the professional help. But a good charity treasurer should be monitoring the level of trading income and should never let his or her organisation get into this position.

Key terms

In any VAT publications you will find the following terms used.

- *Output VAT*: the VAT charged by the charity on goods or services you sell (if you are VAT-registered).
- *Input VAT*: the VAT on the purchases made by the charity (this will be reclaimable if the charity is VAT-registered but only when a purchase relates to an activity where VAT is charged on the income, so most charities end up with considerable amounts of irrecoverable input VAT).

For more detail on VAT issues for charities see *The Complete Charity VAT Handbook* also published by DSC.

VAT and EU law

Most of the framework of VAT is based on EU law, so, in principle, any of the VAT issues in this section could change when the UK finally withdraws from the EU. However, the Treasury will still need revenues from a sales tax such as VAT and it would clearly be much simpler to retain the VAT systems and rules than change to a new tax. Moreover, if the UK leaves the EU in 2019 but remains a member of the Single Market (as a member of the European Economic Area) many VAT principles will still apply. So, major changes are unlikely but changes to thresholds and specific rules are possible.

Charities and corporation tax

Corporation tax is a tax on the trading profits of companies and other business organisations (this includes charities). For any trading activity you have to work out the profit, using the rule:

Profit = Sales − Expenses

Even though the profit is only a surplus to be retained by the charity, in some cases it is subject to tax, otherwise charities would be able to run large commercial businesses on a tax-free basis, competing unfairly with other firms. From 2015, corporation tax is charged at 20% of the taxable profit (higher rates applied in earlier years), although the government has announced plans to reduce this gradually to 17% by 2020. In working out the profit you can only deduct the expenses of the activity concerned (not the expenses of the whole charity), although you can include an element for the cost of voluntary time.

So, for example, a charity that runs a large successful coffee shop with relatively modest expenses could find that, as well as having to charge VAT, a substantial slice of its income might have to be set aside for corporation tax. But there are ways round this, as described below.

Charity exemptions from corporation tax

The corporation tax rules contain a large number of charity exemptions, as follows. They are all subject to the condition that any profit is retained by the charity for the development of the service (but, in a charity, the trustees could not in any case benefit from a profit).

1   *Primary purpose trading.* Where the goods or services are provided directly as part of the charity's objects, there is no liability to corporation tax (though bear in mind that VAT could still apply). This is a very important rule. Some charities waste huge effort in setting up trading subsidiary companies when the activity they want to carry out is part of the charity's primary purpose.

    The liability to corporation tax only arises with trading for fundraising purposes. But even this has many exemptions, as summarised below.

2   *Where the trade is carried out mainly by the beneficiaries of the charity;* for example workshops run by blind people, coffee shops run mainly by people with learning disabilities or a car wash service run by young people. Although such income would be treated as a fundraising trade (rather than primary purpose trading), there is no corporation tax on any profit, provided that those doing the bulk of the work are the people whom the charity exists to support.

3   *Trades that are ancillary to the primary purpose;* for example, accommodation for students or refreshments in an art gallery. These are also exempt from corporation tax. (However, if an art gallery runs a café which is open to the general public – not just those visiting the gallery – it would no longer satisfy the 'ancillary' test, unless you could show that the sales to non-gallery visitors were less than 10% of the total.)

4   *Any small-scale trading and fundraising activities within set limits are also exempt.* This rule is very flexible as, within limits, it exempts any kind of trading for fundraising purposes from corporation tax. The vast majority of fundraising projects by small charities will fit this, even where the activity involves selling something. The condition is that the charity's total income (not the profit) from such activities is:
   • no more than £5,000 in total; or
   • no more than 25% of the charity's total income up to a maximum of £50,000 (for a charity with an income of more than £200,000 in total).

Table 11.1 gives examples. But even when the trade is beyond the limits shown in table 11.1 there are further exemptions for certain types of trading income.

Table 11.1   Examples of small-scale trading exemption

Charity's total income	Maximum trading income for fundraising that can escape corporation tax	
£3,000	£3,000	(Up to £5,000 allowed anyway)
£12,000	£5,000	(£5,000 allowed anyway)
£30,000	£7,500	(25% of income)
£160,000	£40,000	(25% of income)
£250,000	£50,000	(£50,000 upper limit)

5   *Sales of donated goods*; for example jumble sales, charity shops and auctions of donated gifts are exempt from corporation tax (and for VAT, the 0% rate applies).

6   *Fundraising events.* There are also exemptions from corporation tax for other specific fundraising events (provided that they are supported because people know the event is for charity) in the cases of:

   • small events of any kind, provided that the takings do not exceed £1,000 per week;
   • larger events, provided that the charity holds no more than 15 events per year of the same type in any one location.

As well as the profits being exempt from corporation tax, the income from such activities counts as VAT-exempt. This means that you do not have to charge VAT on ticket sales for a fundraising event (but as a VAT-exempt activity you cannot then reclaim VAT costs related to the event, such as catering costs or equipment hire).

Trading outside the concessions – trading subsidiary companies

For most smaller charities, one or more of the above concessions will almost certainly cover your fundraising activities and a liability to corporation tax is thus quite rare. But if you do go beyond these limits, it is up to the charity to make a corporation tax return to HMRC.

However, where a charity would end up paying a lot of corporation tax, a further solution is to set up a non-charitable **trading subsidiary** company (see figure 11.2). For example a charity that raised substantial funds through Christmas cards and catalogue sales could arrange for the scheme to be run by the subsidiary company rather than the charity itself. Although the company is liable to corporation tax on the profit, if it gives the whole of its profit back to the charity as a Gift Aid donation (see chapter 12), no corporation tax is paid.

The subsidiary is then a separate entity – many people would class this as a social enterprise in its own right. However, this means a lot of extra work; the trading subsidiary is a legally separate organisation: it is not itself a charity but a normal profit-making company. So it is usually established as a company limited by shares, with all the shares held by the charity (rather than as a company limited by guarantee as used for non-profit organisations). Some charities like to use the legal form of a CIC for a trading subsidiary to demonstrate that, although it is trading commercially, the trade is for a community purpose: to generate funds for the charity.

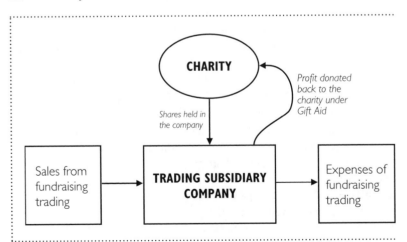

Fig. 11.2 A charity with a trading subsidiary

Because it is a legally separate body, the trading company needs completely separate accounts (both on a day-to-day basis, and separate year end accounts submitted to Companies House). It will need its own directors so that the charity and the subsidiary can enter into meaningful discussions and, of course, separate minutes must be kept for board meetings. (There may be some overlap with the charity trustees, but the Charity Commission recommends that there should always be at least one charity trustee who is not a director of the subsidiary, and at least one director of the subsidiary who is not a trustee of the charity. This is so that proper arm's-length negotiations can take place between the charity trustees and the directors of the subsidiary when needed.)

Because it is not a charity, the subsidiary will typically have to pay normal business rates if it occupies its own premises. Great care is also needed with regard to any expenses met by the charity that relate to the subsidiary. For example, if staff of the charity do work for the subsidiary, or if the charity lets the subsidiary occupy part of its premises, a written service agreement is needed with appropriate charges, otherwise the charity would be subsidising a commercial business. Moreover, it can be very difficult to deal with start-up costs for the company; the charity cannot give charitable funds to the subsidiary, so a commercial bank loan may be needed. Also, at year end, the charity may have to prepare group accounts, consolidating figures for the charity and the subsidiary – see 'Charities with subsidiaries – group accounts', page 118.

However, any type of charity can, if necessary, have a trading subsidiary company. The subsidiary will almost always use the legal form of a company or CIC limited by shares, but the parent charity could be structured as a charitable trust, association, CIO or a charitable company. In such cases people often get confused about the legal structures; part of the task of the treasurer is to make absolutely sure that all decisions, especially financial decisions, are clearly made in relation to the charity *or* the subsidiary – not fudged between the two.

Most large charities have a trading subsidiary – sometimes more than one – but with current concessions (especially the general exemptions in table 11.1), there are very few cases where they are needed by smaller charities. There are one or two situations where a charity is undertaking a venture which is so risky that a separate company is felt to be needed purely to protect the charity, even though there is no saving of corporation tax (the benefit being that the trading subsidiary would have limited liability in its own right). But even so, if a charity's trading company failed leaving bills unpaid, it is likely to cause serious damage to the charity's reputation. Running a separate subsidiary company means a major increase in the workload for the treasurer and finance staff, and only in the most exceptional cases is this justified for smaller charities.

Accounting for partnership arrangements

In recent years the government has placed huge emphasis on partnership working between the statutory and voluntary sectors, and has encouraged voluntary organisations themselves to work in partnership.

There are many arguments for and against partnerships, but it is vital that treasurers and finance officers are fully clear on the financial arrangements between partners, which can sometimes create major VAT liabilities (as well as other complications) if not handled correctly.

The main complications arise when two or more charities make a bid to undertake work on a joint basis. In most cases the funder will require one of the charities to act as the lead agency or **accountable body** – taking overall responsibility for the work, and bringing in the other charity (or charities) as needed. Often the lead organisation will talk about 'sub-contracting' part of a project to a second charity – but this can be dangerous.

Suppose charity A in figure 11.3 is awarded £100,000 funding by its local authority to provide a specific project, but charity B will handle part of the delivery (amounting to £40,000). There are several cases to consider.

- If the work is contract funded, and if A and B are both VAT-registered charities, it is quite straightforward. B will invoice A for £40,000 + VAT and A will invoice the original funder for £100,000 + VAT, reclaiming the VAT charged by B as part of its normal VAT return.

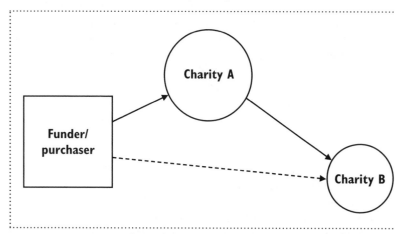

Fig. 11.3 Example of a partnership arrangement

- If, however, the work is grant funded, problems can arise. If B is doing work for A under a sub-contract, then if B is VAT-registered it has to charge VAT to A on the sub-contract work if B's work is for services which are standard rated and B is VAT-registered. So B invoices A for £40,000 + 20% VAT = £48,000. Because the main work is grant funded, A cannot reclaim the VAT it has paid to B, and the grant is likely to be fixed at £100,000 in total. The net effect is that A is left with only £52,000 of the funding to carry out its own share of the work, rather than £60,000 as expected. (This scenario has created £8,000 of irrecoverable VAT, which is lost from charitable funding and transferred to the Exchequer.)

- It follows that if the main work is grant funded, then whether or not A and B are VAT-registered, it would be better for A to offer grant funding to B of £40,000 to carry out its share of the work. However, if this approach is to be used, it must be clear in all the paperwork from the outset – language such as 'sub-contracting' should be avoided. But, a grant agreement from A to B gives the trustees of A much less leverage over B if anything goes wrong, and the trustees of A must be confident that they can trust B to use the grant funding appropriately (they can, of course, require B to treat the grant as a restricted fund, but if the grant had conditions on services which B must supply to A this could be challenged by HMRC that it was, in reality, a contract rather than a grant.)

- Another case – which can often be damaging for smaller charities seeking to work in partnerships – is if the work is contract funded and A is a large VAT-registered charity but B is a small organisation that is not VAT-registered. B will thus invoice A for £40,000 (no VAT) and A will invoice the funder for £100,000 + VAT. However, because B is not VAT-registered, it will have to bear the VAT cost on any purchases it makes – for example, if £12,000 of the £40,000 paid to B is for materials, this will incur £2,400 of VAT at 20%. If A prepared the initial funding bid, knowing the project would be carried out under a VATable contract but without knowing sub-contract arrangements at the time, A will probably have assumed that all VAT on purchases would be reclaimable. So A will typically insist that B has to do its share for £40,000. B will therefore, in effect, only have £37,600 to spend on what was budgeted as £40,000 of work (because £2,400 has gone on irrecoverable VAT). On the other hand, if A agreed to increase the payments to B, it could not then reclaim this extra cost as input VAT – because it is a charge from a non-VAT registered organisation – so A would then be left with only £57,600 (rather than £60,000) for its share So, either way, £2,400 of the funding is lost as irrecoverable VAT. (The problem could be solved if B was willing to register for VAT voluntarily, but that may not be sensible if this is just a one-off short-term project. Alternatively, A and B could perhaps redraft the sub-contract arrangements so that all project materials were bought by A.)

- So if there would be VAT problems and if the funder will agree, it can be more attractive if A and B bid for the work as equal partners in terms of status, rather than one acting as a sub-contractor to the other. But unless there are two separate contracts (between the funder and A, and the funder and B), the two charities would be acting in partnership in the full legal sense and would then be considered 'jointly and severally liable' – that is, A could be sued if B failed to deliver (or vice versa). Often trustees are unwilling to risk this.

So, apart from the first option where the work is funded by VATable contracts at all stages in the chain, irrecoverable VAT is likely to arise at some point and it is important that whoever is preparing the initial bid allows for this in setting the project budgets. Alternatively, if A and B anticipate much partnership working on these lines, it may be worth considering a merger to form a single charity.

Shared services

Sometimes, rather than establishing a partnership arrangement for a particular project, two or more charities agree to set up a separate organisation to provide services on a long-term basis to both organisations. For example, several charities may wish to come together and have a common IT support service, or human resources department, or a common fundraising team.

If they are well designed such arrangements can lead to economies of scale, saving overall costs. The organisation supplying the common service is called a 'cost sharing group' (CSG) whose members are the charities using its services. It could be a charity in its own right, or a normal company or CIC jointly owned by the charities concerned.

However, until recently there was a major problem: unless the CSG was small enough to come below the VAT threshold, it had to charge 20% VAT on the services it provided to the charities concerned. If these charities were funded mainly by grants, donations or VAT-exempt contracts, this left them with a big irrecoverable VAT bill which wiped out any savings the CSG might offer.

But fortunately, under European law (which continues to apply until such time as the UK withdraws fully from the EU – see page 166), VAT is not chargeable on services of this kind, so long as the CSG exists for the purpose of providing necessary services directly for member organisations (such as charities) which are funded mainly by non-business or VAT-exempt income and provided the CSG merely claims from its members the exact reimbursement of their share of the joint expenses. These provisions were implemented in the UK from 2012, so a CSG which meets the criteria can work as a VAT-exempt organisation. The CSG cannot make a long-term profit, but the 'exact reimbursement' rule can be averaged over a number of years (to allow the CSG to buy equipment, for example). However, the CSG must be an independent organisation (the VAT concession does not apply if a charity has spare capacity and sells its own services to other charities).

It follows that charities can now work together to establish CSGs on these lines, without incurring additional VAT. Therefore, provided the activity is substantial enough to justify a new organisation, a CSG is well worth considering when several charities need a similar service. However, the conditions must be followed strictly and professional advice from a specialist in this area will usually be needed.

12 Linking fundraising and accounting

As this book has stressed throughout, the overall management of a charity's finances is a matter for the trustees as a whole. But implementation of the trustees' financial decisions normally falls to two key people or teams:
- the treasurer, together with the bookkeeper or finance officer; and
- the charity's main fundraiser (a trustee or a member of staff).

You may not use the term 'fundraiser', but there must always be someone who takes the lead on submitting grant applications, asking for donations, bidding for contracts or marketing the charity's services. Even if your charity is fortunate enough to have a regular stream of income from investments, those investments must be managed.

An accounting/fundraising team

Some charities also expect the treasurer to handle everything to do with fundraising – just because it relates to money. But this is normally too much for one person, and it is better to find ways of sharing responsibility.

Yet, sadly, in many charities (even in very small groups) there is often too little communication between the fundraiser and the person who handles the accounts – sometimes with disastrous results. This can be partly a matter of personality: fundraisers are often exuberant people who like to grasp opportunities and are frequently networking outside the confines of the charity, but they tend to find accounts rather boring. Treasurers and bookkeepers often have a quieter approach, with an emphasis on detail, and despair of getting others to follow clear procedures.

But unless a charity is successful in generating income, there will be no funds for which the treasurer has to account. On the other hand, fundraisers desperately need the charity to have good accounting procedures, so that once funds are received they are properly managed and used. There is nothing worse for a fundraiser than finding a donor or funder who makes a gift or a grant but who, when approached again, is reluctant to help because they were unhappy at how the first gift was accounted for or were not satisfied with the charity's published accounts.

Here is a checklist of possible areas where you need to work out effective communication and division of responsibilities.

- *Issuing receipts for gifts*: who is responsible? Who writes the acknowledgement letter? With a large-scale appeal, the response handling and accounting for gifts may be the biggest task.
- *Purpose of gifts*: is there a simple mechanism to ensure the treasurer or bookkeeper knows to which fund every grant or donation relates?
- *New restricted funds*: is the fundraiser authorised to invent new projects (which would mean new restricted funds) or must this be approved by others? How does the treasurer or bookkeeper know when to create a new fund in the books?
- *Costing of new projects*: when bidding for funds, who works out what to ask for? What overheads are to be included? And if you do not get all you ask for, who decides whether to continue or whether to drop the project? (See also page 190.)
- *Deciding when to refuse a gift*: every charity needs an ethical policy to clarify when it is right to refuse a gift – who deals with the decisions?
- *Pledges versus actual gifts*: once you have a promise of support, who is responsible for contacting the donor or funder to ensure that the gifts are received? Sometimes a fundraiser feels that an appeal is complete when the target is reached. But it may need four or five years of accounting for regular donations (and issuing reminders where needed) before all the funds are in the bank.
- *Banking of income*: who does what, especially with fundraising events? Is the treasurer expected to have people calling unexpectedly with bags of cash? Or are those who organise cash collections responsible for counting and banking the proceeds? (Remember the need for controls – see chapter 6.)
- *Cash floats*: if you are running stalls and events or need petty cash for the office, what is the procedure for drawing and accounting for cash floats?
- *Showing income on the SOFA (see chapter 7)*: when money comes in from fundraising events, are the trading and donated income distinguished (see chapter 4 for the principles)? If not, how can you get a sensible estimate of the split?
- *Fundraising expenses*: fundraisers need to keep a note of the costs of fundraising activities run by the charity so they can be included correctly in the accounts. Under the SORP, you cannot just show the net income.

- *Paying advance fundraising costs*: if a fundraising activity needs payment up front, for example to hire a venue or print brochures, who approves this? What about cash flow (see chapter 9)?
- *Gift Aid tax claims*: if you have donations from individuals, it will usually be possible to reclaim tax under Gift Aid (see 'Gift aid', overleaf). Who will manage this? Who is responsible for getting Gift Aid declarations completed? Whose task is it to submit the tax claim to HMRC? And if the claim covers gifts for different funds, do you know how to split the tax recovered?
- *Fundraising database*: if you have more than about 20 donors you will probably need a donor database of some kind, to keep track of who has given what, and this will probably link to the Gift Aid procedures. Who is responsible for this? If the fundraiser, is he or she aware of the need for auditability of the information (by both the charity's auditor/ independent examiner and by HMRC)? Who is responsible for the security of the personal data in such records and ensuring they are only used as permitted under the Data Protection Act?
- *Incoming standing orders*: if you have donors making regular gifts by bankers order, who checks the bank statement against the donors' pledges? (It is generally best if the statement first goes to the person who records gifts into the fundraising database, and then to the treasurer with a total for the main books. If this is cumbersome, consider having a separate bank account for incoming standing orders.)
- *Direct debits* are still rare on the income side in smaller charities due to the processes and bank assurances required, but the big difference from standing orders is that direct debits must be requested each month (or as agreed) by the charity. You will almost certainly have an automated system agreed with your bank or an agency – but who is responsible for this system at the charity's end? In particular, what is the procedure for refunds in the event of errors or donor complaints?
- *Online giving*: is your charity happy to use external websites to handle online giving? If so, which provider is to be used and who agrees the charges made? Who is responsible for administering the site on the charity's side?
- *Credit/debit card gifts*: more local charities are starting to accept these in person (not just online). Who is responsible for the procedures?
- *Charities Aid Foundation (CAF) and similar cheques*: CAF has schemes where donors pay into a CAF account on which tax is reclaimed, and the donors can direct funds to any charity of their choice by writing a CAF cheque (or quoting their card number). Who handles this? Do you have a means to ensure such gifts are not erroneously treated as Gift Aid? (Some other agency charities have similar schemes.)

- *VAT*: where goods are sold for fundraising purposes, VAT may be applicable (see chapter 11). Who is responsible for establishing the VAT position and setting prices to allow for this?

- *Funders requiring invoices*: for work done under contracts, the charity will have to invoice the funder – who is responsible? If the amount varies, who is responsible for the invoice figure? Are you clear on the VAT issues (see chapter 11)? If someone other than the treasurer raises invoices, does the treasurer know about unpaid invoices in order to include them as debtors at year end?

- *Loan finance*: sometimes a major project will require the charity to take on a loan to cover initial costs for a new service or a major fixed asset such as a new building. Naturally this will need detailed discussion by trustees, but even if agreed in principle there is much work in applying for a loan – is raising loan finance the responsibility of the fundraiser or the treasurer? Moreover, loans are usually subject to interest – remember to allow for the interest payments (not just the capital repayments) in fundraising plans and project budgets.

- *Subsidiary groups*: how do all these procedures work if the charity has subsidiary groups managing their own books (see chapter 6)? This is especially important with semi-independent fundraising teams – if their events are run on behalf of the charity, both their income and their expenses must appear in the charity's accounts. Or are they independent groups that raise funds and simply pass them on to you as donations?

- *The annual report and accounts*: are the needs of funders and supporters considered when they are being prepared (see chapter 7) or are the accounts seen purely as something required by law? Bids which initially look good to funders can easily fail if the charity's accounts are inconsistent with what is said in the bid.

There are not many charities where fewer than four or five of these issues apply. If you have established a good relationship, with plenty of communication, between yourself and those who bring in the funds, it will make your job much easier and will greatly improve the overall financial management of the charity.

The rest of this chapter addresses some of the above areas.

Gift aid

Gift aid is the government scheme whereby a UK taxpayer gives to charity, and the charity can reclaim the income tax paid by the donor on his or her gift.

Some charities get much of their income through Gift Aid donations, and thus receive a great deal of government support for their work. The big attraction is that Gift Aid applies to *any* organisation with charitable status. (There is also a separate scheme for anonymous cash gifts – the so-called 'Gift Aid Small Donations Scheme' (GASDS) – see page 185. However, this section is about normal Gift Aid by identified donors.)

Regardless of the donor's personal tax rate, the gift is treated as being made net of basic-rate income tax. So to work out how much tax you can reclaim, you have to **gross-up** the gift. With basic-rate income tax at 20% this means you get an extra 25% on all donations made under Gift Aid. For example:

- Sue Brown earns £100. Assuming she pays tax at 20% basic rate, £20 tax is deducted and she will receive £80 after tax.
- If she gives the £80 to charity, and completes a Gift Aid declaration, the charity can reclaim the £20 tax she has paid. So in total, the charity gets £100.
- By completing a Gift Aid declaration, Sue has enabled the charity to gain £20 tax on top of her £80 gift. As £20 represents 25% of £80, the value of her gift to the charity is increased by 25%.

A summary of the conditions to reclaim tax are shown in the box overleaf, but for detailed guidance on Gift Aid rules see www.gov.uk/claim-gift-aid. Also, it is possible that the rules set out here could change in future, as the government has an ongoing review of Gift Aid and charitable giving, especially the rules on donor benefits.

Once you have set up a Gift Aid scheme, it is worth including even quite small donations because it adds very little extra work and with regular gifts the amounts build up. If someone gives £5 a month this is £60 a year, and you will reclaim £15 in tax. With 70 supporters giving at this level, you will add more than £1,000 a year in tax reclaims. You can apply Gift Aid to membership subscriptions, provided that the subscription is largely a donation, where any benefits to the member have little financial value – see rule 6 in the box overleaf (and where different members receive different benefits, special rules apply).

In the case of charities which charge for admission to a property, museum, gallery, nature reserve or similar, Gift Aid is permitted on the amount paid (even though the donor gets the benefit of admission), provided that they *either* pay at least 10% more than the normal price, *or* they are buying an annual season ticket. (There are detailed HMRC rules governing how these issues are measured.) Bear in mind that even though Gift Aid is allowed, a payment for admission will count as trading income and may be subject to VAT (see chapter 11).

Conditions for reclaiming tax on a donation under the Gift Aid scheme

1   It must be a genuine donation from an identifiable individual donor made out of their post-tax income:
    • not a payment for goods or services;
    • not a donation from a business.

2   The recipient must be a charity in UK tax law (this includes exempt or excepted charities). Since 2010, this includes organisations in other EU/EEA countries if they meet the UK tax definition of a charity.

3   Payment must actually be made and evidence of this must be available (i.e. an audit trail of money received).

4   The donor must be a UK taxpayer (paying income tax or capital gains tax – other taxes do not count). The donor must pay enough tax in total to cover the tax being reclaimed by the charity (but the donor's tax rate does not matter).

5   The donor must make a *declaration* that he or she wishes the gift to be treated as Gift Aid. The Gift Aid declaration must cover all issues required by the Regulations, but it can be open-ended to cover all future gifts. You do not have to use specific forms and, provided you follow the required procedures, you can also accept declarations by telephone or Internet.

6   The donor must not get any but the most trivial benefit from the gift – i.e. it must be a genuine donation. If you are considering giving the donor anything in return (e.g. free tickets for an event, or some item of value) make sure you understand the rules, and be sure to keep records. Since 2011, the limit on any benefits to the donor are as follows (although the government has raised the possibility of some further changes from 2017/18):
    • for small gifts up to £100 the maximum benefit is 25% of the net gift;
    • from £100 to £1,000 the maximum benefit is £25;
    • from £1,000 to £50,000 the maximum benefit is 5% of the net gift;
    • for gifts over £50,000, the maximum benefit is £2,500.

7   The charity must publish annual accounts and make them available to HMRC (and anyone else) on request.

8   The charity must be willing to have its books and records for Gift Aid donations subject to HMRC audit (this includes bank statements, Gift Aid declarations and fundraising literature, as well as Gift Aid records and systems).

Gift aid declarations

To operate Gift Aid you need to take care that Gift Aid declarations are properly worded to reflect the rules, as set out in the Regulations and HMRC guidance (see figure 12.1 for an example based on the HMRC model) and completed by all eligible donors. Many charities have launched appeals with literature where the Gift Aid declaration is invalid. Also you must have sufficient information to identify the donor – the absolute minimum is a surname, initial, postcode and house number, and the address must be the *home* address.

Charity Gift Aid Declaration

Boost your donation by 25p of Gift Aid for every £1 you donate
Gift Aid is reclaimed by the charity from the tax you pay for the current tax year. Your address is needed to identify you as a current UK taxpayer.

giftaid it

In order to Gift Aid your donation you must tick the box below:

❑   I want to Gift Aid my donation of £ . . . . and any donations I make in the future or have made in the past four years to:

Name of charity . . . .

I am a UK taxpayer and understand that if I pay less Income Tax and/or Capital Gains Tax than the amount of Gift Aid claimed on all my donations in that tax year it is my responsibility to pay any difference.

My Details

Title. . . . . . . First name or initial(s) . . . . . . Surname . . . .

Full Home address . . . .

. . . .

Postcode . . . . .Date. . . . .

Please notify the charity if you:
* want to cancel this declaration;
* change your name or home address;
* no longer pay sufficient tax on your income and/or capital gains.

If you pay Income Tax at the higher or additional rate and want to receive the additional tax relief due to you, you must include all your Gift Aid donations on your Self-Assessment tax return or ask HM Revenue and Customs to adjust your tax code.

Source: www.gov.uk/claim-gift-aid/gift-aid-declarations (with Gift Aid logo added). This version allows for multiple gifts over a period of time.

Fig. 12.1 Sample Gift Aid declaration

You do not need to use the exact form of words shown in the figure and the declaration does not have to have a signature. But the donor must confirm that they wish their gift to be treated as Gift Aid and they have paid or will pay sufficient income tax (or capital gains tax). For new declarations from 2016 onwards, HMRC requires the wording to make clear that if the donor has not paid enough tax they are responsible. The precise legal requirements are contained in The Donations to Charity (Gift Aid Declarations) Regulations 2016.

The requirement that the donor must pay enough tax to cover the tax reclaimed by the charity is increasingly important with the recent rises in the personal allowance (to £11,500 from 2017/18 and due to rise to £12,500 by 2020). Anyone whose taxable income is less than this cannot give under Gift Aid. Many people who only work part-time have incomes below this. Moreover, in 2017/18 a pensioner would need to receive at least £5,297/year (£442/month) *in addition* to the basic single person's state pension in order to be paying income tax. Many charities have donors who made Gift Aid declarations in the past who are no longer eligible, and if this is uncovered during an HMRC audit the charity could be asked to repay a substantial percentage of their tax reclaims over several years (or donors could be requested to reimburse HMRC for taxes they never paid).

From 2017, Gift Aid declarations can also be given to donor intermediaries such as online giving websites, and the rules allow one declaration to cover gifts to a number of different charities. If so, the intermediary must send the donor an annual statement of his/her gifts unless the total is less than £20. Most intermediaries will also handle the tax claims and pass the tax refunds directly to the charity, less a small charge to cover their costs, although the level of charges varies substantially between different online giving sites.

Reclaiming tax

Claims for repayment of tax under Gift Aid are made to HMRC Charities at Bootle. For charities receiving donations directly (as opposed to via an online giving site), efficient systems and procedures are vital. There is no point in having a Gift Aid scheme unless tax claims are made properly and regularly (at least once a year, though charities receiving extensive Gift Aid donations may claim more frequently). You need someone methodical in charge of the scheme (and with a good respect for donor confidentiality). Moreover, HMRC now requires that claims must be made by a trustee or member of staff who is 'fit and proper' – this is because some people have tried to establish bogus charities in order to reclaim Gift Aid, or have abused legitimate charities for the same purpose.

In the case of a new charity, it is first necessary to apply for recognition of the organisation as a charity for tax purposes, using HMRC's form ChA1. Once recognised, the organisation is given a charity tax reference (this is quite separate from the registered charity number). You cannot claim Gift Aid without this. You must identify one or more 'fit and proper persons' (trustees or members of staff) who are authorised to make claims on behalf of the charity (if you need to nominate a new person, use form ChV1).

The actual process of reclaiming tax has changed significantly since 2013 – former claim forms can no longer be used. HMRC introduced in recent years Charities Online in the hope of streamlining the process for charities to reclaim tax – though the requirements can be challenging. There are three possible approaches:

- For a charity with a very small number of donors, claims can be made using a paper-based form ChR1. This must be filled in methodically by hand with one character in each box so it can be scanned by HMRC. Every time you need a ChR1 you have to contact HMRC to request one (they are personalised to the charity concerned). With a continuation form ChR1CS up to 90 Gift Aid donations can be submitted in one claim. However, it is *not* possible to make claims under GASDS (see 'The Gift Aid Small Donations Scheme (GASDS)' on page 185) if you use this approach.

- For charities claiming up to 1,000 donations at a time, an online form can be used. The charity needs to register for Charities Online (see www.gov.uk/claim-gift-aid-online) which means first applying for a Government Gateway account (you have to wait for an activation code by post) then registering for HMRC Online, and then specifically for Charities Online. You can then log on to make a repayment claim which involves uploading a spreadsheet created by the charity showing details of each donor and the amounts given. The spreadsheet must be in '.ODS' format which means you will need Microsoft Excel 2010 or later or the free software Libre Office 3.5 or later. However, the rules on the formatting of the spreadsheet are very strict: HMRC provides blank spreadsheets which you can download and enter the necessary information. A claim under GASDS can also be submitted using the same system.

- The third possibility is to use giving database software which communicates directly over the Internet to Charities Online in order to make the claim. You still have to register for Charities Online (as just outlined) but claims are then made using your own software. The HMRC website lists more than 20 software providers producing systems which meet their requirements. In practice, most charities with more than (say) 100 donors will want to use a database of some kind to keep track of giving so it makes sense to choose software which is compatible with Charities Online. As the charity is registered with Charities Online, GASDS claims can also be made. As well as making the claims, a key role of such systems is to assist with the long-term records needed for HMRC audits (particularly important if you have donors giving regularly, where several weekly or monthly gifts may be combined for a claim).

Your trustees need to be aware that HMRC normally pays tax claims as submitted but retains the right to inspect your books and, if problems are found on a Gift Aid audit, the charity could have to repay large amounts of tax reclaimed. On average, a charity claiming Gift Aid will have an HMRC audit roughly every three years, but the frequency can vary enormously – charities perceived as low risk may go for a very long time without an audit. So it is crucial to ensure that Gift Aid declarations are well stored. If you have an audit, HMRC will typically choose a small sample of gifts to review in detail, where in each case you will need to produce the Gift Aid declaration and records such as bank statements, credit card receipts or numbered envelopes to show the money was actually received from the donor concerned.

However, if you can only produce full records for (say) 92% of the gifts in the sample, HMRC may assume that only 92% of tax was validly reclaimed, and hence the charity could be required to repay 8% of all the tax reclaimed for the last four years (though you should be given a chance to remedy the situation before any penalty is imposed). People often remain loyal to charities for decades, and a Gift Aid declaration completed in 2001 could in theory still be needed for a Gift Aid audit in 2050!

Other issues for maximising Gift Aid donations

Gift aid means that any charity that is able to generate gifts from individuals can get further help from the government. But to operate it effectively needs careful coordination between fundraisers and treasurers.

In addition to the tax reclaimed by the charity, donors who pay higher rates of tax (40% or 45%) can get further tax relief, so if you are seeking substantial donations it is worth bearing in mind these rules. However, the higher rate relief goes to the donor, not the charity, so if you want the charity to benefit you have to persuade the donor to give more in the first place, as shown in the following example.

Jane Smith is willing to give £100 to charity – she is a higher rate (40%) taxpayer and wants her gift to be as tax effective as possible.

She should actually make a Gift Aid donation of £133. The charity will reclaim £33 tax from HMRC making the gift worth £166. But Jane will also get higher rate relief of £33 (20% of £166), so the gift only costs her £100 as intended.

The Gift Aid Small Donations Scheme (GASDS)

Many charities have long complained that it is difficult or impossible to get all donors to complete Gift Aid declarations, particularly in situations where gifts are normally collected in cash. Moreover, as we noted above, many donors may be non-taxpayers and hence ineligible for Gift Aid.

To address this, the government introduced GASDS from 2013, with further changes from 2016 and 2017, allowing charities to reclaim an amount similar to Gift Aid on cash donations, though it has significant limitations. The main features are as follows:

- GASDS allows a charity to make a claim on cash gifts up to £8,000 (previously £5,000) each tax year. The amount repaid is 25% of the cash received up to this limit – so if you collect £400 in cash you can reclaim a further £100. A charity which has £8,000 (or more) of cash donations in a year can reclaim 25% of £8,000 – i.e. £2,000.
- It only applies to gifts in cash or, from April 2017, contactless payments by card or mobile phones (but not cheques or other methods) and no more than £20 per donation (so if someone puts a £50 note in your collecting box it is ineligible). However, no donor information is needed and the donors do not have to be taxpayers.

- Gifts can be in any currency, but they must be deposited in full in an account held by the charity at a UK bank or building society (don't use them as a float to make cash payments).
- The charity must have made normal Gift Aid claims in the same tax year on gifts totalling at least 10% of the amount being claimed under GASDS. So, to claim GASDS on the maximum £8,000 of cash gifts, at least £800 of normal Gift Aid donations must have been received and claimed for that tax year. This means charities which do not have any taxpaying donors cannot operate GASDS even if they get plenty of cash gifts.
- Until recently, charities had to have made normal Gift Aid claims for at least two prior years, but that rule is removed from the 2017/18 tax year.
- The donor must not get any benefits at all, other than a lapel badge or sticker (if used). So GASDS cannot be used on subscriptions, admission charges and so on – it must be a genuine donation. A suggested donation is fine (e.g., 'We ask each visitor to give £5') so long as it is genuinely optional.

There are complex rules for connected charities (to stop a charity splitting up in order to make more claims). However, a charity with multiple community buildings can claim separately for up to £8,000 of cash given in each building, subject to strict criteria.

Claims under GASDS must be made using Charities Online (see page 183) – so the scheme cannot be used by a charity which only makes Gift Aid claims using the paper form.

To maximise GASDS you may want to consider a sign on the lines of that shown in fig 12.2 on your collecting box. (However, this shows the difficulties of the scheme.)

So the scheme has significant limitations and many charities have concluded it is not worth the effort. Under the current rules it will never generate more than £2,000/year of additional income to any charity (or possibly £2,000 in each building). For most charities, getting taxpaying donors signed up to normal Gift Aid will generate much more income. But to a small charity which can meet all the rules, GASDS can be a useful boost.

Fig. 12.2 Maximising GASDS

Fundraising regulation and ethics

A charity's reputation can easily be ruined by inappropriate forms of fundraising and, unless there is a specific trustee with oversight of fundraising, the treasurer will often have a key role in this. For example, the treasurer or finance officer should certainly be involved in approval of literature where donors are promised that their gifts will be used in a specific way, to ensure that systems are in place to track such gifts and allocate them to the correct restricted funds.

The Charities Act 2006 included provisions allowing the government to regulate fundraising of any kind in England and Wales. These powers were extended by the Charities (Protection and Social Investment) Act 2016 in response to some fundraising scandals which came to light in 2015 (mainly linked to large charities using commercial fundraising agencies that were acting improperly).

The government remains keen to avoid using these powers and instead to encourage a self-regulatory approach. But the former Fundraising Standards Board (FRSB) was felt to have insufficient powers, and in 2016 it was replaced by the Fundraising Regulator (FR) (see 'Useful addresses'). For larger charities in England and Wales with over £100,000 of annual fundraising costs on generating voluntary income, registration with the FR, and payment of a levy towards its costs, is effectively compulsory. Smaller charities are also strongly encouraged to register with the FR under a voluntary scheme which started from 2017 costing just £50/year.

Registration with the FR means that the charity commits to abide by the *Code of Fundraising Practice* which is the key ethical and professional code.[10] It has detailed sections covering many different types of fundraising. The Code also provides guidance on issues such as the acceptance and refusal of donations and payment of fundraisers on a commission basis, as well as matters such as safety and respect for the environment in fundraising events. Originally developed by the Institute of Fundraising, the Code is now controlled by the FR. Charities who register agree to accept the decisions of the FR in the event of fundraising complaints (but the FR can also investigate complaints regarding other charities).

The FR will also operate a Fundraising Preference Service (FPS) from 2017 enabling people to contact the FR and ask to be removed from the contact lists of a range of specified charities (rather than having to contact each charity individually). Most FPS requests are likely to come from those receiving excessive communications from larger charities, but even a smaller charity may receive a request from the FR to stop sending materials to particular named persons.

While the FR remains a non-statutory body it has an agreement with the Charity Commission to refer the most serious cases for possible action by the Commission within its powers under the Charities Act 2011 (which were considerably extended by the 2016 Act). This includes powers to disqualify trustees who are acting inappropriately, or in extreme cases, to wind up a charity. Likewise, complaints which amount to breaches of data protection laws can be referred by the FR to the Information Commissioner.

A slightly different arrangement applies to charities registered solely in Scotland where a Scottish Charity Fundraising Complaints Hub has been set up (see 'Useful addresses') – this is administered by the Scottish Council for Voluntary Organisations working closely with OSCR. However, the *Code of Fundraising Practice* remains the key basis for considering complaints. At the time of writing, arrangements for Northern Ireland remain under discussion.

While a treasurer will rarely be a fundraising expert, the crucial links between fundraising and accounting mean that treasurers need to be aware of this Code and treasurers will often be more aware than other trustees of the impact of regulation such as this.

Investments

For charities which have significant **investments**, the arrangements for investment management are crucial if the charity is to have the income needed and is to be able to sustain its work for future years. Although investment management is not usually seen as part of fundraising, costs of investment management are classified by the SORPs as part of the 'Expenditure on raising funds' line on the SOFA.

Investment management for charities is a major issue beyond the scope of this book. However, there are various firms of investment managers with special experience of work with charities who are able to provide expert help. (In fact, this is an area where trustees *must* take professional advice if they do not have the relevant expertise themselves.)

The involvement of the treasurer and/or finance officer in investment decisions will vary considerably between charities, but if the trustees have an investments sub-committee the treasurer will usually be a member and will often play a leading role when decisions are taken from time to time on the appointment of investment managers.

The treasurer and finance officer also need to be active in helping the trustees to agree an **investment policy** – for example, in clarifying timescales for holding investments in relation to the various funds of the charity, the levels of income needed and the relative importance of income and capital growth. Also, many charities now have an ethical investment policy, to ensure that the charity only invests in companies whose work does not conflict with the charity's objects. Such policies must be stated in the trustees' annual report (see 'Presentation of the report and accounts' on page 95).

Some charities also make use of **social investments** as a means of undertaking their work; for example, making loans to beneficiaries on subsidised terms, or supporting other charities with investments that only have to be repaid if a project succeeds. When a charity makes a social investment it hopes to get *some* financial return (unlike a grant where funds are given away completely) but the expected return is less than with a conventional financial investment.

Charities have been undertaking social investments for many years (even if they did not use that term) but in some cases there were legal doubts as to whether the charity had the necessary powers. However, for most charities in England and Wales, the Charities (Protection and Social Investment) Act 2016 has given a specific power to make social investments, provided the trustees follow certain principles. In particular, the loss of income or the risks of not getting the capital repaid (as compared to a commercial investment) must be justified by anticipated outcomes linked to the charity's objects. However, trustees considering social investments should clearly debate the risks and benefits (including considering the Charity Commission's guidance). Clearly documented policies are needed and naturally the treasurer needs to be fully involved. The FRS102 SORP 2015 (module 21) includes specific guidance on the treatment of social investments in the trustees' report and accounts.

Costing projects and fundraising bids, and refusing gifts

Not all offers of money are helpful to a charity. Donations subject to very tight restrictions may be simply too much work to justify a restricted fund for one specific gift. Also, some restrictions might break your own policies or even be illegal. For example, under the Equality Act 2010 a charity could not accept a gift with conditions on the race of beneficiaries, unless it was a project addressing specific racial disadvantage.

Just as damaging are offers of funds that require the charity to do something but which do not cover the full costs, including relevant overheads and management time (see 'Managing core costs' in chapter 4, page 50). Sometimes the trustees will feel that the project is sufficiently central to their objects to justify subsidising it with a contribution from general funds. But very often treasurers find out too late that someone has committed the charity to a new project that had not been properly costed, and which will prove a net drain on the charity's general funds.

Issues of costing and budgeting have been addressed in several chapters. The time to work out costs is when a new project is first being considered, and this needs close liaison between the fundraiser and treasurer or finance officer to ensure everything is included. It is all too easy to forget the VAT, the professional fees, the employer's NI, the cost of salary increments over the life of the project, the recruitment costs, the premises overheads, the maintenance and annual depreciation of capital items, the increase in accountancy costs, the management time to supervise a project, and all the other elements involved.

If you tell a funder, 'We need £40,000 to do this', you may get what you ask for. Even if you do not, you have only lost the cost of the time spent on the proposal. But if you say you can do it for £30,000, get the go ahead and then come back asking for more money, most funders are likely to refuse and will also regard the charity as less than competent when it comes to future requests. The lower bid may succeed, but at a net cost to the charity of £10,000. If the funder could really only find £30,000 it would be better to refuse to do the project (or to propose something smaller where £30,000 would cover everything).

Charity finance as a whole

In this book we have looked at a vast range of financial issues, from basic bookkeeping to the legal requirements for charity accounts, to considerations of charity tax, and implications for fundraising. You will have seen how these issues need to be considered as a whole, and the idea that a treasurer or finance officer is just someone who keeps the books does not make any sense, even in the smallest charity.

In order to make this a handbook that can be read in a few hours, there are many topics only mentioned in passing and, if such issues affect your charity, you will need to refer to further sources or seek professional guidance. Also, the field of charity finance is constantly developing, with new legislation, new versions of the SORP, changing tax rules and new initiatives in government policies towards the third sector. There will clearly be further changes ahead that will impact on charities as the government negotiates the UK's exit from the EU, and possible changed relationships between Scotland, Northern Ireland and the rest of the UK. But if you have a good general understanding of the topics covered here, you will be very well placed to support your charity in its management of finance.

Being an effective charity treasurer or finance officer is partly about good accounting procedures and partly about understanding the legal requirements, so that you can advise and support your trustees. But it is also about recognising the privilege of managing resources that are not your own, which have been given to your charity in the hope of making the world a better place – that's the heart of the public benefit requirement. If, by taking on the finance role, you can enable your charity's funds to be used effectively for the cause set out in its objects, you will be making a major contribution to society.

Appendix: Differences for accounting years that began prior to January 2016

In this book the various legal requirements for charity accounting are explained (at least at an overview level) based on the rules that apply as at 1 January 2017.

However, while there have been changes to areas such as Gift Aid in 2016/17 (see chapter 12), the latest major change regarding the *presentation* of charity accounts took effect in all parts of the UK for accounting years starting on or after 1 January 2016. The main chapters of this book thus deal with the charity accounting rules effective from 2016. Nevertheless, most charities are only filing their first set of accounts under these requirements during 2017 or early 2018.

It will thus be some time before all sets of accounts are prepared under the regulations which apply from 2016, so if you are preparing accounts for earlier years, or if you are reading the accounts of other charities, you will certainly need to be aware of the previous requirements. This appendix summarises the main issues which apply around the years of transition to the new rules – points to consider if you are dealing with charity accounts for a financial year which began in 2015 or earlier.

Receipts and payments accounts

As explained in chapter 7, the SORP only applies to accounts prepared on an accruals basis. So, if your charity is producing receipts and payments (R&P) accounts there are no fundamental changes from 2016.

However, even if you do not need to follow the SORP for your accounts, you still need to consider the appropriate regulations which determine what has to be included in the trustees' annual report and specify the duties of your auditor or independent examiner.

At the time of writing, charities in England and Wales are still subject to the Charities (Accounts and Reports) Regulations 2008, so there are no recent changes in the regulations.

Charities registered in Scotland are subject to the Charities Accounts (Scotland) Regulations 2006 (as amended). These regulations were further amended from 2016, but the latest changes do not affect R&P accounts. However, remember that for Scottish charities, the regulations even specify the content of R&P accounts.

For charities registered in Northern Ireland, the accounting regime under the Charities Act (Northern Ireland) 2008 only took effect for years starting on or after 1 January 2016. For charities which were registered with CCNI prior to that date, interim reporting arrangement applied under which accounts had to be filed with CCNI as part of the annual return process, but the formats were not prescribed. CCNI made clear that either R&P accounts or accruals accounts were acceptable (but no specific thresholds applied). The details are in CCNI publication ARR06 (see 'Further reading'). Independent examination or audit was encouraged but an external scrutiny was not mandatory except for very large charitable companies.

Where a registered charity in Northern Ireland still has to file accounts for a year subject to the interim reporting arrangements, it would be simplest – and also best practice – to follow the new rules that apply from 2016 (as explained in chapters 2 and 7) even though the full framework was not mandatory for earlier years. This would also be the best approach for charities in Northern Ireland that are still on the **deemed list** and not yet registered with CCNI, although specific formats are not mandatory except for charitable companies which must always produce accruals accounts (R&P accounts are never allowed for companies).

Accruals accounts under the SORP 2015 regime

Charities preparing accounts on an accruals basis must follow the appropriate version of the Charities SORP. This is now compulsory for charities throughout the UK with more than £250,000 income and for charitable companies of any size (although in Northern Ireland this only had statutory force from 1 January 2016).

However, as explained in chapters 2, 7 and 10, the Charities SORP has undergone several changes in recent years. In particular, there are *two separate changes* to the SORP, the first from 1 January 2015 and then a further change from 1 January 2016.

The implementation of those changes differs between the three UK jurisdictions – England and Wales, Scotland, and Northern Ireland – and also between charitable companies and non-company charities such as trusts, associations and CIOs. Table A.1 summarises which SORP or SORPs may be followed in each case.

For years beginning in 2015, all but the largest charities have a choice of the SORP 2015 (FRSSE) or the SORP 2015 (FRS102); however, for financial years starting in 2016 or later only the SORP 2015 (FRS102) remains current, as explained in chapter 2. But, as discussed in chapter 7, for non-company charities in England and Wales, there is also a case for keeping with SORP 2005 which is the standard referred to by the Charities (Accounts and Reports) Regulations 2008, even though it is now out of date, unless the trustees feel it is appropriate to depart from the regulations using the principle of a 'true and fair override' (see page 109). It seems likely that at some point the 2008 Regulations will be updated by the government, to remove this inconsistency.

It was expected when the 2015 SORPs were issued that the Regulations would have been updated to take effect for years starting from 1 January 2015; an update on these lines was made for Scottish charities. For Northern Ireland the new regulations effective from 2016 referred directly to the latest SORP. But for England and Wales, no update had been made even after two years. So at 1 January 2017 – the date used in this book to explain legal requirements – the 2008 Regulations remain applicable for the accounts of non-company charities in England and Wales.

These changes are all linked to the *starting date* of the relevant accounting year – so, for example, if you are dealing with a financial year 2015/16 (ending 31 March 2016) the year began on 1 April 2015, so follow the requirements in the table for years starting in 2015.

Occasionally charities prepare final published accounts for years or periods which are not exactly 12 months. This is particularly the case when a new CIO or charitable company is formed, when the first set of accounts must start from the date the body was incorporated (the date of charity registration in the case of a CIO). So, for example, a CIO which was registered on 23 November 2015 might prepare its first set of accounts for the period of just over sixteen months running from 23 November 2015 to 31 March 2017. Also, from time to time, years may be altered because of a change of accounting date. In these cases it is still the starting date of the accounting year (or 'accounting period' as it should be called if not 12 months) which determines the SORP to follow.

In the case of charities registered with more than one regulator, it makes sense to follow the most demanding or most up-to-date framework, which in practice will usually be the Scottish regime.

Table A.I – Which SORP to follow for charities preparing accruals accounts				
Accounting years beginning:	**Charitable companies (any part of the UK)**	**Non-company charities in England and Wales**	**Non-company charities registered in Scotland**	**Non-company charities in Northern Ireland**
2014 or earlier	SORP 2005	SORP 2005	SORP 2005	No mandatory regime, but SORP 2005 was best practice
2015	SORP 2015 (FRSSE),[1] or SORP 2015 (FRS102)	SORP 2005 according to the 2008 Regulations – but by application of 'true and fair override',[2] SORP 2015: FRSSE SORP,[1] or FRS102 SORP can be used	SORP 2015 (FRSSE),[1] or SORP 2015 (FRS102)	No mandatory regime, but use of one of the 2015 SORPs was best practice (whether or not the charity was registered with CCNI)
2016 onwards	SORP 2015 FRS102 *as amended by FRS102 SORP Update Bulletin 1 (Feb 2016)*	SORP 2005 according to the 2008 Regulations – but by application of 'true and fair override',[2] SORP 2015 FRS102 can be used *(with Update Bulletin 1)*	SORP 2015 FRS102 *as amended by FRS102 SORP Update Bulletin 1 (Feb 2016)*	SORP 2015 FRS102 *as amended by FRS102 SORP Update Bulletin 1 (Feb 2016)*[3]

See 'Further reading' for sources of the SORPs mentioned.

[1] The FRSSE SORP was permitted for years starting in 2015 for charities that met *at least two* of the following criteria:
- Income – not over £6.5 million
- Assets – not over £3.26 million
- Employees – no more than 50

[2] See the text above on the issue of departing from the regulations to give a true and fair view.

[3] In Northern Ireland, the SORP regime is only compulsory from 2016 for registered charities, but in practice all Northern Irish charities preparing accruals accounts are strongly encouraged to use it.

Practical issues for changing to the new SORP

Although it is vital that the notes to the accounts show which SORP is being used, many of the detailed requirements in SORP 2015 are similar to those in SORP 2005. For example, the requirements to prepare a SOFA, balance sheet, and appropriate notes have applied for many years (right back to SORP 1995). Many of the accounting policies remain unchanged.

But there are a number of important differences, so it is essential to refer to SORP 2005 if you are working on a year which started prior to January 2015, or on a subsequent year in the case of a non-company charity in England and Wales which has chosen *not* to override the Regulations.

Here are some of the differences:

- SORP 2005 is based on the former Generally Accepted Accounting Practice in the UK (UK GAAP) – as set out in various standards (primarily FRS1 to FRS27 – see Appendix 2 of SORP 2005). Alternatively, it was also permissible for all but the largest charities – generally those with less than £6.5 million income – to follow the old FRSSE (see chapter 10 for explanations). But there are only a few places where SORP 2005 specifies different approaches for those charities following FRSSE. There was just one SORP 2005 – rather the choice (from 2015) of the FRSSE SORP and FRS102 SORP.

- The format specified in SORP 2005 for the SOFA – in particular the headings needed – was somewhat different to SORP 2015. Specifically, under 'Resources Expended' SORP 2005 requires a separate line for 'Governance Costs'. It also specifies three separate categories to be identified under 'Cost of Generating Funds'. So, if preparing a SOFA under SORP 2005, be sure to refer to the layout specified (SORP 2005 Table 3).

- A number of recognition and measurement rules were different in SORP 2005 – so the actual figures in the accounts could be different. For example, there was no requirement to recognise the value of donated stocks before they were sold.

Many of these differences are quite technical, and most charities will need advice from an experienced charity accountant (often their auditor or independent examiner). But it is important to appreciate that the choice of which SORP you are using for a given set of accounts is critical: be absolutely clear for any accounting year whether SORP 2005 or SORP 2015 is used (and if SORP 2015, be clear whether you are using the FRSSE SORP or FRS102 SORP).

For most charities, the year when you switch from SORP 2005 to SORP 2015 will mean changes to the layout of your accounts, and quite possibly changes to figures as well. This may mean re-computing figures on the balance sheet, and adjusting prior year figures on the SOFA. Changes of this kind should be explained in the notes to the accounts – linked to the change of accounting policies.

Glossary

The following terms are shown in **bold** at their first main use in the book or chapter concerned. Please note that this glossary seeks to explain the use of terms in a charity accounting context – some terms may have other meanings when applied to commercial accounts. In most cases this glossary seeks to give a plain English explanation of the typical usage in a charity context, rather than a legal definition of the term. (Some of these terms are defined more formally in the glossary or in the relevant module of the *Charities SORP* – see 'Further reading').

Accountable body: Where funding is agreed for work involving a partnership of two or more organisations, or where one charity is passing on funding to other charities, the accountable body is the lead charity which is accountable to the funder for ensuring the use of the funding as agreed, or accountable for the overall service provision. (The term is mainly used in relation to public sector funding, but it could apply to funding from any source.)

Accounting period: The period of time used for a particular set of accounts. For *annual accounts*, the period is normally 12 months, but *management accounts* may be prepared for shorter periods such as a month or quarter.

Accounting policies: See *true and fair view*.

Accounting records: The formal term for the basic books of the charity, where every transaction – every receipt, payment or other entry – is recorded individually. The term also includes supporting documents such as invoices, payslips, donation forms, etc., whether paper-based or electronic. In general, charities must keep accounting records for the current year and six prior years.

Accounting standards: An accounting standard is a document used with *accruals accounting* which sets out principles to be used in the preparation of *financial accounts* to assist in ensuring that they give a *true and fair view* and to introduce consistency between the accounts of different organisations. Accounting standards are generally divided into general-purpose standards that apply to any industry or type of organisation – for which the key standard at the time of writing is *FRS102* – and sector-specific standards – which for charities is the Charities *SORP*. General-purpose standards are issued in the UK by the Financial Reporting Council (FRC). The FRC then authorises appropriate sector bodies to prepare

SORPs, subject to FRC approval that a SORP does not depart from the principles in the relevant general-purposes standards.

Accrual: An entry in the books of an organisation to allow for costs applicable to a particular accounting year that are not yet paid by year end. (It is the opposite of a *prepayment* – see chapter 10 for further details.) Accruals may include expenses that are known to apply even if no bill has been received by year end – for example, for fuel which has been consumed up to year end (if material) even though next bill may not be expected until several months into the following year. Accruals normally appear on the balance sheet under the heading 'Creditors due within one year'.

Accruals accounting: Charity accounts prepared on the accruals basis show all income earned during the accounting period (the accrued income) and all expenses incurred in running the charity for that time (the accrued expenditure). This is contrasted with *receipts and payments accounting* which only accounts for money received and paid out. Final charity accounts on the accruals basis must be presented in *SORP* format. Accruals accounting is considered essential for accounts to give a *true and fair view*. (See chapter 10 for more details.)

Aggregate gross income: The total income of a charity group comprising a charity with one or more subsidiaries preparing *consolidated accounts*. It is calculated as the income of the charity, plus the income of the subsidiaries, but deducting income received by the charity from subsidiaries to prevent double counting.

Annual accounts: The final year end published accounts of a charity, as approved by the trustees, sometimes called the *financial accounts*. All charities must publish annual accounts and in most cases they must be sent to the relevant charity regulator (Charity Commission, OSCR or CCNI). A report from an auditor or independent examiner should usually be attached, and they should normally be accompanied by the *trustees' annual report* (see chapters 2 and 7 for specific rules).

Annual report: See *trustees' annual report*.

Annual report and accounts: See *financial statements*.

Articles of association: The *governing document* of a charitable company (in the past, charitable companies had two governing documents known as the 'memorandum and articles of association' but, since 2009, provisions that were in the memorandum are treated as part of the articles).

Asset: Any money, object or resource which is owned by the charity or its trustees for the work of the charity (or to which the charity or the trustees have legal entitlement). Assets must be shown on the charity's *balance* *sheet, statement of assets and liabilities* or *statement of balances*. The assets are usually divided into *fixed assets* and *current assets.*

Asset lock: Certain organisations such as charities and community interest companies (CICs) are subject to a framework which makes it illegal for money or other resources to be removed from the organisation except for expenditure directly related to their stated purposes. (In the case of CICs, up to 35% of profits can be paid to investors, but otherwise the assets remain locked.) By contrast, a normal company limited by shares generally has no asset lock, and assets can be used to pay dividends to private shareholders.

Auditors: A firm of accountants holding the status of a registered auditor, appointed to report on the *annual accounts* of a charity in accordance with applicable legislation – in particular, with *accruals accounts* to state whether the auditors consider that the accounts give a *true and fair view.* (However, for many small and medium-sized charities, it is possible to appoint an *independent examiner* rather than auditors.)

Audit trail: A trail of information which enables an auditor or examiner to verify how any figure in the accounts was reached. A key element of any audit trail is a list of all the transactions entered into the charity's books, usually broken down under the account headings used. With manual accounting, a cashbook is central to the audit trail. Most computer-based accounting systems automatically create an audit trail of transactions entered (but this is not the case with spreadsheets). See chapter 5.

Auto enrolment: The requirement that all employees in the UK (with limited exceptions, such as those earning under £10,000) must be automatically enrolled in a pension scheme (most commonly the government's NEST scheme) unless they specifically request otherwise. This includes charity employees. Once enrolled, both the employer and employee make pension contributions based on a percentage of earnings. See chapter 5.

Balance sheet: One of the two *primary statements* (the other is the SOFA) in any set of charity accounts prepared on the *accruals accounting* basis. The balance sheet shows the various *assets* and *liabilities* of the charity at year end totalled to a figure for net assets which must equal the total of the charity's *fund* balances at year end. The required format for the balance sheet is set out in the Charities *SORP.* (See chapter 7 figure 7.2 for an example of a charity balance sheet.)

Balancing off (or closing off): In any bookkeeping system, whether manual or computerised, at the end of an accounting period the two sides of any account must be deducted from one another to give a net figure, leading to the final balance on the account. This is often called 'balancing off'. The difference between the two sides, plus the opening balance (if applicable) at the start of the period, is then carried forward to the following period. For example, on a particular fund, payments may be deducted from receipts to give a balance of net receipts to the fund over that period. Or, on a debtors account, credits may be deducted from debits to give the net movement in debtors over that period: this is then added to the opening balance of the debtors account at the start of the period to give the final debtors balance. See chapter 5.

Budget variance: The difference between the actual figure on a particular account and the budget that was set. It can be expressed as an absolute difference in pounds, or as a percentage. See chapter 9.

Capitalisation limit: In general, with *accruals accounts*, *fixed assets* will be *depreciated* over a number of years. However, to avoid keeping track of depreciation on small items, it is normal to set a capitalisation limit below which the entire cost of an item is charged at the time of purchase (even for items expected to last several years) where it would not make a *material* difference to someone reading the accounts. The same principle can be used with *receipts and payments accounts* to decide whether or not an asset is included in the *statement of assets and liabilities* (or *statement of balances* in Scotland).

Cash flow forecast: A financial report, normally prepared for internal use by trustees or staff (or as part of a funding bid) showing the likely movements of money for some time ahead, either for the charity as a whole or for a particular project. Particularly for activities where costs may be incurred before the corresponding receipts (such as a project paid in arrears) a cash flow forecast is vital to consider whether the charity has sufficient cash *reserves*, or whether borrowing is required. Depending on the activity, a cash flow forecast may relate to a short period such as a few weeks, or may cover a period as long as several years for a project which has extensive start-up costs that will take time to recover. (This should be distinguished from a *statement of cash flows* which provides historical cash flow information.)

Charitable association: An unincorporated structure used by many charities where members come together under the terms of a *constitution*. Usually the members elect a committee and those who serve on the committee are the *charity trustees*.

Charitable company: A charity which is formed as a company with charitable aims (almost always a company limited by guarantee) which is also recognised as a charity. Charitable companies are subject both to company law and charity law.

Charitable incorporated organisation (CIO): A type of charity with corporate status and limited liability, but governed solely by charity law (thus giving many of the advantages of a *charitable company* but without being subject to company law). A CIO is formed by registration with the relevant charity regulator (Charity Commission or OSCR, or CCNI in the future). In this book, use of the general term 'CIO' includes Scottish CIOs (*SCIOs*) unless otherwise stated.

Charitable trust: The simplest structure for a charity: an initial donor (the *settlor*) makes gift of money or other property and appoints initial trustees. Most charitable trusts are governed by a *trust deed* but a charitable trust can also be established through the terms of legacy (sometimes called a 'will trust') or by a *Scheme* of the Charity Commission (a legal document created under the powers of the Charity Commission).

Charities SORP: See *SORP*.

Charity: An organisation with exclusively charitable aims established for public benefit, as defined in the relevant *jurisdiction* (slight differences in the definition apply between England/Wales, Scotland, Northern Ireland and the definition for tax law). Registration requirements vary, but particularly in England and Wales many charities are *exempt* or *excepted* from registration with the Charity Commission.

Charity fundraising: The process of raising or securing the necessary income to support the work of a charity. Sometimes the term is used only to refer to funds provided by individual donors, but in this book the term 'fundraising' refers to the process of generating income from any sources that may support the work of a charity.

Charity regulator: A body with statutory responsibility for the oversight and regulation of charities: in the UK the term includes the Charity Commission (for charities in England and Wales), OSCR (for Scottish charities) and CCNI (for charities in Northern Ireland).

Charity trustees: The persons charged with the governance of a charity. Some charities use other terms such as 'committee members', 'directors', 'members of the council', etc. – but, in law, those who have the authority to make formal decisions on behalf of the charity are charity trustees (whether or not that term is used) and thus have duties in relation to charity accounting as explained in this book. The *treasurer* is normally one of the trustees, but decisions must be taken by trustees collectively. (Note that some charities have *holding trustees* or a *custodian trustee* as well as charity trustees.)

Community benefit society (CBS): A corporate body, sometimes called an incorporated society or a bencom, which is established for purposes which benefit the community. Available throughout the UK, a CBS can be recognised as a charity, but the primary regulator is the Financial Conduct Authority. CBSs are established under the Cooperatives and Community Benefit Societies Act 2014 (and previously under the Industrial and Provident Societies Acts). In England and Wales, a charitable CBS is currently an *exempt charity*. (Note that this book does not cover the specific accounting rules for CBSs or other exempt charities.)

Consolidation: When an organisation has one or more subsidiary bodies which maintain their own accounts, the term 'consolidation' refers to the process of bringing the separate sets of accounts together into an overall account. Sometimes the subsidiary bodies are simply groups or branches within the structure of one charity (see 'Subsidiary groups' in chapter 6) so, the charity is only required to produce one set of *annual accounts*. However, in the case of a charity which has a *trading subsidiary* company or where a charity controls subsidiary charities, each entity must produce *individual accounts* which are then consolidated to produce *group accounts* (see 'Charities with subsidiaries – group accounts' in chapter 7).

Constitution: One of the most common forms of *governing document* for a charity setting out its objects and rules for members and trustees. The term 'constitution' can be applied to any kind of governing document, but is most commonly applied to the rules of a charitable association or a CIO.

Contract: An agreement between two or more parties where one party agrees to provide goods or services to the other in return for 'consideration' (normally the consideration is a payment of money – generally described as a *fee*). Where a charity receives income from contracts or fees it should be classed as *trading income* in the accounts.

Creditors: Persons or organisations to which the charity owes money or other resources.

Current asset: An *asset* which is either in the form of money or which can be readily converted to money within 12 months. Current assets typically include: cash at bank, cash in hand (i.e. petty cash or cash receipts not yet banked), *debtors* (where the receipt of the amount due is expected within 12 months), *prepayments*, stocks (if *material* for the charity concerned) and short-term investments such as deposit accounts with less than 12 months' notice.

Current liability: A *liability* for which the charity expects to make payment within the next 12 months (otherwise it would be a *long-term* liability). Current liabilities generally include trade *creditors* (where due within 12 months), *accruals* and *deferred income*.

Custodian trustee: See *holding trustee*.

Debits and credits: See *double-entry bookkeeping*.

Debtors: Persons or organisations which owe money or other resources to the charity.

Declaration of trust: See *trust deed*.

Deemed list: A list of bodies in Northern Ireland which are not yet registered with CCNI, but which had been recognised as charities for tax purposes (by HMRC) as at February 2011. They are deemed to be charities for the purposes of CCNI oversight until such time as CCNI makes a formal decision on whether or not they should be registered.

Deferred income: This is the technical term for income received in advance of the year in which it should be recognised, although when it arises it is best to use a more meaningful explanation such as 'Subscriptions received in advance' or 'Grant only to be used next year'. Such amounts normally appear on the balance sheet under 'Creditors due within one year' because, at the end of the year concerned, the charity is not yet entitled to use the amount held in its bank balance.

Deficit: A deficit arises when the expenditure was more than the income in a given year – either for a particular *fund*, or for the charity as a whole.

Depreciation: In *accruals accounting*, the process of spreading the cost of a *fixed asset* over a number of financial years. In each year's *SOFA*, only that year's depreciation appears as expenditure.

Designated fund: A fund holding resources set aside by the trustees, usually to provide for future significant expenditure that may arise in future years. However, a designated fund is not a *restricted fund* as there is no external restriction on its use, so designated funds are included within *unrestricted funds* in a charity's *annual accounts*.

Direct payments: Payments made to a charity to provide support to a particular individual, normally paid directly by the individual concerned or by those responsible for his/her care.

Donated income: Income which is given to the charity with no expectation of anything in return other than a receipt or acknowledgement and possibly feedback on how it was used: it is given to advance the charity's aims, not for any benefit to the donor. The term 'donated income' generally includes donations from individuals (including tax recovered under Gift Aid), legacy gifts, and *grants* from other organisations.

Donation: A gift to charity, usually made by an individual. The donation may be given for the charity's general work (an *unrestricted* donation) or for a specific project or appeal (a *restricted* donation). (If the donor is an organisation it is more usual to describe the gift as a *grant* but sometimes companies and smaller grant-making charities prefer the term 'donation'.)

Donor: A person (or organisation) making a donation to charity.

Double-entry bookkeeping: The process of bookkeeping where every transaction is recorded against two accounts, one side known as a 'debit' and the other side as a 'credit'. This makes it much easier to verify the resulting figures than with single-entry bookkeeping (see chapter 5). Double-entry bookkeeping is more or less essential with *accruals accounting*, but even with *receipts and payments accounting* it is very much recommended if the charity has several funds and/or several bank accounts. Most computer-based accounting systems automatically use double-entry bookkeeping principles.

Dual regulation: The situation where a charity is subject to more than one charity regulator. For example, if a charity established in England has regular activities in Scotland it will be typically be subject to regulation by both the Charity Commission and OSCR.

Endowment fund: A *fund* which is given to the charity on terms where the fund itself cannot be normally spent. Typically the endowment is invested and the resulting investment income is allocated to another fund to support the work of the charity, but the capital cannot be spent. In some cases an endowment fund may comprise property rather than *investments* – such as a historic building, village hall or place of worship – which is to be retained permanently for the operational work of the charity. If the endowment can never be spent it is called a *permanent endowment*, but where the trustees have the authority in certain circumstances use the capital (or to sell the property) for other charitable expenditure it is called an *expendable endowment*.

Excepted charity: A charity in England and Wales which is excepted from registration with the Charity Commission – but it remains subject to the authority of the Commission and is subject to the accounting requirements in the Charities Act 2011. The definition currently includes most English and Welsh charities (other than *CIOs*) with incomes of up to £5,000, and many Christian churches (in specified denominations), Scout and Guide groups and certain armed forces charities with incomes of up to £100,000.

Exempt charity: A charity in England and Wales which is exempt from the direct oversight of the Charity Commission, for example academy schools, most English universities, and charitable *community benefit societies*. Many, but not all, exempt charities are subject to a principal regulator which has oversight in terms of their charitable status. (Note that this book does not cover the specific accounting rules for exempt charities.)

Expendable endowment: See *endowment fund*.

Extended trial balance: See *trial balance*.

Fair value: In *accruals accounting* under IFRS principles (this includes charity accounts prepared under the FRS102 SORP 2015), assets and liabilities are normally shown in the accounts at fair value – that is, the value that would be placed on them in an arms-length transaction between unconnected parties. Sometimes the computation of fair value can be quite complex – see the example in chapter 10 (table 10.1) regarding the valuation of a multi-year grant commitment.

Fee: See *contract*.

Financial accounts: This term usually refers to accounts which are prepared for external use (as with a charity's *annual accounts*) in contrast to *management accounts* which are only for internal use within a charity.

Financial statements: The financial and related documents which a charity is required to publish at year end. For most charities, the financial statements comprise: the *trustees' annual report*, the *annual accounts*, and the report of the *auditor* or *independent examiner*.

Fixed asset: An *asset* which the charity intends to hold for at least 12 months. Fixed assets are generally divided into *tangible assets* (for example buildings, equipment or vehicles used in the operational work of the charity) and *investments* which are held purely to generate an income to support the charity's work (provided the intention is to hold them for at least 12 months). However, other types of asset are possible including *heritage assets* (such as paintings owned by an art gallery or artefacts in a museum), or *intangible assets* (if, for instance, the charity had acquired some form of valuable intellectual property which needed to have a value on the *balance sheet*). Some charities also have programme-related investments, more commonly known as *social investments.*

Fixed asset register: A record of all the charity's *fixed assets* generally including details such as a description and location of the item, serial or registration number (if applicable), supplier and price paid, and possibly warranty or insurance details. In the case of fixed assets subject to *depreciation* with *accruals accounting*, the fixed asset register should be updated to show the depreciation charged each year. To avoid recording numerous small assets, newly acquired fixed assets are generally not added to the fixed asset register if their cost or value is below the *capitalisation limit* that the charity has set. The fixed asset register is an important part of the charity's accounting records, although for straightforward cases a copy of the supplier's invoice for the fixed asset may provide most of the information needed. (Even for a charity using *receipts and payments* *accounting* a fixed asset register of some kind is needed in order to produce a *statement of assets and liabilities* (SOAL) for the annual accounts.)

FRS102: See *accounting standards*. (See also further discussion in chapter 10.)

Full cost recovery: When an external body is funding a particular service provided by a charity (whether under a grant or a contract) the charity will usually wish to agree a level of funding which at least should cover the full costs of the service including an appropriate share of the charity's overheads. (In some cases, with contract funding, the trustees may require sufficient funding to provide a surplus in addition to the full cost.) Where the funder will not agree to pay the full cost, trustees have to consider whether to undertake the work at a lower price (by subsidising the project from other income) or whether to decline the work.

Fund: A pool of money or resources held by a charity for particular purposes. For more details see *unrestricted funds*, *designated funds*, *restricted funds*, and *endowment funds*.

Fund accounting: The process of maintaining *accounting records* so that all transactions involving income or expenditure are allocated to specific *funds* within the charity's books. Fund accounting is one of the most significant issues that distinguishes charity accounting from most commercial accounting. Where a charity has any *restricted funds* the trustees are likely to be committing a breach of trust if they do not use fund accounting to keep track of the separate funds. Transfers between funds require use of an *inter-fund transfer* transaction.

Funds transfer: This term normally refers to an *inter-fund transfer* in the charity's accounting records. (However, sometimes the term is used to describe the transfer of funds between bank accounts or investments. But to avoid confusion, this type of transaction is better described as an 'asset transfer', as it is a transfer between *asset* accounts – it does not involve a transfer between the funds of a charity.)

General fund: The main unrestricted *fund* of a charity which is also undesignated – so it is available for the general work of the charity. Every charity should have a general fund (to be used at least for miscellaneous income and expenses, even if most of the income is allocated to *restricted funds*).

Governing document: Every charity requires a formal document which sets out the basis on which it is established. The governing document will include the charitable objects, how trustees are appointed, how decisions are made, and normally a clause to say what happens if the charity is dissolved. The governing document can take various forms – most commonly a *constitution*, *trust deed*, or *articles of association*.

Grant: A gift or *donation* made to a charity, or made by a charity to an external recipient. A grant (as opposed to a *contract*) has no requirement for anything to be provided back to the donor or funder other than an acknowledgement and possible feedback/monitoring information. (There is no legal distinction between a grant and a donation, but the term 'grant' is more frequently used when it is made by an organisation rather than an individual.) Many grants are made to charities for specific purposes, and in such cases the grant must be allocated to an appropriate *restricted fund*. If a grant has conditions such that the charity is only entitled to receive the grant subject to achieving specific outputs or service levels it should be treated as a *performance-related grant*.

Gross-up: In a charity context, the term 'to gross-up' is mainly used in relation to Gift Aid donations: it involves converting the net value of a gift to the gross value including tax reclaimed. With income tax at 20%, the gross value of a gift is the net value plus 25% (see chapter 12).

Group accounts: In cases where a charity owns a trading subsidiary company (see chapter 11) or in a few rare cases where one charity is a subsidiary of another, there may be a legal requirement to prepare group accounts – accounts based on *consolidating* the figures from the charity and its subsidiary (or subsidiaries) together. The group accounts must generally be prepared in addition to the *individual accounts* for the separate entities – though often the group accounts and individual accounts for the parent body are shown together in the same document, with columns headed 'group' and 'charity' respectively.

Heritage assets: See *fixed assets*.

HMRC: The body responsible for assessment and collection of the vast majority of taxes in the UK (although Scottish devolved taxes are administered by Revenue Scotland).

Holding trustee: An unincorporated charity cannot hold property in the name of the charity, so holding trustees or a *custodian trustee* may be appointed to hold the legal title to property held for charitable purposes. In some cases the holding trustees are the same persons as the charity trustees, but it is common to appoint a smaller number of people who will hold the property on a long-term basis. The holding trustees must act on any properly taken decisions of the charity trustees with regard to the property. If a corporate body is appointed to hold property (for example, a larger charity structured as a charitable company or CIO) the term *custodian trustee* is normally used.

Impairment: In *accruals accounting*, impairment is the process of reducing or 'writing down' the value of an asset, usually for exceptional reasons. It generally refers to a reduction in the value in excess of the normal *depreciation* that would be charged, for example if the asset has become out of date or damaged and has less potential for future use than previously anticipated.

Incorporated charities: This term refers to charities which have 'legal personality' – in other words, a charity which is recognised in law as a person in its own right. An incorporated charity can hold property in its own name, and can sue or be sued in the courts. The main forms of incorporated charities include *CIOs*, *charitable companies*, and *community benefit societies*.

Independent examiner: A person appointed to provide an independent report on the *annual accounts* of a charity. Independent examination is an option for most small and medium-sized charities if there is no requirement for a report by *auditors*. There is a detailed legal framework for independent examination of accounts, with separate rules in each of the three UK jurisdictions. For some charities, the independent examiner must be professionally qualified, but in other cases the trustees can appoint anyone to be independent examiner who is suitably independent of the charity and provided they are satisfied that he/she has the necessary skills and experience for a competent examination. (See chapter 8 for details.)

Individual accounts: The accounts for a single charity or other entity (in contrast to *group accounts*).

Intangible assets: See *fixed assets*.

Inter-fund transfer: An entry in the books of a charity recording a transfer of resources from one *fund* to another (expenditure of one fund which becomes income to another fund). With *accruals accounting*, inter-fund transfers appear on a special line on the *SOFA*. In most cases, where the resources of several funds are held in the same bank account, an inter-fund transfer is purely a book entry – it does not relate to any movement on the bank account. Where restricted funds are involved, inter-fund transfers must only be entered with appropriate authorisation within the relevant restrictions and they must therefore be explained by *notes to the accounts* (this is mandatory with *accruals accounts* and good practice with *receipts and payments accounts*).

Investment: An asset held by the charity with the expectation of a financial return. See *fixed assets, current assets* and *social investments*. (See also 'Investments' in chapter 12.)

Investment income: Income to a charity from investments of any kind, for example bank interest, share dividends, or rental income from investment properties. (Note that capital growth on investments is *not* investment income, but is shown on a separate part of the *SOFA* as an 'investment gain' – however, the presentation of gains and losses on investments are not directly covered in this book.)

Journal: A specialised entry in the accounts – an unusual *transaction* – which is more complex than those entered on a regular basis. In *double-entry bookkeeping*, a journal may involve a number of debits and credits, and in a computer-based accounting system it is normally possible to enter a journal using any combination of debits and credits across different accounts. Journals are commonly used for entries such as salary payments (if split across multiple accounts with possible *creditors* for tax, NI and pension amounts), *depreciation*, capitalisation of a *fixed asset* purchase which was initially entered as normal expenditure, recharging income or expenditure between projects or funds, and possibly for *inter-fund transfers*. Also, an accountant preparing the *annual accounts* for a charity may identify journals needed in order to adjust figures from the charity's internal books to reach the figures needed for the final accounts – for example if the treasurer or bookkeeper had not entered depreciation, or had posted some income to the wrong fund. However, it is essential that any journals proposed by an external accountant are referred back to the charity's treasurer or bookkeeper for approval (or for rejection if there was a misunderstanding). Journals of this kind also need to be notified so they can be recorded in the charity's own accounting records – otherwise the charity's books will not agree to the final accounts.

Jurisdiction: A country or territory where a particular legal system applies. In the UK there are three jurisdictions each with a separate framework of charity law: England/Wales, Scotland, and Northern Ireland.

Liability: An obligation which the charity has towards a third party such as an amount due to a supplier which has not yet been paid (a *creditor*) or the outstanding balance on a loan made to the charity. A liability is the opposite of an *asset*. Liabilities are treated as having a negative value on the *balance sheet*, *statement of assets and liabilities* or *statement of balances*: liabilities are deducted from the assets to give the *net assets* of the charity. They are usually divided into *current liabilities* and *long-term liabilities*.

Long-term liability: A liability for which the charity does not expect to have to make any payment until more than 12 months in the future – for example, the value outstanding on a mortgage where capital does not have to be repaid for several years. (However, if any part of the capital is due to be repaid in the next 12 months, that part of the mortgage should be treated as a *current liability*.)

Management accounts: Accounts which present financial information in a form for internal decision making by trustees or managers (as opposed to *financial accounts*).

Material: With *accruals accounting*, estimates and judgements have to be made in determining the specific amounts to include in the accounts and deciding which amounts should be *recognised* (see *true and fair view*). However, sometimes the relevant amounts are so small that it would make no material difference to the reader of the accounts which of the alternative approaches were used. For example, in a charity with £400,000 income, it is immaterial whether an outstanding staff expense claim for £3.50 at year end is treated as a *creditor*, or simply left to be treated as expenditure in the following year. Auditors and independent examiners are not required to report on minor concerns that something might have been wrongly classified in the accounts which would be immaterial to most readers of the accounts (although fundamental discrepancies such as missing transactions or suspected theft of charity funds would almost always be material no matter how small the amount). There is no fixed percentage for measuring what is material – a judgement must be made on what would be relevant to someone carefully reading the charity's accounts.

Non-business use: This term is most commonly used in relation to VAT accounting (see chapter 11), especially with regard to buildings. Even if a building is used exclusively for charitable purposes, it will be classed for VAT purposes as 'business use' if most of the work undertaken is supported by fees, contracts or other *trading income*. To be classed as 'non-business use', at least 95% of the work undertaken in the building must generally be funded by *donated income* or *investment income*. However, the interpretation of these terms and the apportionment of use can be complex and it is usually worth seeking specialist advice.

Non-charitable trading income: See *trading for fundraising purposes*.

Non-profit/not-for-profit: An organisation or activity which is not intended to make a profit. All charities are not-for-profit organisations, but the term also includes many other organisations in the public sector and third sector. A charity may well make a profit on a particular activity or fundraising event, or it may have a *trading subsidiary* that makes a profit. But it is never appropriate to speak about the profit of a charity as a whole. Where the income of a charity is more than the expenditure, the accounts will show a *surplus* to support the ongoing work of the charity.

Notes to the accounts: Information that is included as part of the *annual accounts* in addition to the *primary statements*. So, with *SORP* accounts, the notes include all information additional to the SOFA, balance sheet and (where applicable) the statement of cash flows. In the case of *accruals accounts*, the regulations in each jurisdiction and/or the SORP require many specific disclosures to be made by way of notes (see chapter 7). In the case of *receipts and payments accounts*, the requirement for notes is more limited (though still good practice) but for Scottish charity accounts and with *CIOs* in England and Wales, a number of notes are required even with R&P accounts. (See chapter 7 for more details.)

Performance-related grants: A *grant* where the charity only becomes entitled to the income to the extent that particular services are carried out. Often such grants are expressed in terms of an amount of grant that will be paid for each unit of work undertaken (for example, a grant of £x per client per night). Performance-related grants are frequently linked to *service level agreements* (SLAs) specifying the precise services to be provided by the grant funding; however, care is needed to distinguish performance-related grants from *contract* funding.

Permanent endowment: See *endowment fund*.

Prepayment: A prepayment arises when a charity pays in advance for a cost which should only be recognised as expenditure in the year ahead. (It is the opposite of an *accrual* – see chapter 10 for further details.) Prepayments normally appear under the 'Debtors' heading on the balance sheet.

Primary purpose trading: *Trading income* is classed as being for the primary purpose of the charity where a charge is made or a *fee* is paid for services or goods which are directly provided as part of the charity's objects. Common examples include course fees charged by educational charities, or sales of theatre tickets by performing arts charities. Trading which is not undertaken for the primary purpose must be treated as *trading for fundraising purposes*.

Primary statements: The key financial reports within a statement of accounts (as opposed to supporting information which is provided in *notes to the accounts*). In the case of *accruals accounts* under the Charities *SORP* the primary statements are the *SOFA* and the *balance sheet*. With *receipts and payments accounts* the primary statements are the *R&P account* and the *SOAL* (or *statement of balances* in Scotland).

Public benefit requirement: To be a charity, an organisation must be established for public benefit (as well as having purposes or objects which fall within the specific headings) but the precise definition and interpretation of the public benefit requirement varies slightly between England/Wales, Scotland and Northern Ireland. Key issues include whether or not the purpose (objects) of the charity are inherently beneficial, and whether there are undue restrictions on who can benefit (the class of beneficiaries) – for example if there are substantial charges to access the charity's services a *charity regulator* may decide the public benefit requirement is not met. If a charity ceases to meet the public benefit requirement it could lose its charitable status. Trustees are required to consider the public benefit requirement in the decisions they make. In England/Wales and Northern Ireland this includes considering the specific public benefit guidance from the Charity Commission or CCNI (see 'Further Reading') and the *trustees' annual report* must explain how the activities of the charity during the year were carried out for public benefit.

Qualified accounts/report: The accounts of a charity are said to be 'qualified' when the report of the *auditor* or *independent examiner* contains some reservations or qualifications. In other words, the auditor or examiner was unable to give a clean report on the accounts. (See chapter 8 for further details. Note that this term has nothing to do with the professional qualifications of the auditor or examiner.)

R&P account: One of the two primary statements (the other is the *SOAL* or *statement of balances*) in any set of charity accounts prepared on the *receipts and payments accounting* basis. The receipts and payments account (R&P account) shows the various categories of receipts and payments, normally over a 12-month period. Where the charity has multiple funds, the accounts must either provide a separate R&P account for each fund, or use multiple columns to distinguish the funds (as with a SOFA in *accruals accounting*). In Scotland the categories to be used in the R&P account are specified in the Charities Accounts (Scotland) Regulations 2006. In England/Wales and Northern Ireland there is no prescribed format for an R&P account, but the Charity Commission and CCNI both publish guidance (see 'Further Reading'). (See chapter 7 figure 7.1 for an example of an R&P account.)

Receipts and payments accounting: Charity accounts prepared on the receipts and payments basis (sometimes called the 'cash basis') just show money received and paid out in the main *R&P account*. However, accounts on this basis must also contain a *statement of assets and liabilities* (in England/Wales or Northern Ireland) or *statement of balances* (in Scotland). This is contrasted with *accruals accounting* which shows income earned and expenses incurred. Charity accounts on the receipts and payments basis are *not* subject to the accounting requirements of Charities *SORP* and do not generally give a *true and fair view* even though they should be factually correct. (However, even when using the receipts and payments basis, the financial statements must normally include a *trustees' annual report* and the SORP guidance may be useful for that.)

Recognition (of income or expenses): With *accruals accounting*, recognition involves deciding the point in time when the charity is entitled to the income or liable for the expenditure, which therefore determines the financial year in which the income or expense should be included. With a simple donation, recognition occurs at the time when the gift is made, but with more complex items there can be considerable debate – for example with legacy income where a person had died leaving part of their estate to charity, but where it is unclear when the charity will receive the legacy, or where the amount is uncertain. Similarly, the recognition of expenditure involves policy decisions such as the period of depreciation for different types of fixed assets.

Registered charity: A charity which is registered with the relevant *charity regulator* (Charity Commission, OSCR or CCNI) and allocated a registered charity number. (Note that not all charities are registered and some charities may be dual-registered – see chapter 1.)

Reserves: The reserves of a charity are the resources available at a given point in time that could be spent at the trustees' discretion on the short-term work of the charity (without, for example, selling assets which are essential to the charity's activities, and without approaching funders for permission to use restricted funds outside the terms on which they were given). The reserves figure is normally therefore calculated as the balance of unrestricted funds less any tangible fixed assets that form part of the unrestricted funds. Where part of the unrestricted funds comprises designated funds, these are usually also excluded if they include amounts set aside for specific future expenditure which the trustees consider fundamental to the long-term sustainability of the charity's work.

Reserves policy: A policy set by the trustees for the level of *reserves* they consider to be needed. The reserves policy must be stated (even by small charities) in the *trustees' annual report*. It is often expressed in terms of a number of months: the period of time for which the trustees consider the charity should be able to survive even if all income suddenly ceased. (See chapter 4.)

Restricted fund: A *fund* where there is some external condition (beyond the trustees) on how the fund can be used. The condition could arise either because the charity invited *grants* or *donations* for a specific purpose, or because of an explicit condition imposed by a funder or *donor*. Strictly speaking the term 'restricted fund' can include either a *restricted* *income fund* or an *endowment fund* (but in most cases it refers to the former).

Restricted income fund: The official name for a normal *restricted fund* where the income can be spent (within the terms of the restriction), as opposed to an *endowment fund* where the fund itself cannot normally spent.

Scheme of the Charity Commission: See *charitable trust.*

Scottish charitable incorporated organisation (SCIO): A *CIO* incorporated under Scottish charity law, registered with OSCR. (However, the legal framework for SCIOs has a number of important differences from CIOs registered with the Charity Commission for England and Wales.)

Section 167 register: A register to be maintained by CCNI of external charities operating in Northern Ireland. The legal basis of the register is s. 167 of the Charities Act (Northern Ireland) 2008. (However, at the time of writing the section 167 register is not yet in operation.)

Service level agreements (SLAs): An agreement with a funding body on the level of services to be provided by a charity as a condition of the relevant funding. Note that an SLA is not itself a funding agreement (so one cannot say 'we are funded by an SLA') but either a grant agreement or a contract for services could incorporate an SLA as one of the conditions. (Sometimes the funding agreement begins with the SLA, and the grant or contract funding is only mentioned at the end.)

Settlor: The initial *donor* who makes a gift or money or property creating a new *charitable trust.*

Social investment: An *investment* made by a charity which is not expected to give a commercial return, but where the making of the investment will support the charity's objects and hence the trustees agree it is appropriate to accept a lower return than with a conventional investment. A charity can also be the recipient of a social investment. (See 'Investments' in chapter 12.)

Statement of assets and liabilities (SOAL): In a set of charity accounts prepared on the *receipts and payments basis* in England/Wales or Northern Ireland, the SOAL provides a list of the *assets* and *liabilities* of the charity at year end. In the SOAL, bank balances should be reconciled to the *fund* balances (from the *R&P account*) and other assets and liabilities should then also be listed: for example, *fixed assets, debtors, creditors.* In Scotland, the equivalent is a *statement of balances.* (See chapter 7 figure 7.1 for an example of a SOAL.)

Statement of balances: The equivalent of a *statement of assets and liabilities (SOAL)* in *receipts and payments accounting* by Scottish charities.

The categories to be used in the statement of balances are specified in the Charities Accounts (Scotland) Regulations 2006.

Statement of cash flows: In a set of charity accounts prepared on the *accruals accounting* basis, a statement of cash flows shows the movements of money (cash) through the charity over the financial year. It forms an additional statement, usually presented immediately after the *SOFA* and *balance sheet.* For charities following SORP 2015 (FRS102), for financial years starting in 2016 or later, a statement of cash flows is required for charities with an income of more than £500,000 (below this it is optional).

Statement of financial activities (SOFA): One of the two *primary statements* (the other is the *balance sheet*) in any set of charity accounts prepared on the *accruals accounting* basis. The SOFA shows the income and expenditure, normally over a 12-month period, broken down into columns for *unrestricted, restricted* and *endowment* funds, totalled to a final balance at year end on each type of funds. The SOFA may also show *inter-fund transfers* and other gains and losses The required format for the SOFA is set out in the Charities *SORP*. (See chapter 7 figure 7.2 for an example of a SOFA.)

Statement of Recommended Practice on Accounting and Reporting by Charities (SORP): The Charities SORP is the accounting standard which explains how charities preparing *accruals accounts* should set out their *financial statements*, including the *SOFA, balance sheet, statement of cash flows* (if applicable), *notes to the accounts* and *trustees' annual report.* The Charities SORP exists in various versions applicable at different dates: the latest version at the time of writing is the SORP 2015 (FRS102) as supplemented by the *SORP Update Bulletin 1* (but some charities may need to follow earlier versions as explained in chapter 7 and in the appendix). See also *accounting standards.*

Surplus: A surplus arises when a charity's income was more than the expenditure in a given year – either for a particular *fund,* or for the charity as a whole.

Tangible assets: See *fixed assets.*

Total return: Total return is a specific method of investing by a charity (usually in relation to a *permanent endowment fund*) where both the capital growth and the investment income are considered together to determine the amount available for charitable expenditure. In England and Wales, the trustees can adopt such an approach under the Charities Act 2011, subject to very strict safeguards, compliance with Charity Commission guidance and provision of specific disclosures in the trustees' annual report. (The details of total return investing are outside the scope of this book, but chapter 4 provides some further explanations of the principles.)

Trading for fundraising purposes: When a charity sells goods or services in order to raise funds the activity is classed as trading for fundraising purposes (as opposed to *primary purpose trading*). Trading for fundraising purposes (also known as *non-charitable* trading) includes sales of tickets for fundraising events, sales of gifts and souvenirs, sales of refreshments or donated goods purely to raise funds, and sales of the charity's core services where they are not being purchased on behalf of beneficiaries, such as a charity renting out its training room to a commercial business. Charities are allowed limited concessions regarding trading for fundraising purposes (see chapter 11) but beyond those limits, the profits of the activity may be taxable.

Trading income: Income to a charity which arises from making some kind of charge for a product or service (as opposed to *donated income* and *investment income*). Trading income is divided into that which derives from *primary purpose trading* and income from *trading for fundraising purposes*.

Trading subsidiary: A non-charitable company established as subsidiary of a charity, normally to undertake *trading for fundraising purposes* (i.e. non-charitable trading) which would be taxable if it were undertaken by the charity itself (see chapter 11). The profits of the trading subsidiary are donated back to the charity.

Transaction: A financial event requiring an entry in the books of a charity such as a receipt, a payment, receiving or issuing an invoice (this is still a transaction even if it will not be paid immediately), *depreciating* a fixed asset, posting an *inter-fund transfer*, recording a *prepayment* or an *accrual*.

Treasurer: The person, normally a trustee, who takes the lead on financial matters within a charity. This will typically include taking the lead on any recommendations to trustees with regard to accounting procedures, budgets, *annual accounts*, communication on behalf of the trustees with the *auditors* or *independent examiner* and generally supporting the trustees with all decisions of a financial nature. However, the treasurer has no power to make financial decisions alone: all decisions are for the trustees as whole (or for staff where the trustees have authorised them to take decisions within pre-agreed budgets). In a very small charity, the treasurer's role may also include the day-to-day bookkeeping and payment of bills, etc.

Trial balance: In *double-entry bookkeeping*, after *balancing off* each account, a list of every account showing its final debit or credit balance is prepared at the end of each accounting period and is called a 'trial balance'. Because the debits and credits on every transaction should balance, the total of the debits and credits across the whole charity should balance – if not, there has been an error in the double-entry recording of transactions. (In a computer-based accounting system, the trial balance is generated automatically and unless there has been a malfunction in the system, the debits and credits will always balance.) The trial balance is often used as the starting point for preparing the *SOFA* and *balance sheet* in the annual accounts. A simple trial balance just has three columns, with the name of each account, a column for debit balances and a column for credit balances. However, it can be helpful to prepare an *extended trial balance* where, rather than just having debit and credit columns, the account balances are allocated to various columns according to where they will appear in the final accounts.

True and fair view: Where *accruals accounting* is used, the aim is always that the final accounts should give a true and fair view of the financial strength of the charity in terms of its income, expenditure, *assets* and *liabilities*. For this to be possible, suitable accounting policies must be chosen to deal with issues such as *recognition* of income and expenditure, *depreciation of fixed assets*, and valuation of assets of liabilities, so that all *material* figures in the financial statements are meaningful and appropriate. It is also essential that all figures from the books are properly categorised on the *SOFA* and *balance sheet* (including analysis between different funds). However, simply presenting a *SOFA* and *balance sheet* on their own would not be sufficient to give a true and fair view: *notes to the accounts* are also needed, to allow the reader to understand the breakdown of major figures, and the accounting policies used and to disclose details such as transactions with trustees. Compliance with relevant accounting standards (in particular, the Charities *SORP*) is generally considered to be a fundamental requirement for accounts to give a true and fair view. *Auditors* will state whether in their opinion the accounts give a true and fair view (but this is not part of the duties of an *independent examiner*, although an independent examiner must still review the accounting policies and the presentation of the accounts and state if any concerns have arisen). However, the responsibility for ensuring the accounts give a true and fair view rests with the charity trustees – *not* with the charity's auditor or independent examiner. (See 'Concepts of accruals accounts' in chapter 10 for more on the principles.)

Trust deed: The usual governing document of a *charitable trust* (or the document may be called a *declaration of trust*).

Trustees' annual report: The annual report of the charity trustees which, for most charities, must accompany the *annual accounts* in order to provide a full set of *financial statements*. The report will include legal and administrative information such as the name and objects of the charity, details of the governing document, and names of trustees who served during to year. It must also include a report on the work of the charity during the year (taking account of the *public benefit requirement*) and details of key policies set by the trustees – in particular a *reserves* policy. The precise requirements vary between England/Wales, Scotland and Northern Ireland, and between smaller and larger charities. (See chapter 7 for more on the principles and refer to module I of SORP 2015 for details.)

Unincorporated charities: This term refers to charities which do not have their own 'legal personality' – in other words, the charity only exists by virtue of individual trustees coming together. Any property must be held in the names of the individual trustees (or possibly in the names of *holding* trustees) and any agreements are made by the trustees as individuals (so they do not have the benefit of limited liability in the event of a dispute). The main forms of unincorporated charities are *charitable trusts* and *charitable associations*.

Unqualified accounts/report: Charity accounts where the report of the *auditor* or *independent examiner* contained no qualifications or reservations in the wording: in other words, accounts with a clean audit/independent examination report which raised no concerns. All charities subject to audit or independent examination should aim for an unqualified report on their accounts. (See chapter 8 for further details.)

Unrestricted fund: A *fund* of the charity which has no external restriction: the trustees can use the resources of the fund as they consider most appropriate to support the charity's objects. The unrestricted funds can include a *general fund* and possibly also *designated funds*.

Zero-based budgeting: The process of preparing a budget for a charity where nothing is based on the previous year – all budgets are set from first principles (in effect, starting from zero).

Notes

[1] This quote is from the Charity Commission's publication *Charity Reporting and Accounting: The essentials November 2016 (CC15d)* (section 6) – similar comments also appear in many other Charity Commission documents.

[2] For details of accounting requirements in the Church of England, see *PCC Accountability: Incorporating SORP 2015* (Church House Publishing, 2017).

[3] Charities Act 2011, s. 130; Charities Accounts (Scotland) Regulations 2016, reg. 4; Charities Act (Northern Ireland) 2008, s. 63.

[4] For more on the concept of 'value for money' when public sector bodies are procuring services from external providers (including charities), see *Managing Public Money* (HM Treasury 2013, revised 2015) – also known as 'The Green Book'. One of the standards listed is that all public services must 'achieve value for money'.

[5] In exceptional cases a charity may wish to avoid one or more trustees' names being made public if it could put individuals at risk. For example, if a woman who is a survivor of domestic abuse became a trustee of a charity working in that field, she might be tracked down by a former perpetrator if her status as a charity trustee was made public in the charity's annual report. Similar issues might apply in a charity undertaking work which was very unpopular in a particular locality where threats of violence might be made against its trustees.

In circumstances of this kind, the charity can apply to the relevant charity regulator (Charity Commission, OSCR or CCNI) for permission to exclude such information from the annual report (if this is granted, the annual report should explain that the charity has a formal authorisation not to show trustees' names). In England/Wales or Northern Ireland, the request should also ask that the relevant trustees' names are not shown on the online Register of Charities (OSCR does not publish trustee names on the Scottish Charity Register). Such requests can apply to all trustees of the charity or just some.

If necessary, a request can also be made to omit the charity's address, but this makes it very hard for anyone to contact the charity: it is usually better to have a PO Box address.

If the request to omit trustee names from the annual report is agreed, the authorisation would be made by the Charity Commission under the Charities (Accounts and Reports) Regulations 2008, reg. 40(4); by OSCR under the Charities Accounts (Scotland) Regulations 2006, sch. 2 para. 5 (which refers back to s. 3(4) of the Charities and Trustee Investment (Scotland) Act 2005); or by CCNI under the Charities (Accounts and Reports) Regulations (Northern Ireland) 2015, reg. 32(4).

However, there is little point in making such a request for a charitable company because the details of the directors/trustees will still be available from Companies House (there are very exceptional cases where names can be omitted even from the Register of Companies, but this is much more complex to achieve). It follows that it is usually better to structure a charity as a CIO or as an unincorporated body rather than as a charitable company if you wish to be able to avoid disclosing trustee names.

In all cases, you must have formal permission from the relevant charity regulator to omit trustee's names: in other cases, the names of all trustees who served during the relevant year and up to the date of approval of the report must be shown.

[6] See, in particular: G. G. Morgan and N. J. Fletcher (2011), *Public Benefit Reporting by Charities* (Charity Commission research study ref. RS25), appendix C.2, table L; Charity Commission (2016), *Accounts Monitoring Review: The quality of charity accounts.*

[7] See J. Kemp and G. G. Morgan (2017), *Incidence and Perceptions of 'Qualified' Accounts Filed With the Regulator by Small Charities* (paper presented at British Accounting and Finance Association Annual Conference, Edinburgh, April 2017).

[8] Charities Act 2011, s. 145; Charities Accounts (Scotland) Regulations 2006, reg. 11 and Charities Act (Northern Ireland) 2008, s. 65.

[9] Charities (Accounts and Reports) Regulations 2008, regs. 24–6; Charities Accounts (Scotland) Regulations 2006, reg. 10; Charities (Accounts and Reports) Regulations (Northern Ireland) 2015, regs. 20–22.

[10] The Fundraising Regulator's *Code of Fundraising Practice* can be found at www.fundraisingregulator.org.uk.

Further reading

Charity Commission for England and Wales publications

The Charity Commission for England and Wales (the Charity Commission) produces a wide range of guidance publications for charities. They are available from the Charity Commission's website, in most cases both as web pages to read online and as PDFs which can be downloaded and printed. In almost all cases they apply to excepted charities in England and Wales as well as registered charities.

The following guidance is particularly relevant to treasurers and finance workers and is most quickly accessed by searching online for 'Charity Commission Publications'.

CC3   – *The Essential Trustee*

CC8   – *Internal Financial Controls for Charities*

CC11   – *Trustee Expenses and Payments*

CC12   – *Managing a Charity's Finances: Planning, managing difficulties and insolvency*

CC14   – *Charities and Investment Matters: A guide for trustees*

CC15d – *Charity Reporting and Accounting: The essentials*

CC16   – *Receipts and Payments Accounts Pack*

CC17   – *Accruals Accounts Pack*

CC19   – *Charity Reserves: Building resilience*

CC25   – *Charity Finance: Trustee essentials*

CC20   – *Charities and Fundraising: A guide to trustee duties*

CC29   – *Conflicts of Interests: A guide for charity trustees*

CC32   – *Independent Examination of Charity Accounts: Directions and guidance for examiners*

CC35   – *Trustees, Trading and Tax: How charities may lawfully trade*

The specific guidance on public benefit (which trustees *must* consider by law) is available at www.gov.uk/government/collections/charitable-purposes-and-public-benefit. The revised guidance from 2013 comprises three publications:

PB1 – *Public Benefit: the public benefit requirement*

PB2 – *Public Benefit: Running a charity*

PB3 – *Public Benefit: Reporting*

Note: For the Charities SORP (jointly published by the Charity Commission and OSCR) see 'Accounting Standards' on page 226.

Publications from the Office of the Scottish Charity Regulator

The Office of the Scottish Charity Regulator (OSCR) has a wide range of guidance for Scottish charities (generally published as PDFs).

The specific accounting guidance is available at www.oscr.org.uk/charities/managing-your-charity/charity-accounting which explains the principles and has drop down options for further details. Major publications for download include:

Scottish Charity Accounts: An updated guide to the 2006 Regulations

Receipt and Payments Accounts (work pack with templates)

Independent Examination: OSCR guidance for charities and independent examiners

The OSCR website also includes a range of examples of charity accounts and trustees' reports.

OSCR's key guidance on charitable status in Scotland including the Scottish approach to public benefit is available at www.oscr.org.uk/charities/becoming-a-charity/meeting-the-charity-test and includes:

Meeting the Charity Test: A brief guide

Meeting the Charity Test: Full guidance

Note: Many of the principles in the Charity Commission's publications (if not the legal details) are also relevant in Scotland.

For the Charities SORP (jointly published by the Charity Commission and OSCR) see 'Accounting Standards' on page 226.

Publications from the Charity Commission for Northern Ireland

The Charity Commission for Northern Ireland (CCNI) has issued a wide range of accounting guidance, all available as PDFs to download at www.charitycommissionni.org.uk/manage-your-charity/annual-reporting. The key publications are as follows:

ARR01 – *Charity reporting and accounting overall summary*

ARR02 – *Charity reporting and accounting the essentials guidance*

ARR03 – *Receipts and payments accounts guidance*

ARR04 – *Accruals accounts guidance*

ARR05 – *Annual monitoring return guidance*

ARR07 – *Guidance for independent examiners*

ARR08 – *The trustees annual report and public benefit reporting*

Note that CCNI's *Guidance for Independent Examiners* included mandatory *Directions* which must be followed by anyone undertaking an independent examination of the accounts of a registered charity in Northern Ireland (they have similar status to the Directions made by the Charity Commission in CC32 for independent examiners in England and Wales, but they are not identical).

For accounting years that began before 2016, when interim reporting arrangements applied in Northern Ireland (see the appendix on page 193), refer to:

ARR06 – *Charity reporting: Interim annual reporting arrangements*

CCNI's key guidance on charitable status in Northern Ireland, including the statutory guidance on public benefit which *must* be considered by trustees of Northern Irish charities is available at: www.charitycommissionni.org.uk/manage-your-charity/register-your-charity/the-public-benefit-requirement. Key publications include:

PBR1   – *The public benefit requirement*

PBG   – *Public benefit glossary*

EG016 – *Registering as a charity in Northern Ireland guidance*

In addition, CCNI has detailed guidance in relation to each of the main categories of charitable purposes (PBSD01 to PBSD12).

Note: Many of the principles in the Charity Commission's publications (if not the legal details) are also relevant in Northern Ireland. In general, charity law in Northern Ireland is closer to England and Wales than to Scotland, so in the absence of specific CCNI guidance, the relevant guidance from the Charity Commission will normally be more relevant than guidance from OSCR.

Legislation on charity accounts

ACTS

Charities Act 2011 [as amended – primarily by the Charities (Protection and Social Investment) Act 2016]

Charities and Trustee Investment (Scotland) Act 2005 [as amended – primarily by the Public Services Reform (Scotland) Act 2010]

Charities Act (Northern Ireland) 2008 [as amended – primarily by the Charities Act (Northern Ireland) 2013]

SECONDARY LEGISLATION

Charities (Accounts and Reports) Regulations 2008

Charities Accounts (Scotland) Regulations 2006 [as amended]

Charities (Accounts and Reports) Regulations (Northern Ireland) 2015

Note: Legislation is available to purchase from bookshops or can be accessed free online from www.legislation.gov.uk. However, published versions (whether in print or online) may only give the legislation as originally enacted. Statutes (i.e. Acts) are generally updated on www.legislation.gov.uk when they are amended, but this often takes some time after the amendment is made – look for the notes on each Act regarding amendments outstanding. This updating does not, however, apply to secondary legislation which is currently only available in original versions. So, for example, while charity accounting in Scotland remains subject to the 2006 Regulations (as amended), the full legal details can only be obtained by taking the original 2006 Regulations together with the Charities Accounts (Scotland) Amendment Regulations of 2007, 2010, 2014, and 2016.

TERTIARY LEGISLATION (by charity regulators)

Regulations made by charity regulators (rather than by the Parliaments or the Northern Ireland Assembly) are not available from www.legislation.gov.uk but can be obtained from the websites of the charity regulators themselves. This includes the Charity Commission's Directions to Independent Examiners, which are in the Charity Commission's publication CC32 (see page 223), and those of CCNI which are in publication ARR07 (see page 225).

Accounting standards

Charities SORP (FRS102) (effective 1 January 2015)
Charities SORP (FRS102) Update Bulletin 1

The latest SORP, plus various explanatory helpsheets, are jointly published by the Charity Commission and OSCR and are available from the SORP microsite www.charitysorp.org. This site also allows a charity to download a tailored SORP containing only the modules required. Printed versions of the 2015 SORPs are published by CIPFA (see page 234).

FRS 102: The Financial Reporting Standard applicable in the UK and Republic of Ireland, Financial Reporting Council, FRC Publications, 2015 (also available online from www.frc.org.uk).

See also the guidance listed above on charity accounting from the Charity Commission, OSCR and CCNI.

There are also a number of documents that amplify the SORP in relation to particular types of charities – see 'Groups for treasurers in specific types of charities' on page 233.

As explained in chapter 2 and in the appendix on page 193, earlier versions of the SORP will continue to be relevant in certain cases.

Accounting and Reporting by Charities: Statement of Recommended Practice Charities SORP 2005, reissued May 2008 (available online, including supplementary bulletin, from www.gov.uk/government/publications/charities-sorp-2005 or in printed copies from CCH Publications).

Charities SORP (FRSSE) (effective 1 January 2015) (available online from www.charitysorp.org or in printed copies from CIPFA – see page 234).

Preparing published charity accounts

Charities: A CCH industry accounting and auditing guide (6th edn), Anthony Epton, David Duvall, Susan Singleton, and Michael Steed, Croner CCH, 2013

Charity Accounting and Taxation (5th edn), Buzzacotts LLP Charity Team, Bloomsbury, 2010

Charity financial management

Income to Impact: Financial stewardship of public sector and not-for-profit organisations (2nd edn), Adrian Poffley, Directory of Social Change, 2010

Full Cost Recovery: Version II and full cost business planner, ACEVO, 2011

Good Guide to Financial Management (4th edn), Paul Palmer, Fiona Young, Neil Finlayson and Yogita Rajani, NCVO Publications, 2014

A Practical Guide to Managing in a Downturn: Staying solvent and surviving well, Kate Sayer, Ian Oakley-Smith, Stephen Lloyd and Margaret Bennett, Directory of Social Change, 2009

A Practical Guide to Financial Management: For charities and voluntary organisations (3rd edn), Kate Sayer, Directory of Social Change, 2007

Charities and tax issues

Charities, Trading and the Law (2nd edn), Stephen Lloyd and Alice Faure Walker, Jordans, 2008

The Complete Charity VAT Handbook (4th edn), Alastair Hardman and Kate Sayer, Directory of Social Change, 2016

Value Added Tax – Charities, HMRC VAT Notice 701/1 (revised August 2014), available at www.gov.uk/government/publications/vat-notice-701 1- charities (this explains the main VAT rules specific to charities, though various supplementary notices may also be applicable)

Charity law and legal structures

Charitable Incorporated Organisations, Gareth G. Morgan, Directory of Social Change, 2013

Charitable Status (6th edn), Julian Blake, Directory of Social Change, 2008

The Charity Trustee's Handbook (revised 2nd edn), Mike Eastwood, Directory of Social Change, 2011

The Russell-Cooke Voluntary Sector Legal Handbook (3rd edn), James Sinclair Taylor and the Charity Team at Russell-Cooke, Sandy Adirondack ed., Directory of Social Change, 2009

Bookkeeping and accounting in general

There is a wide range of introductory books on accounting and bookkeeping in general, which clearly explain issues such as double-entry bookkeeping, methods of depreciation, cash flow forecasting and the understanding of published accounts. The following publications are examples written for the UK context and they are suggested because they specifically focus on broader issues of financial reporting – not just bookkeeping. However, most accounting books base their examples on commercial traders and companies and do not therefore cover charity-specific issues in any detail.

Accounting and Finance: An introduction (7th edn), Peter Atrill and E. J. McLaney, FT Pearson/Prentice Hall, 2014

Financial Accounting (2nd revised edn), Michael Jones, Wiley, 2014

Introduction to Accounting for Non-Specialists (2nd edn), Len Hand, Carolyn Isaaks, Peter Sanderson, Cengage, 2010

AUDITING ISSUES

There are many books on the principles of audit and review of accounts, most of which focus on commercial entities. However, one of the most comprehensive audit texts does include helpful discussion of charities:

The Audit Process: Principles, practice and cases (6th revised edn), Louise Crawford, Iain Gray and Stuart Manson, Cengage Learning, 2015

Other government guidance

Improving Financial Relationships With the Third Sector: Guidance to funders and purchasers, HM Treasury Publishing Unit, 2006

Financial Relationships with Third Sector Organisations: A decision support tool for public bodies in England, National Audit Office (a web-based tool that can be found on www.nao.org.uk/guidance/better_funding)

Useful addresses

Statutory and regulatory bodies

Charity Commission for England and Wales

All enquiries should be addressed to:

Charity Commission Direct, PO Box 1227, Liverpool, L69 3UG
Tel: 03000 66 9197 (mornings only)
Website: www.charitycommission.gov.uk

Charity Commission for Northern Ireland (CCNI)

257 Lough Road, Lurgan, Craigavon, BT66 6NQ
Tel: 028 3832 0220
Website: www.charitycommissionni.org.uk

Office of the Scottish Charity Regulator (OSCR)

2nd Floor, Quadrant House, 9 Riverside Drive, Dundee, DD1 4NY
Tel: 01382 220446
Website: www.oscr.org.uk

Fundraising Regulator (FR)

2nd floor, CAN Mezzanine Building, 49–51 East Road, London, N1 6AH
Tel: 0300 999 3407
Website: www.fundraisingregulator.org.uk

HM Revenue and Customs (Charities)

HMRC, Charities, Savings and International 2, BX9 1BU
Tel: 0300 123 1073
Website: www.gov.uk/charities-and-tax

Note: The HMRC office now covers charities throughout the UK and deals with charity-specific issues both for direct tax questions (such as Gift Aid) and indirect taxes (such as VAT). All the requirements for applying for charity tax recognition and operation of Gift Aid schemes are available from the website above.

Professional bodies concerned with charity finance

The following professional associations are established specifically for those working with charities. (They are all charities in their own right.)

Association of Charity Independent Examiners (ACIE)

ACIE provides support, training and a qualification for independent examiners, and a referral service for charities seeking an independent examiner.

The Gatehouse, White Cross, South Road, Lancaster, LA1 4XQ
Tel: 01524 34892
Website: www.acie.org.uk

Charity Finance Group (CFG)

CFG offers a range of services relevant to finance managers in charities of all sizes. It includes a section specifically for community accountants.

15–18 White Lion Street, London, N1 9PG
Tel: 0845 345 3192
Website: www.cfg.org.uk

Honorary Treasurers Forum

The Honorary Treasurers Forum provides online support and regular meetings to support treasurers in the important work that they do, to share expertise and promote best practice.

Cass Business School, 106 Bunhill Row, London, EC1Y 8TZ
Tel: 0207 0408781
Website: www.treasurersforum.org.uk

Institute of Fundraising (IoF)

Although IoF members are normally fundraisers rather than treasurers and finance staff, some of its work – for example on tax-effective giving – is also of relevance to treasurers (see chapter 12).

Charter House, 13–15 Cartaret Street, London, SW1H 9DJ
Tel: 020 7840 1000
Website: www.institute-of-fundraising.org.uk

Groups for treasurers in specific types of charities

There are also a number of networks and associations of treasurers or finance staff within particular types of charities. Some of these produce quite detailed guidance on accounting but do check that it is accurate and up to date in terms of complying with charity law. If your local charity is part of a national network, contact the central office to find out if there is any specific support for local treasurers.

Other professional bodies

Many more general professional bodies have a charity-specialist group or special newsletters for those working with charities, including the ICAEW, ACCA, CIPFA, ICAS and ICSA (see overleaf). These bodies can also be used to help find accountants. Firms of registered auditors will always be regulated by ICAEW, ACCA, ICAS or Chartered Accountants Ireland.

Association of Accounting Technicians (AAT)

140 Aldersgate Street, London, EC1A 4HY
Tel: 0845 863 0800
Website: www.aat.org.uk

Association of Chartered Certified Accountants (ACCA)

110 Queen Street, Glasgow, G1 3BX
Tel: 0141 582 2000
Website: www.accaglobal.com

Chartered Accountants Ireland

Belfast office: The Linenhall, 32–38 Linenhall Street, Belfast, BT2 8BG
Tel: 028 9043 5840
Website: www.charteredaccountants.ie

Chartered Institute of Management Accountants (CIMA)

The Helicon, One South Place, London, EC2M 2RB
Tel: 020 8849 2251
Website: www.cimaglobal.com

Chartered Institute of Public Finance and Accountancy (CIPFA)

77 Mansell Street, London, E1 8AN
Tel: 020 7543 5600
Website: www.cipfa.org

Institute of Chartered Accountants in England and Wales (ICAEW)

Chartered Accountants Hall, Moorgate Place London, EC2R 6EA
Tel: 020 7920 8100
Website: www.icaew.com

Institute of Chartered Accountants of Scotland (ICAS)

Chartered Accountants House, 21 Haymarket Yards, Edinburgh, EH12 5BH
Tel: 0131 347 0100
Website: www.icas.org.uk

Institute of Chartered Secretaries and Administrators (ICSA: The Governance Institute)

Saffron House, 6–10 Kirby Street, London, EC1N 8TS
Tel: 020 7580 4741
Website: www.icsa.org.uk

Index

What else can DSC do for you?

Let us help you to be the best you possibly can be. DSC equips individuals and organisations with expert skills and information to help them provide better services and outcomes for their beneficiaries. With the latest techniques, best practice and funding resources all brought to you by our team of experts, you will not only boost your income but also exceed your expectations.

Publications

With over 100 titles we produce fundraising directories and research reports, as well as accessible 'how to' guides and best practice handbooks, all to help you help others.

Training

The voluntary sector's best-selling training – 80 courses covering every type of voluntary sector training.

In-house Training

All DSC courses are available on your premises, delivered by expert trainers and facilitators. We also offer coaching, consultancy, mentoring and support.

Conferences and Fairs

DSC conferences are a fantastic way to network with voluntary sector professionals whilst taking part in intensive, practical training workshops.

Funding Websites

*DSC's funding websites provide access to thousands of trusts, grants, statutory funds and corporate donations. You won't get more funders, commentary and analysis anywhere else. Demo our sites **free** today.*

Trust**funding**.org.uk
Government**funding**.org.uk
Company**giving**.org.uk
Grantsfor**individuals**.org.uk

Visit our website today and see what we can do for you:

WWW.**dsc.org.uk**

**Or contact us directly:
publications@dsc.org.uk**

 **@DSC_Charity**
For top tips and special offers